In Memoriam
Robert Mantle
Able linguist and writer, thorough historical researcher, amusing raconteur and trusted friend – sorely missed by the whole team.

This is an extremely thorough 4 volume guide to the regimental march tunes and other parade music which inspired loyalty, pride and battlefield motivation for generations of Germans over three centuries. Built around a translation of the previously unpublished works of two great German military music historians, the late Lieutenant Colonel Joachim Toeche-Mittler and Lieutenant Colonel (Retd) Werner Probst, it describes the history of every march in the official collections sanctioned by successive kings of Prussia, German Emperors, and later by Chief Inspectors of Music of the German Republic and Third Reich.

In these descriptions one discovers that the collections are not just German, but a pan-European treasure trove of labyrinthine musical influences. The books detail how even today these tunes are still used by German armed forces units, providing the only officially permitted link between them and the military history of the German nation. They describe how the use of this superb parade march repertoire spread around the world, far beyond Germany's borders; it can often be heard in use today especially in Britain and America. The authors detail how modern regimental military music began to develop during the reign of Frederick the Great of Prussia in the mid-18th Century, before its development reached its zenith during the German Empire established by Bismarck from 1871 to 1918. They also trace the potent cultural influences on the march composition styles of the Stahlhelm, Wehrmacht, Kriegsmarine and Luftwaffe of the 20th Century.

This work is no apology or eulogy for a militaristic culture now long gone amongst the German people, but a description of the international and home sources for the march repertoire, and the personalities involved in composing, commissioning, and dedicating marches to the leading personalities of the age, and their adoption as regimental music by the fighting units of Prussia and the other Old German States, Imperial Germany, and the later German Reich and Post War Republics of East and West Germany.

The series will provide information about how the regimental bandsmen and signaller musicians on fife, drum and bugle paraded and performed this repertoire, the manufacture and embellishments of their instruments, Schellenbaum 'Jingling Johnnies' and Drum Majors' Staffs, and their employment and deployment in the ranks of the fighting units on parade and in battle.

The detailed text and appendices are supported by a huge number of rare black & white and colour images showing all aspects of German military music.

Much more than a series of books about music, the volumes will together provide a definitive guide to a colourful and tuneful aspect of Germanic culture, whose lasting influence is still with us, and is about the stirring sounds that can still be heard on parade around the world today. The very concept of cataloguing a collection of parade marches encompassing music gathered over centuries emanated in the early 19th Century from a country abolished by the Allies in 1947 as the fount of German militarism; this music is however Prussia's legacy to the world - indeed, Prussia's Glory!

After a short introduction Volume 1 concentrates on the vast official Royal Prussian collection of 'regimental' and 'neutral' quick marches. Translated from previously unpublished original research by the late Luftwaffe Lt. Col. Joachim Toeche-Mittler, it provides a definitive description for each march, its composer, and how and by whom it was used, in many cases on campaign as well as on parade. With only one exception before 1914, every Prussian, and most non-Prussian regiments, had their regimental march from within this collection.

TUNES OF BLOOD AND IRON

GERMAN REGIMENTAL AND PARADE MARCHES FROM FREDERICK THE GREAT TO THE PRESENT DAY

Volume 1

Infantry Part 1

by Luftwaffe Lieutenant-Colonels
Joachim Toeche-Mittler and Werner Probst

Edited and translated by Antony Dean, Robert Mantle, David Murray and Ian Smart

Helion & Company

Published in 2013 by:

Helion & Company Limited
26 Willow Road
Solihull
West Midlands
B91 1UE
England
Tel. 0121 705 3393
Fax 0121 711 4075
Email: info@helion.co.uk
Website: www.helion.co.uk
Twitter @helionbooks
Blog http://blog.helion.co.uk

Designed and typeset by Farr out Publications, Wokingham, Berkshire
Cover designed by Euan Carter, Leicester (www.euancarter.com)
Printed by Lightning Source Ltd, Milton Keynes, Buckinghamshire

ISBN 978-1-909384-23-1

British Library Cataloguing-in-Publication Data.
A catalogue record for this book is available from the British Library.

For details of other military history titles published by Helion & Company Limited contact the above address, or visit our website: http://www.helion.co.uk.

We always welcome receiving book proposals from prospective authors.

Contents

List of illustrations

Foreword

'No German marches today! Scotch tunes only!'
Thus said Lieutenant Colonel John Douglas of the 79th Cameron Highlanders to Band Sergeant MacLaren as the regiment fell in outside Victoria Station to march to St John's Wood Barracks in June 1857, prior to the presentation of the first Victoria Crosses by Queen Victoria in Hyde Park. It would appear that even then it was accepted that the best marches were being composed in Germany.

These volumes take us directly into the fascinating world of German military marches. Tony Dean and his contributors treat their subject as a serious and important aspect of the German cultural heritage, attracting as it did not only the attention of military musicians but of conventional composers as well. The whole history of the Military Band tradition in the German Army from the re-organisation that followed the defeats at Jena and Auerstädt in 1806 right up to the reunification of Germany in 1990 is covered. It is a veritable treasure house of musical and military folklore. Of particular interest to enthusiasts in the field of military music will be the translations by Tony himself of the biographical notes and historical descriptions made on the collection of approved marches – the *Marschsammlung* – by that doyen of writers on the subject, the late Joachim Toeche-Mittler, whose seminal three volume work *Armeemärsche* aroused so much interest when it appeared in stages from 1966-75. For the first time his notes on quick marches are now available in English. In addition, Tony has translated similar notes by Werner Probst, to appear in Volume 4 of this project, on all the quick marches which were added in the later *Heeresmärsche* collection of the 1930s.

This book is timely, appearing as it does when both the German and British traditions in military music are struggling to survive. The regiments themselves are now divorced from the bands that were once their pride and their glory. And not only that; the sound of the 'cheerful fife' and its accompanying drum is now rarely to be heard; the bugle is all but silent; and even the highland bagpipe, flourishing though it is the world over, has only just survived in the military context.

Tony Dean and his colleagues take us back to those glorious days when music and soldiering were two sides of the same coin, the days when the German battalion of the Legation Guard in North China in 1909, meeting their British counterparts on the line of march, would break into the 'Parade step', while the British 'marched to attention' with arms sloped and eyes turned right, both with bands playing!

Lieutenant-Colonel David Murray
Last Commanding Officer, 79th Cameron Highlanders
and author of *Music of the Scottish Regiments*
DJSM
Herriotshiels,
Lauder

A very rare 1907 photograph of The Band and Fifes and Drums of the German Legation Guard, China, provided by the III.See-Bataillon (The 3rd Sea Battalion of the Imperial German Marines). (Eagle & Lyre Archive)

Editor's Acknowledgements

My thanks go out first to everyone who has contributed to this four-volume work. For lack of space, not everyone can be mentioned by name, but the thanks are no less sincerely given. In responding to my article on the fifes and drums of the Prussian Guards, which appeared in 1997 in *Drummers Call* magazine (the Journal of the Corps of Drums Society, a registered UK charity for the preservation of traditional drum, fife and bugle music), I must thank Lt. Col. David Murray for alerting me to the existence of published books on German military music written by the late Oberstleutnant der Reichsluftwaffe, Joachim Toeche-Mittler. Thanks are due to my co-author, Ian Smart, for lending me copies of these books at that time, until I could obtain my own. David Murray has been kind enough to write the Foreword to this series of four volumes and has helped with translation work, and in numerous other ways throughout over 15 years of this project. These volumes owe much to his constant encouragement and practical assistance, for which I am very grateful. At about the same time my other co-author, the late Robert Mantle, introduced me to the unpublished roughly typed-up notes on German parade marches by Joachim Toeche-Mittler and Oberstleutnant a.D. Bundeswehr, Werner Probst, which were circulated with a privately issued set of records produced for the *Schallplattenfonds*, a group largely found from the then *Arbeitskreis Militärmusik*, now the German Military Music Society (DGfMM). Around a translation of these notes, this book is assembled. Major (Retd) Richard Powell (a former Piper, Scots Guards, and later a commissioned officer in the Royal Logistics Corps) has been a tower of strength with his extensive knowledge of military music matters, having organized so many parades and tattoos during his professional career. Richard's jovial company and his wife Teresa's hospitality are legendary, as is his practical help for friends embarking upon military music projects. I thank him sincerely for reading through my early drafts, making useful suggestions, and encouraging me to rigorously double-check all my facts. Richard also introduced me to Werner Probst, who in turn generously gave his permission for his writings to be published in translation in this series of books, and arranged for permission of those of the late Joachim Toeche-Mittler to be used likewise. Werner has answered my many enquiries by email, provided me with photographs, and has always made time to answer my questions fully despite his own busy schedule and ever present deadlines. I thank him too for introducing me to Herr Wolf-Hubertus Toeche-Mittler, son of the late author, who kindly furnished me with long out-of-print copies of his father's other published works, which for reasons of copyright are not translated here, but nevertheless proved to be indispensable background reading. Similarly, I thank the Chairman of the German Society for Military Music (DGfMM), Alexander Fühling for his help and generous permission to freely use all the resources of the DGfMM picture archive for illustrating this series of books.

In 1992, a letter was published in the *Military Modelling* magazine in which I asked for information about the regiments of the Prussian Guards and their music. To my astonishment, I received over two dozen replies in total, from Britain, Italy, Russia and Germany, but as many as eight were from the United States! William L. McCaughey of Centreville, Virginia and Steven H. Smith of San Gabriel, California, in particular, went to enormous trouble to search out information for me held in the archives of The Library of Congress, for which I am ever grateful. Four people closer to home also deserve special mention. Alan S. Caton of Lutterworth, Leicestershire sent extensive details about the Prussian Guards, and the late Mr. Belmont-Maitland of Tradition Ltd., Piccadilly, who had spent his early childhood in Wilhelmine Berlin, spent some considerable time correcting some of my then misconceptions, for which I am most thankful. Mr. A. Williams of Weston-super-Mare, Somerset, sent me a vast amount of handwritten information reflecting a lifetime's research into the regimental distinctions of the Imperial German armies. That he shared this so freely with someone he has never met, quite astounded me. At this time, I also received a response from Brian D.N. Stevens. Brian invited me to his home in Llandrindod Wells, Mid-Wales and threw open his large private library to me. Over the years since 1992, I have occasionally gone back to Brian to ask for his help, which he has unfailingly given no matter how busy his own research schedule. Many details about the Prussian Guards and their band establishments would not appear in this volume if it were not for Brian's help. A 'thank you' to Mr. Williams and Brian Stevens seems so inadequate, but is none-the-less sincerely given, as are my thanks to all those who replied who, for reasons of space, I cannot name here.

In 1997 I travelled to Berlin and Potsdam to further my research into German military music. I thank the very helpful staff of the Prussian Cultural Foundation, the Berlin State Library and, in particular, Herr Dietze of the Military Historical Research Office located in the former Crown Prince's Riding Hall in Potsdam. Herr Dietze found and photocopied for me valuable and little known information about the military fife, bugle and drum tradition in Imperial Germany. I will never forget his helpful manner and the spontaneous amiable hospitality in his private office while we chatted about my plans. His coffee and cigars were excellent and quite unexpected, for which, along with his valuable advice, I thank him heartily. It seems appropriate here to thank my old friend Wolf-Egbert Rosenzweig, who over the past forty years has always provided me with a home from home in Germany. Indeed, in 1972, it was whilst staying in his then recently deceased father's room that my fascination for Prussian military history and German march music was kindled. The room was full of the most exquisitely painted and constructed model dioramas of the victories of Frederick the Great created by his father Gerhard Rosenzweig, who was born the son of a Prussian officer in 1911. Wounded in the opening campaign of the Second World War, Gerhard Rosenzweig became a journalist, a profession he pursued until his untimely death in 1971. His son Wolf gave me his record collection of German marches, and the rest, as they say, is history. I am thankful for Gerhard Rosenzweig's posthumous influence, for developing in me a lifelong interest, and to his then surviving widow Gertrude for her wonderful hospitality, and Wolf's wife Brigitte for likewise a lifetime of hospitality, friendship and laughter! In Britain, I must thank the staffs of The British Library, St.Pancras and the Library of The National Army Museum, Chelsea for their ever-cheerful help in finding old and often obscure foreign titles deep in the archives in both institutions. Thanks are due to Philip Mather, former Newsletter Editor of the International Military Music Society (UK 'Founder' Branch) who found many rare recordings of German marches for me, and just in time for this publication, fascinating details about the unusual 'Drum Dogs' of Prussian Infantry Regiment Nr.43. Also, many thanks are due to both John Kroes, Knight of Orange-Nassau, and Colin Dean, Band Secretary to HM Irish Guards, both at a critical period chairmen of the IMMS International Committee and IMMS UK Committee respectively, for their years of friendship, good company and encouragement, and especially introductions to useful contacts. I must thank warmly Jean-Pierre Maingam of the Editorial Board of 'Les Tambours de'89' (The French Drum and Fife Association). Jean-Pierre is also a leading member of the French Branch of the International Military Music Society. He provided me with many hard-to-find recordings of German and Austrian military music, and much else besides, including his generous hospitality when I visited the Historic Brass Society's International Symposium in Paris in 1999. Whilst there I met and had a brief but valuable discussion about 19th century Prussian band instruments with the renowned international instrument expert, Dr. Herbert Heyde (formerly of the Musical Instrument Museum, Karl Marx University, Leipzig, and since 1994 Associate Curator, Metropolitan Museum of New York). I am very grateful to Dr. Heyde for his knowledgeable advice and for illuminating further avenues of investigation and study, including allowing me to use detailed information in articles by him.

I extend my sincere thanks to Udo Poepel (late of the *Bundesgrenzschutz*, the German Federal Frontier Guards) of Stuttgart for generously making CD copies of his rare 78rpm record collection of early 20th century German military band recordings, a gift I will always treasure. I am indebted to over one-hundred-and-fifty people for sending me contemporary postcards and photographs of Imperial German era bands and fife and drum corps, some of which appear in these volumes. In this regard, my debt to the late and much lamented Robert G. Schiller of Lebanon, Pennsylvania, is incalculable. His wonderful generosity in allowing me to use anything from his rare collection of Imperial German band photographs, and in addition, when on a visit to London his kindly lending me his priceless and very rare antiquarian book, a history of the Prussian First Foot Guards 1871-1914, which contained much information not seen elsewhere. Bob Schiller also urged me to get on with this project at moments when the task seemed daunting and overwhelming. For his unstinting support and encouragement I owe him a great debt. That he died of a heart attack and will never see these volumes finished, and that he looked forward to them so much, grieves me a great deal. I was also astonished by the generosity of a former senior American diplomat of German descent, who wishes to remain anonymous, who hearing of this project allowed me to use many pictures from his extensive private collection. Although I cannot name him, he will know from reading this that my thanks are heartfelt.

In Germany, I must thank Thomas Brackmann of Hirschberg and Hermann Schmelzer of Rüsselsheim for generously allowing me to use many images from their photographic collections. This is particularly generous as their own photographic guide to Imperial German uniforms *Unter den Fahnen* is soon to be published bilingually in German and English in several volumes. A pioneering work, it is eagerly awaited by collectors and students of the period alike. Thomas too has helped me with many enquiries and acted on my behalf in many transactions with German book and photograph dealers, help for which I am extremely grateful. Katharina Lattke of Leipzig not only found for me many images for this book by scouring postcard dealers' trays in her native Saxony, but also helped me cure my computer problems just as I was about to give up in despair. I express my warmest thanks to her. Many thanks are due too to Holger and Jörn Fickert of Idar-Oberstein who gave me first refusal on a large number of postcards of Imperial German bands they find at the postcard fairs they so enjoy. Likewise, Sven Hübler of Kehl, Thomas Faust of Dettenheim and Frank Schiborr of Radevormwald have between them found for me over one-hundred photographs and postcards depicting Imperial era German bands, many of which appear in these volumes. My sincere thanks are due to all of them. Last, but by no means least in Germany, I thank Rolf Selzer and Christiane Teschauer of Herborn for their unbelievable help and encouragement. Rolf and Christiane motorcycled all the way from their home in western Germany to the mountains of the Thuringian Harz one weekend, just because they had seen a very rare Imperial German Musikmeister's Instruction Manual in an antiquarian bookseller's shop a few weeks before whilst on holiday there. I mentioned I would like to own it, and they went to all this trouble to hunt it down again for someone they knew only via E-mails. Rolf Selzer is a well-known military history expert, particularly for his articles on bayonets in the well-respected *Zeitschrift für Heereskunde* journals. He and Christiane have also found for me some superb pictures, which appear in these books. A plain thank you for such selfless generosity and kindness seems completely inadequate.

In the Low Countries, two people deserve my thanks. David Vercruysse of Lennik, Belgium has provided me with many local First World War postcards depicting German bands in the trenches. USAF Major Howard Christie, stationed in Luxembourg, searched through his extensive collection to find similar images for me, some rare original snap-shot photographs too, which he let me buy from him at a peppercorn price, generosity for which I am most grateful. In Japan, Yasuo Ohfuji of Tokyo, a member of the German Military Music Appreciation Society in Japan, has been an endless source of encouragement, guiding me to rare items, which have appeared for sale, and holding back himself to allow me to obtain them. I express my many thanks indeed to him.

In Britain's Corps of Drums Society there are many I must thank. Firstly, Peter Hart, the Editor of *Drummers Call*, who has spent many hours on the photographs for this book and for putting many of them into a digital format. Without his cheerful and generous help, this project would have been impossible. Similarly, Stephen Sellwood, former long-time picture archivist of the society for regularly alerting me to images relevant for this book. I thank too Reg Davis, the Hon. Secretary for his help and encouragement and for putting me in touch with many people and organisations vital to the research for this book and his wife Maggie for all her hospitality. I thank my good friend Peter Foss (late Scots Guards, and former Senior Drum Major, HM Household Division), and his wife Joan, for many years of friendship, and their hospitality when visiting the north-west of the country. Also, to Peter for sharing his detailed working knowledge of Guards' ceremonial, and for pointing out detail differences and similarities between the Prussian and British Guards traditions. Interestingly, in the late 19th century, Peter's paternal grandfather was a German immigrant from Wittenberg, given conscription his ancestors would have thus served in both the Saxon, and after 1815, the Prussian Army! Soldiering must be in the blood! I must thank another fellow member of the Corps of Drums Society, Major Mike Hall (late Coldstream Guards). A former Drum Major and first ever Officer Commanding the then new Army Drums Training Company, now The Infantry School of Ceremonial, Mike, whilst still a serving officer, took time to teach me how to play the military side-drum with all its accompanying drill. Knowing of my interest in the German tradition, he introduced German style beatings into my learning routine through using the *Wanderliedermarsch*, the parts for which he had obtained whilst serving in Germany. That he gave many hours of his time so freely to someone simply keen to learn displays a rare generosity of spirit for which I am ever thankful. I seem throughout my life to have benefited from the instruction of Guards Drummers and Musicians, serving and retired, a fact which enabled me, a civilian, to approach this subject with some insight.

I owe a great debt of gratitude to my French horn tutor Mr. Frank Watson (a former horn player in the Band of the Grenadier Guards) who began my serious interest in military music during his lessons at the Pimlico Music Centre between the years 1968 and 1973. It is to my eternal regret that I did not follow his advice and pursue a career in Army music. In 1995, after a twenty-year gap from music making, whilst teaching at a Primary School, the visiting brass teacher who had heard I once was a brass instrument player suddenly approached me. He thrust a euphonium into my hands and told me I had six weeks to blow my lip in before the school Christmas concert! I can never thank David Edwards (late Royal Artillery (Mounted) Band and later State Trumpeter, The Life Guards) enough for re-introducing me to the joys of music making. We have remained firm friends ever since, and his constant encouragement in this project, amongst many others, and advice on historic military brass instruments and military music performance techniques has given me an insight when writing these volumes which I otherwise would not have had. Thank you to David and his wife Julie, again, seems utterly inadequate. Some years ago, I became aware that another author was working on a book about German military music. After so many years of research, this initially alarmed me. I need not have worried, as Brian Matthews has been the most co-operative and friendly of potential competitors. Since he was concentrating on the music services of the Third Reich era, we were not, in the event, in competition with one another whatsoever. Indeed, Brian's friendly help and general encouragement, and sound commercial advice, has proved to be very beneficial in completing this project, for which I thank him most sincerely. His book *Military Music & Bandsmen of Adolf Hitler's Third Reich 1933-1945,* published by Tomahawk Films, is a masterpiece of original research, and I recommend it to anyone wishing to further their knowledge about marching songs and military band concert music as an aspect of popular culture during the Third Reich, as it is an area quite different to that covered by these volumes.

To conclude, I must thank the members of my family who have helped with this project. I owe a great debt to my father, the late Revd. F.J. Michael Dean M.A. (Oxon), who gave me considerable time in the early nineties during the early planning stages. Having toured Germany extensively in the 1930s, and introduced me to Germany as a small boy in the 1960s, his influence has been profound. These volumes bear his hallmark, as I have closely followed his advice as to the way the various contributions are organised, and the overall format in which these volumes appear. I regret that he is no longer with us. Needless to say, my debt to him for this, and much else besides, is incalculable. I am indebted to my brother Christopher for suggesting to me that I ask my late mother, Deirdre Gillies, to help with this project. She was a very busy PA to a Professor at Guy's Hospital in London, but in an act beyond the call of maternal affection, typed up not only my barely legible manuscript, but also those of several contributors. She worked phenomenally hard, including having to double-check many words in a foreign language with which she was not that familiar. That she did it all so cheerfully, willingly and at break-neck speed was an answer to a prayer. This work would not have appeared at all if it were not for her help and guidance. I am sad that she will now never see the result of all the hours she lovingly dedicated to these volumes. I also thank my wife Jen for her encouragement, support and tolerance throughout this long exercise. I realize that it has often left me absent in mind, if not always in person, and this requires, at times, extreme forbearance on the part of the partner of a writer and translator. That we are still happily together after so many years of this project is testament to her incredible forbearance. Finally, I thank my step-daughter Vicky, especially for tolerating many hundreds of hours listening to a form of music not the first choice of most young women in their late teens and twenties!

Antony Dean

Editor's Notes

Translation Note

The translation technique used, particularly in the case of the writings of the late Joachim Toeche-Mittler, do not follow normal translating methodology, where by convention expressions are completely altered to convey comparative 'best fit' meaning. In my opinion this modern method often loses much of the original writer's or speaker's language form and turn of phrase. I have attempted to retain, more closely, the flavour of the language used by someone who wrote in an old fashioned Germanic style, as if he were addressing an audience in English but using Germanic expressions and sentence construction. Germanic sentence order and words with a common related root to an English word, frequently work in English, but sound archaic. However, as this gives 'an old Prussian feel' to the writing, I felt it was appropriate to execute the translation in this way. It can be readily seen that the translation of the writings of Werner Probst are in a more modern vernacular, which befits the more modern academic post-war style of his writing.

False Friends and Misunderstandings

Anyone who has studied the German language will be well aware of the pitfalls for the English speaker. Although over eighty percent of the words in our language have a German root, over the fifteen-hundred years since our Saxon forbearers left the German mainland our languages have grown apart, but left us with numerous words which sound almost identical but have quite different nuances in meaning. These words are known as 'False friends'. These words frequently lead to fairly major and fundamental misunderstandings. For example the opening words of the first verse of the Deutschlandlied "*Deutschland, Deutschland über alles*" has been taken since the days of the Great War to imply that the German people were stating a desire for overlordship... "*...über alles*" sounding like "over all" or "over everyone" in English. This is a fundamental historic misunderstanding. In German the words were sung and meant "above all else", it was a hymn appealing to Germans to put their country before the then powerful local or regional loyalties. The sentiment of the Deutschlandlied is therefore more akin to the British anthem "I vow to thee my country" rather than a German equivalent to "Rule Britannia!" Another word which has been fundamentally misunderstood, especially since 1945, is the word 'Reich'. In English it has come to imply an 'expansive dictatorial militarist German empire'. 'Reich' has become a bogey word in English. However, its precise and true meaning is nothing more than the word 'Realm', as in 'The Queen's Realm'. Deutsches Reich means the 'Realm of the Germans', and 'Kaiserreich' means 'The Kaiser's Realm', nothing more! It does not imply any particular form of government. The democratic Weimar Republic was a Deutsches Reich. Modern Germany is not a Reich because the Federal Republic does not encompass all the territories which were the historic home or 'Realm of the Germans'. It is worrying how entrenched misunderstandings caused by mistranslations of language can affect mutual perceptions between peoples over many generations.

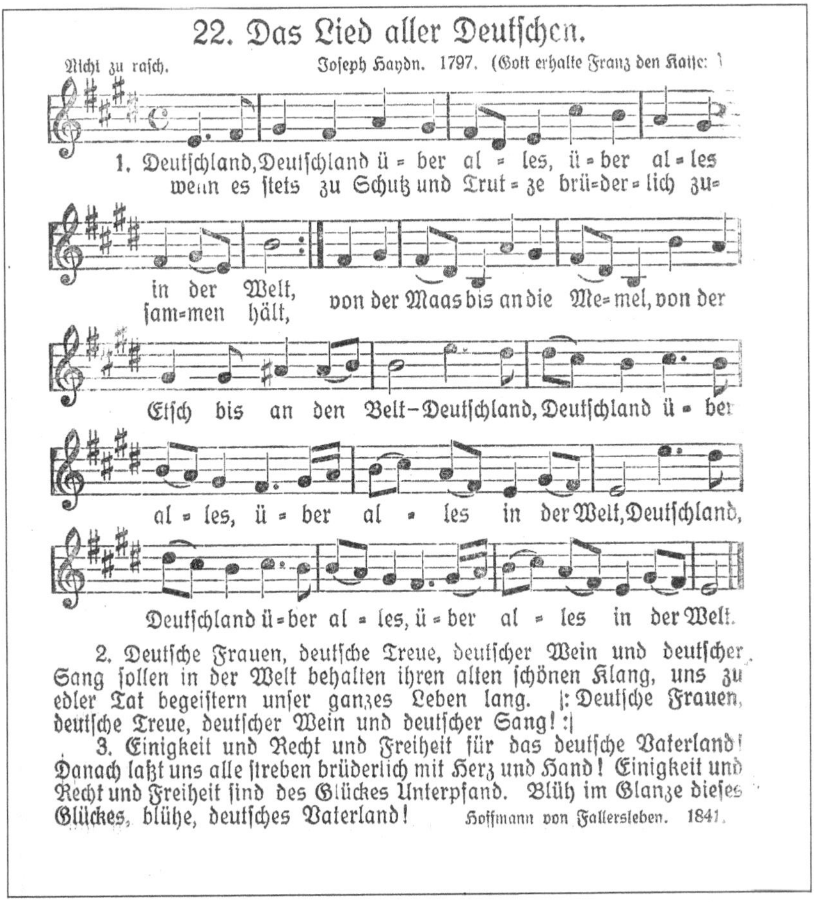

Deutschlandlied – Das Lied aller Deutschen – Sung patriotically by Germans throughout the late 19th and early 20th century, it did not become the official national anthem of Germany until 1922. From 1922 to 1945 the first verse was sung. Since the Second World War the third verse is sung instead, but only because the first verse alludes to an historic Germany from the rivers Maas to Memel which are today far outside the frontiers of modern Germany. The words "über alles" meant "above all other loyalties" rather than lording it 'over all others' – a common misinterpretation in the English speaking world!

Place Names Policy

These volumes focus primarily on the period of the German Empire before 1918. Prior to that date Germany was almost double the territorial size it is today. Many places referred to then had officially, naturally enough, German names. We have retained the names of places as they were known then. This is not in any way to be taken as a revanchist attitude. Since the 1991 German-Polish Friendship Treaty, vast former German homeland territories (in total equal in size to all of England) have legally under international law become an integral part of Poland. Between 1945 and 1991 these territories were placed under provisional Polish sovereignty pending a treaty between a re-united Germany and Poland. This has now happened, and the situation is regularized under international law, and must be accepted as such. This is despite how this originally came about through the illegal brutal ethnic cleansing of the former German population of between 9 and 12 million in these territories, at Stalin's insistence, *after* hostilities had ended in 1945! At Potsdam the Western Allies agreed to an orderly, slow, and natural population transfer. It did not happen in that way, and for many decades the expellees had a legitimate grievance under international law. With the Polish-German Friendship Treaty of 1991 any outstanding matters are now to be settled in a spirit of friendly co-operation and mutual respect. It is therefore usual and proper to use only the Polish names for these places today. However, when writing about a period prior to 1918 this clearly would be nonsensical. This is the only reason the German names have been used throughout these books. Any reader wishing to find out the current name and location of any of these places can type the German name from this text into an internet search engine and the modern Polish (or Russian, in the case of the small former northern half of East Prussia) will appear, often with interesting links to town coats-of-arms (largely unchanged since the 19th century) and pictures of the town in question. Hours of interesting research and expanding one's knowledge can be had in this way!

Opinions Disclaimer

The views expressed by any one contributor to this work are not necessarily shared by any of the other contributors. In some places moderately contentious views are expressed, which will most certainly not be shared by the other contributors. No one contributor is legally responsible for the opinions expressed by another contributor.

Glossary and Guide

How to use these volumes – a message from the Editor-in-Chief, Tony Dean

None of these four volumes are meant to be read cover-to-cover. Indeed, it would be a painful exercise to do so. The introductory chapters, and in later volumes the translations of instrumental and drill regulations, written or translated by my colleagues, the late Robert Mantle, Lt. Col. David Murray, Ian Smart or me, can be read through in order to understand the history and context in which the notes on each march were written. These march notes give information about every march in the various German march collections, and were originally penned by either the late Lt. Col. Joachim Toeche-Mittler or Lt. Col. Werner Probst as a guide to a long series of privately produced march recordings. Their sections contain sometimes necessarily repetitive comments, and are translated and printed here in an edited form as a useful guide for those seeking information on an individual march in isolation. As such it is hoped it will be useful to both academic and amateur music historians, concert programme organisers and CD booklet writers. These sections of the volumes should thus be regarded as encyclopaedic, rather than for reading through cover-to-cover.

Where to find marches in the four volume series of *Tunes of Blood & Iron*

Throughout these volumes readers are sometimes directed to marches listed elsewhere using the march collection identifying letters (see below), followed by the volume within that collection (rendered in Latin numerals), and after a comma the march number (using Arabic numerals) e.g. *AM III, 72*. This methodology was used at the time and these derive from the official collections described as follows:

AM – AM was the abbreviation for Armeemarsch (Army March). The special designation 'Army March' in Prussia denoted a march placed in his official Royal Prussian Army March Collection by successive Kings of Prussia from 1817 to 1918. This was continued by the Weimar Republic's all-German Reichswehr until a new Collection was created in 1933 (see HM below). All Prussian troops, and after 1918 all German troops, were restricted to using just these marches at all formal parades. All other marches from whatever source could only be used at informal events and on the bandstand, but were forbidden on parade. There were 4 volumes of AM, denoted as follows:

AM I

(Slow marches and later General Salutes for Presenting Arms – covered in Volume 2 of *Tunes of Blood & Iron*)

AM II

(Quick marches – the Royal period 1817-1918 covered in Volume 1 of *Tunes of Blood & Iron*. The Weimar Republic period 1918-1929 covered in Volume 2 of *Tunes of Blood & Iron*)

AM III

(Cavalry & Artillery marches – both Royal and Republican periods covered in Volume 2 of *Tunes of Blood & Iron*)

AM IV

(Fife & Drum music, and a few band marches missed in previous sections – AM IV was a provisional addition to the Royal Collection – covered in Volume 2 of *Tunes of Blood & Iron*)

HM

HM was the abbreviation for Heeresmärsche (Army Marches) used as the prefix for marches in the official collection of 1933-1945. Like the old AM collection there were sections as follows:

HM I

(General Salutes for Presenting Arms – covered in Volume 2 of *Tunes of Blood & Iron*)

HM II

(Quick Marches for use by the Transition Army of 1933-34 and the Wehrmacht 1935-45 – covered in Volume 4 of *Tunes of Blood & Iron*)

HM III A & B

(Cavalry and Panzer Marches for use by the Transition Army of 1933-34 and the Wehrmacht 1935-45 – covered in Volume 2 of *Tunes of Blood & Iron*)

MdLw (FlM)

Marsch der Luftwaffe (Fliegermärsche) was a selection from both the AM and HM collections, plus a few additional marches with special arrangements (including for the first time saxophone parts) for use by the Luftwaffe 1935-1945. (Covered in Volume 4 of *Tunes of Blood & Iron*)

Bundeswehr Marschsammlung

A selection of marches approved for use in 1961 for modern Germany's Bundeswehr 1955-2013+. All three sections therein are covered in Volume 4 of *Tunes of Blood & Iron*)

Glossary

Musician Ranks and Appointments

Musikinspizient – Music Inspector (Chief of the Music Service)

Stabshoboist – (literally: Staff Oboist) – Bandmaster – a senior NCO. All musicians, whether woodwind, brass or percussion players, were styled 'Oboists' after the all-woodwind quartets of the 18th century. Stabshoboisten could be awarded further honorific titles and were thereafter addressed as such. For example Musikdirigent or Musikdirektor, but these were due to professional qualifications gained and not a rank; bandmasters remained forever NCOs. In 1908 the rank Stabshoboist was abolished and renamed Musikmeister, with a promotion possible to higher pay as an Obermusikmeister after several years service. Sometimes the civilian title Kapellmeister (lit: chapel master; originally a bandmaster at a royal or ducal court chapel) was used to describe a Stabshoboist, often as Militärkapellmeister (lit: Military chapel master).

Hoboist – Musician or Bandsman (regular establishment NCO musician). About two-thirds of most regimental bands were composed of Hoboisten. From 1908 the rank was renamed Musiker.

Hilfshoboist – (lit: Helping Oboist) – a conscript or regular soldier from the company ranks seconded to augment the band and awarded Acting NCO rank for doing so. About one-third of regimental bands were composed of Hilfshoboisten. From 1908 the name was changed to Hilfsmusiker.

Regimentstambour – Senior Regimental Drum Major – the most senior of the three battalion drum majors of a regiment he was a senior NCO who wore a sword (never drawn). He did not belong to the band but led the Spielleute (lit: playing people; singular: Spielmann), a generic name for the Hornisten and Trommler (see below) when massed as a bugle, fife and drum corps which always marched ahead of the band. He signalled with a Drum Major's Staff on parade and with a bugle held aloft on manoeuvres and campaign.

Bataillonstambour (vernacular: 'Tambourmajor' or just 'Tambour') – Battalion Drum Major. He did not belong to the band but led the Spielleute of his battalion. He had junior sergeant rank and wore a bayonet like the rank-and file. He likewise signalled with a Drum Major's Staff on parade and with a bugle held aloft on manoeuvres and campaign.

Hornist (plural: Hornisten) a Spielmann – Bugler of an infantry battalion company, also trained on the fife. Some regiments had a Stabshornist who was the leading Bugler of the regiment on the HQ Staff. He acted as the Commanding Officer's Bugler and had responsibility for the musical training of Buglers/Fifers throughout the regiment.

Trommler, a Spielmann – Drummer from an infantry battalion company

Stabswaldhornist – (lit: Staff Woodland-hornist) – Bandmaster of a Jäger or Schützen (Rifles) band. Sometimes Stabwaldhornist was confusingly abbreviated to a colloquial use of Stabshornist, even by officialdom, but Bandmaster role here was entirely different to the Stabshornist of the infantry of the line who was the CO's bugler (see above).

Waldhornist – Musician or Bandsman of a Jäger or Schützen band.

Bataillonshornist or Bataillonssignalhornist – Battalion Bugle Major of Jäger or Schützen in charge of company Buglers

Signalhornist – Bugler of a Jäger or Schützen battalion company.

Stabstrompeter – (lit: Staff Trumpeter) – Bandmaster of a Mounted Band.

Trompeter – Musician or Bandsman of a Mounted Band. They were also the signal trumpeters of their respective squadrons. Just as there were Hilfshoboisten in the infantry, so the cavalry had Hilfstrompeter seconded to the band from the ranks.

Bataillonsmusiker – an unofficial term to describe either a Spielmann or musical volunteer from the ranks who, playing a variety of instruments, helped form a small unofficial battalion band (Bataillonsmusikkorps). These were common in the 3rd battalions of regiments. These had previously often been independent Füsilier-Bataillons until amalgamated as a 3rd Battalion of a Line regiment, but wished to perpetuate their all brass band musical tradition. Sometimes these little bands were string ensembles. They had no official status and should not be confused with the official Regimental Band.

Introduction

"Klingling, bum-bum, tschingdada"

Although written tongue in cheek, this opening line from a poem written in 1901 by Detlev von Liliencron, a former Prussian officer turned poet, perfectly conveys the combinations of sound so unique to German military bands of old. The "kling-ling" chimes of the lyre-glockenspiel, its little brightly coloured horse tail plumes dancing with every step. The "bum-bum" of the booming bass drum, which was so enormous it was worn at an acute angle across the body. It was struck by a large padded stick, wielded by the right arm in a series of outstretched flourishes. The left hand did not play, but grabbed a leather strap near the right wooden hoop, in order to hold the weight of its massive structure. The "tsching" of the great hollowed-out Chinese cymbals, not flat like other nations, but thick and heavy and shaped as if a pair of broad-brimmed brass hats, mandarin style. They were whirled in the air after clashing, glinting in the sun. The punchy "da-da" which was at the end of every phrase of the otherwise twittering woodwind and the rasping brass. At the front was the Bataillonstambour (Battalion Drum Major), rhythmically bouncing his varnished wooden staff with its playful woollen tassels dancing high in the air. Behind him were his battalion bugler-fifers and drummers. Called Spielleute, they were company signallers with their bugles, fifes or small, shallow, metallic-sounding "rang-a-tan" side-drums. The old Prussian style of march music was in keeping with its crisp and clipped drill. German bands are still renowned for their snappy drill. Every musician's instrument is held absolutely still when at rest and not being played, there is no fumbling around or warming their instruments up. (Well, on parade at least!) At attention or on the march at the Drum Major's or bandmaster's signal, in one brisk movement, all instruments are raised or jolted sideways with a snap to their mouths, just moments before the sound blares out. Likewise, when the music stops, the instruments are crisply jerked either downwards or sideways to the carry position, on the next step after the last note. In the Kaiser's day all this snap precision drill and crisp playing was emphasised by the stomp of high-kicked hobnail boots pounding the flat grey *Pflasterstein* cobblestones in time to the "crash" of the side-drums. The drums were literally hammered from above the right shoulder in order to keep the men in step, the Drummers at the front striking their drums on each word of command "*Links,* (pause) *Links,* (pause) *Links-Rechts-Links!....* from beginning to end of the march tune, and often drowning out the band! Behind the Drummers and Fifers, beside the proud bandmaster, the Schellenbaum, that towering tree of glinting metal with jingling bells and star-shaped pendants hanging from its branches. This "Jingling Johnny", a Turkish style crescent on a pole, copied from the Jannissaries of old Ottoman, was topped with a fearsome silver eagle, and grasped by both hands, down below, under a large silver or brass bell, also decorated with hanging pendants of little stars and bells. With long, flowing horse-tail plumes in state colours hanging either side of the crescent, it was carried not by a musician, but by the tallest man in the regiment. When the band broke into the '*Paradeschritt*', the 'parade-step' (sometimes called the 'Exerzierschritt', the 'drill-step') – known to us as the 'goose-step', it became a glittering, bouncing, unstoppable musical machine. The horse-tail plumes on the *Schellenbaum* and lyre-glockenspiel, the fringes on the swallowsnest wings of the Drum

Homburg vor der Höhe on 4 September 1897, and the Spielleute (Drums & Fifes) of III Batl. Füsilier-Regiment von Gersdorff Nr. 80, followed by the Band of Infanterie-Regiment Kaiser Wilhelm (2.Grossherzoglich Hessisches) Nr. 116 lead Kaiser Wilhelm II and King Umberto I of Italy back from a parade. (Eagle & Lyre Archive)

Major and Bandmaster, and in regiments of the Prussian Guards, the fringes on every musician's *Schwalbennester*, (flat swallowsnest-shaped musicians-wings), kinked and jerked madly with each crashing, bounding, high-kicking step! A German regimental band, with a battalion's fifes and drums on parade in the Kaiser's era, was indeed an imposing sight, and a delight to the ears for all who appreciated truly *martial* military music.

'Goose-stepping' needed a different playing technique

A totally different method of articulation, tonguing and breath control, and a very different mental approach to the playing style of march music in general was required. This playing style became a habit, even when playing marches on the bandstand. The style was particularly marked when marching in packed 'close order' formations, and when 'goose-stepping' and playing at the same time. It was a method which produced completely different intonation, rhythm, flourishes and elongated pauses between phrases. It was achieved by maintaining correct march tempo but clipping each note shorter than written, creating a powerful jolting effect, especially in the *fortissimo* passages. It also involved holding the pauses an instant longer. Both aspects of the technique involved departing a whisker from the music 'as written', but its effect exaggerated the impact, strength and sheer swagger of a march. Bands today hold onto their notes longer and play marches more smoothly, for impact they might use a 'flowing' *crescendo* to give strength and resonance, but even on parade they are performed in a musician's classical symphonic music style, as befits their modern non-militaristic tastes and training methods, rather than clipped in the more exciting old

The Kaiser Alexander Garde-Grenadier Regiment Nr.1 march past Kaiser Wilhem II outside the Zeughaus in Unter-den-Linden, Berlin, in Winter greatcoat order, circa 1913. They are led by their Regimentstambour (Senior Drum Major) and his Spielleute (Drummers & Bugler-fifers). Behind them in front of the regimental band led by Fritz Brase, who is just out of view, the eagle and flag of the Schellenbaum towers above their tall brass-fronted mitres. The mitres were worn only when the Kaiser or their Royal Colonel, Tsar Nicholas II, was present. (Eagle & Lyre Archive)

military soldier-bandsman music style of the Kaiser's day. The old playing style survived both world wars and could still be heard in West Germany when the old pre-war bandmasters were still in charge. The names Wilhelm Stephan, Johannes Schade and Heinz Schlüter immediately come to mind. In the mid 1970s these *"Alte Knochen"* ("Old Bones") retired, and the crisp style gradually disappeared. Their recordings are sometimes re-released in CD format, and are recommended for superb performances of German march music in the traditional style.[1] During the 1950s the Musikkorps der Schutzpolizei Berlin (West Berlin Police) under Heinz Winkel were also known for their hard parade style when playing traditional marches. These have just been re-released on a series of six CDs and are highly recommended for those who enjoy a thumping parade style.[2] In East Germany, which retained the goose-step to July 1990, just three months before re-unification, the clipped parade-style of playing could be heard right up until then. Although many of their marches were new compositions, they did play some of the old repertoire.[3] In British military bands

1 Most recent is a five CD boxed set BCD7278 'Deutsche Armeemärsche und der große Zapfenstreich' re-released by Bauer Studios GmbH, Markgröninger Strasse 46, D-71634 Ludwigsburg, Germany (Email info@bauerstudios.de)

2 JUBAL Musikverlag Berlin, Hildegard Strasse 21, D-10715 Berlin, Germany. (E-Mail: jubalmusic@t-online.de)

3 For their best performances look out for CD re-releases of the Zentrales Orchester der NVA conducted by Gerhard Baumann, re-released by Barbarossa Musikverlag, Sperberfeld 45, D-14532 Kleinmachow, Germany. (Email: barbar@t-online.de)

The regimental band of Füsilier-Regiment von Gersdorff Nr. 80 play their battalions column past, en route to the Front, late 1914. Their regimental quick march was an arrangement made in 1840 by Bandmaster Hübner of tunes from the opera Les Huguenots by Giacomo Meyerbeer. In peace time this band was famous for providing music for Guard Mounts at the Kaiser's Summer Court at Homburg vor der Höhe, and the regiment was as a result nicknamed the 'Sommergarde'. (Eagle & Lyre Archive)

A Prussian column led by its Drums and Band marches through St. Avold, then in German Lorraine, c. 1915-16, to the amusement of local children. By now the leather helmet has given way to the massed produced wartime felt version. (Eagle & Lyre Archive)

before the early 1960s this clipped playing style (but not the goose-step of course!) was also common practice, and the technique was known semi-officially as 'Playing Short'. In the USA it was known as 'Spacing the notes' as described by Frank Simon, solo-cornetist in the Sousa band. Lt. Col. Werner Probst and the famous German composer and march arranger, Hans Ahrens, have together discussed this phenomenon and designated the term 'Straffes Spiel' (literally 'taut playing') to describe a similar crisp and snappy technique when used by German bands. The spritely and somewhat triumphalist style can instantly be recalled when one thinks of a march accompanying an old Pathé News cinema newsreel. It is a style no longer performed in either the USA, Britain or, with a few exceptions, Germany, and many would argue that military march music is the poorer for its discontinuance.

German Military Music in Battle – Great War 1914-1918

Before the age of 'smart'-weapons and ultra-modern hi-tech warfare, military music always played a vital role in battle, as well as being used, as today, for ceremonial purposes. It is a mistake to think that wars of the type fought in the 20th century were devoid of music in battle. Even as late as the Korean War (1950-53) the bugle was still in use as a battlefield instrument. Indeed, in Korea, Drum Major Phillip Buss of the I Bn. Gloucestershire Regiment once played his trusty bugle all night long, in order to confuse the thousands of Chinese infantrymen who had surrounded his battalion's position! Since ancient times military music has been vital for both signalling and for morale in battle, and to the Germanic peoples especially so. Tacitus tells us in his *Germania* written in 98 A.D. that the Germans sang of their heroes and then chanted as they went into battle. This the Romans found extraordinary, as they had not met this phenomenon before. Although almost 2,000 years later by the time of the Great War of 1914-18 German bandsmen had been trained as

Bavarian infantry about to march from their home garrison to the front c. 1915-16, led by their fine-looking over regulation strength band. (Eagle & Lyre Archive)

medics, they nevertheless frequently played their battalions into the most forward positions. This was especially true of the drummers and bugler-fifers of the battalion companies, but on occasion the regimental bands also. Early in the war, during the Battle of Le Cateau on 25 August 1914, the 2nd King's Own Yorkshire Light Infantry were blocking the high road along which the Germans needed to advance. Surrounded on three sides and shelled by German field guns at just 900 yards range, to their astonishment they heard the German buglers repeatedly blowing the British call "Cease Fire" in an attempt to confuse the British Light Infantrymen. Two months later at the appalling 'Kindermord von Ypern' – the massacre of the innocents, the hastily trained and deployed youngsters of the German Reserve Divisions at Ypres on 22 October 1914, a British Tommy recalled that...'About 4.30 am three battalions of Germans assaulted our position. They came on with two Colours flying and a band, and they were all singing. We emptied ten rounds a man rapid into the approaching mass...' On a happier note an amusing musical tale was recalled by Private Frank Caulton, 2nd (City of London) Bn. (Royal Fusiliers) London Regiment.[4] When, as part of 29th Division his company captured Noyelles on 29th November 1917, they found a German band had left their instruments behind during a hasty retreat. The instruments gave his comrades several hours of hilarious amusement. However, the instruments were left behind when the Germans counter-attacked, and were presumably reclaimed by the German band who had involuntarily lent them out! Incredibly, given the effect of the ever present machine guns, endemic to trench warfare, as late as 1918 bands were still in front line service. During the Germans' last advance of the war, the 'Kaiserschlacht' of Spring 1918, Private George McKay, I.Bn. NZ Rifle Brigade was amazed when he peeped over a ridge to see thousands of Germans marching forward with a band playing out in front.[5]

4 Quoted in full in MacDonald, ., *They Called It Passchendaele*, (Penguin: 1993)

5 MacDonald, ., *1918 – To the Last Man.*

An unidentified German band leads a company through a town thought to be near the French-Belgian border, early in the First World War. It must be before the 1916 issue of the Stahlhelm, as the old Pickelhaube is still worn by the band. (Eagle & Lyre Archive)

In the Kaiser's Navy too, the bands went with the ships to war. The later Grand Admiral Dönitz recalled in his memoirs how, as a young naval lieutenant aboard the SMS *Goeben*, he had the ship's band play spirited marches to encourage the men during the exhausting work of re-coaling at Messina. Speed was vital despite the roasting Mediterranean summer sun. This was during the first two days of the war, 4th to 6th August 1914, when the SMS *Goeben* was desperately trying to gain time to avoid being trapped by the British fleet. The band did its work of encouraging the men, and the SMS *Goeben* got away. These stories all demonstrate the important role military music played in the First World War on the German side, however, other nations undoubtedly benefited from the work of their own bands during the conflict. Although rarely admitted since 1914, even on the Allied side the bands owed much to mid 19th century German example. However, towards the end of that century Britain and the United States had developed playing techniques and arrangement styles of their own, which remain rather different to central European practice. Nevertheless, in the centuries before the Great War it was to Germany that other nations looked when establishing and expanding their own military band services.

Worldwide impact of German Bands – c.1500-1900

Many of the key evolutionary changes of the military band from a group of late Renaissance shawms, through the oboe and bassoon quartet of woodwind players from the late 17th century onwards, to the addition to the oboes of trombones, natural horns and trumpets to create the *Harmoniemusik* of the late 18th century, and on to the full wind-band we know today, began in either Austria or Germany. This is true of both the combinations of instruments used, and their technological development. These developments within German realms led to German pre-eminence in the world of military music. Thanks to

Sometime between 1908 and 1914; a band still in full dress blue tunics practices playing on the march at the Elsenborn Training Ground near the Belgian border. (Eagle & Lyre Archive)

new musical instrument technology introduced to Prussian bands by Wilhelm Wieprecht in the 1840s, this pre-eminence lasted until the early twentieth century. All over Europe, and indeed further overseas, countries not only copied developments in Germany, but also employed German bandmasters, and in many cases the ordinary musicians from Germany for regimental bands of their own armies. Well into the third quarter of the 19th century this was especially true in both Britain and the United States. Until the early twentieth century, Switzerland, Sweden, Norway, Japan,[6] Turkey, Ireland[7] and Spain all had the benefit of German military music inspectors or advisors. For example, Turkey's famous *Vatan-Marşi*, which uses the patriotic-revolutionary "Young Turk" Freedom Song as its trio, was composed by Paul Lange (1865-1920), who hailed from Kartzow near Potsdam, whilst he was Director of Court Music in Istanbul, and Colonel of the Sultan's Naval Military Music Service from 1909 to 1918. He had the honour of being made a Bey (an Ottoman knight), and in 1920 was given a state funeral! Even the famous Hawaiian tune "*Aloha Oe*" was composed by Heinrich Berger (1844-1929), who hailed from Coswig in Anhalt, trained as a bandmaster whilst serving in the Prussian 2nd Foot Guards in Berlin, and then became Director of the Royal Hawaiian Band in Honolulu from 1872 to 1915, following a request from King Kamehameha V to Wilhelm I for a German bandmaster. However, if looking for German influence today we must look to the non-aligned states of South America, and in particular Chile, who from the earliest times of their republic have had Prussian or German military advisors. The first German General Inspector of

6 The German Navy bandmaster from Kiel, Franz Eckert, re-arranged the Japanese National Anthem, *Kimigayo* into western notation

7 The official "Irish Army March" was composed by Fritz Brase, late Bandmaster of the Kaiser Alexander Garde Grenadier Regiment in Berlin, and from 1920 to 1940 Colonel commanding the Irish Army Music Service

A Royal Saxon regimental band plays on a route march in 1913 near the Training Ground at Neuhammer am Queis, just outside Saxon territory in Prussian Lower Silesia (Today, Świętoszów in Poland)

the Chilean military music service was Richard Hüttenrauch, appointed in 1896. He was formerly *Musikmeister* of Infanterie-Regiment Nr. 169 in Lahr, and after his period in Chile, between 1926 and 1936, helped establish military bands in the German image in several central American republics, before returning to Germany as *Stabsmusikmeister* der Luftwaffe Fliegerhorstkommandantur Brandis in Saxony. As bandmasters in Chilean service Hüttenrauch was assisted by *Musikmeister* Paul Müller and *Musikmeister* Bügelsack. A remarkable visual survival of their German influence appears annually to this very day in Chile at the "Dia de Glorias" parade each September. The fifes and drums, band and rifle companies of the Chilean NCO College "Bernardo O'Higgins" goose-step past using pure Imperial German era drill. They wear the pre-1914 design full-dress Prussian-blue uniforms cut in the tight Prussian style, with correct regulation summer white cotton trousers. They wear brass spiked, black leather 'Pickelhauben' helmets identical to the original Prussian pattern, with the correct grenadier's white, or musician's red parade plumes fixed over their spikes. All this is accompanied by spirited renditions of Prussian military music, as to this day they still have German military music advisors. As the last Imperial German Crown Prince, Wilhelm, once remarked on an official visit to Chile:

"Ha ha! Unbelievable! I have travelled half way around the world, and what do I find? A sight identical to a 'Kaiserparade' on the Tempelhoferfeld in Berlin!"

It remains so in 2012.

1

From Tilsit to Versailles, from Blücher to Bismarck

A short history of Prussian military music from 1807-1871 by Robert Mantle

Prussian bands during and immediately after the Napoleonic Wars

The campaign of 1806-1807 against Napoleon had disastrous consequences for the Prussian Army; the Treaty of Tilsit limited its strength to 42,000 men. The reform and reorganization of the army after 1807 had, as its primary objective, the building up of a force that could be quickly expanded in time of war and military music had a very low priority. Nevertheless, military bands continued to exist. The Prussian General Staff's official history of the army at this period states that the Foot Guard Regiment had twenty-four bandsmen at this time, while the other infantry regiments had ten in addition to their drummers, fifers and buglers.[1] Cavalry bands consisted of twelve trumpeters under a trumpet major, while the Jäger and Schützen battalions had eight horn players under a Stabshornist. We also learn that the Guards band consisted of two flutes, a piccolo, two oboes, four clarinets, a serpent, two bassoons, a contra bassoon, two horns, two trumpets, four trombones, a side drum, a bass drum, cymbals and a triangle. The line regiments made do with a largely woodwind ensemble and a brass quartet (two horns, trumpet and trombone). When we come to the repertoire of the time, however, the evidence is almost completely lacking for the period 1807-1814. (Much of the old regimental music had been lost with the old regiments – only seven infantry regiments survived 1806-7 out of sixty – and was not rediscovered until the end of the nineteenth century.) Some marches have been identified, notably Beethoven's *March in F Major* composed for the Bohemian Militia in 1809, which became associated with the I Army corps in 1813 and became known as the *Marsch des Yorck'schen Korps,* or simply the *Yorck'scher Marsch*. It has remained popular ever since. Another march from this era, the *Marsch der Freiwilliger Jäger* was played by the Guards Jäger Battalion for a century before it became part of the official collection. Evidence of music played on the battlefield is equally elusive. British eyewitnesses state that when Blücher met Wellington on the evening of 18th June 1815, a Prussian band played *God Save the King* (ignoring the fact that Prussian anthem, *Heil Dir im Siegenkranz* had the same tune); and that is virtually all. The greatest influence on Prussian military music during the 1813-1815 campaigns and for a long while afterwards was the Russian Army. The Russian Guards had impressive bands which since 1809 had been supervised by the German Bohemian Anton Dörfeldt (1781-1829) the Director of the School of Military Music at St Petersburg. King Friedrich Wilhelm III of Prussia was impressed by many aspects of Russian music; the establishment of military choirs was a direct result of the Russian tradition of 'Singers to the Front', while

1 *Das preußische Heer der Befreiungskriege: Das Preussische Heer im Jahre 1812* (Berlin, 1912) pp. 371-374.

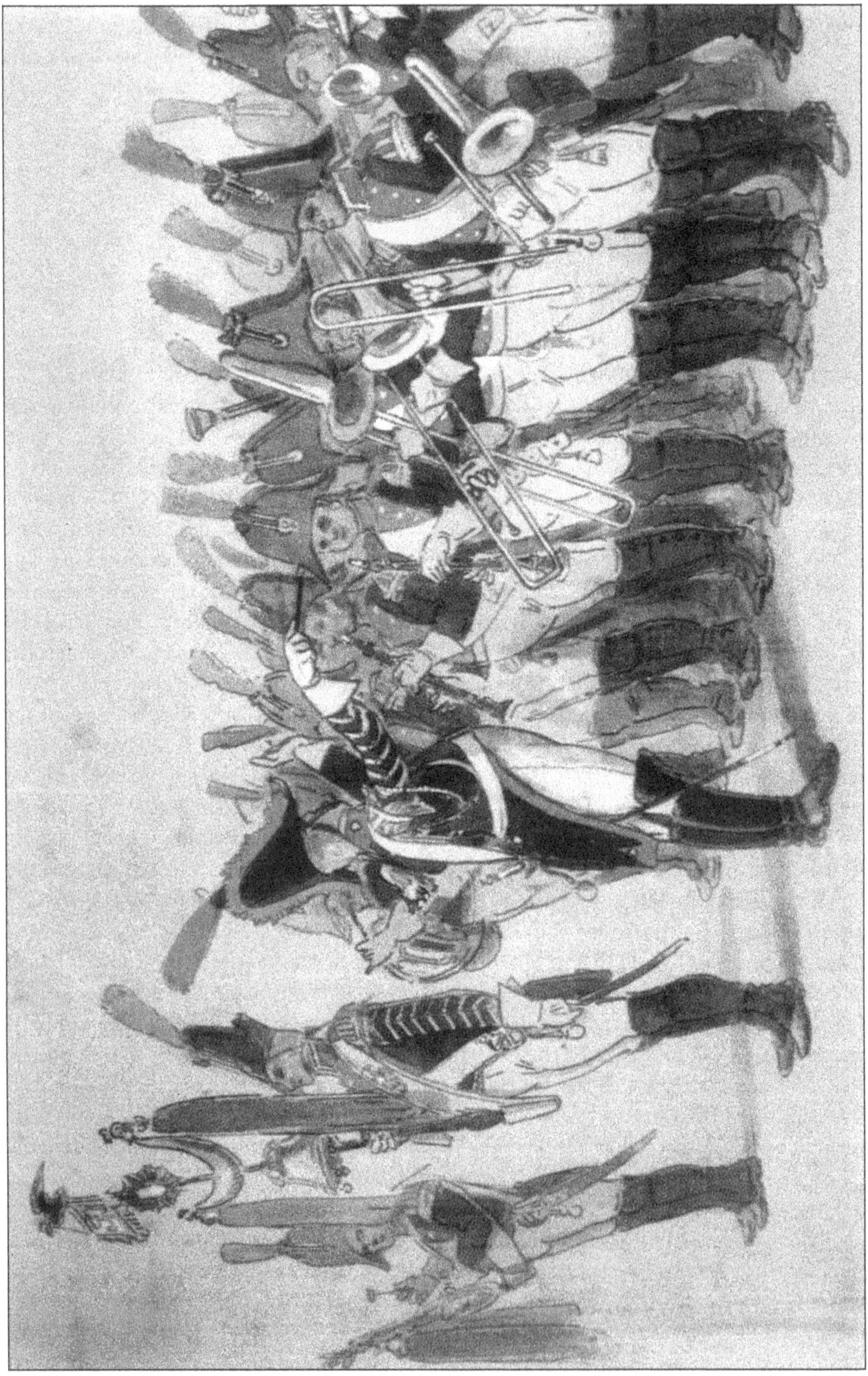

A Prussian military band circa 1807.(Eagle & Lyre Prints Archive)

German Bohemian Anton Dörfeldt (1781-1829), the Director of the School of Military Music at St Petersburg (Pen and ink sketch by Caroline Wood)

the Prussians adopted the Russian ceremony of Tattoo (with Hymn by Bortnanjski) as the *Grosser Zapfenstreich*. By the end of 1814, moves were afoot to put Prussian military music on an organised footing. After the interruption of the Hundred Days Campaign, Prussia's army had expanded and the coming of peace meant that there would be more need for music for ceremonies and parades. A basic repertoire was essential and here Dörfeldt came to the rescue; he had compiled a collection of slow and quick marches and by 1815 there were around seventy pieces in each category. Tsar Alexander I introduced Friedrich Wilhelm to the collection when he visited Berlin in October 1815 and a commission was soon established to select marches for the Prussian Army. On 10th February 1817, the King issued a decree:

> To assist regiments in choosing good military music, I have had a selection of good marches compiled and each regiment will be given a copy of this collection. In order to improve the troops' repertoire, it is my wish that only music from this collection should be played on future occasions and at large scale reviews and parades, especially those where I am present.
>
> Friedrich Wilhelm

This was the origin of the Prussian Army March Collection, which was to continue until 1929. The original collection was in two volumes; Volume I contained thirty-six slow marches and Volume II thirty-six quick ones. All were scored for the infantry band of the time. The original thirty-six quick marches are briefly described later in this book; most had fallen out of favour (or never been taken up by bandmasters) within twenty years and new compositions were added to the collection. When they were recorded in the early 1980s many had been unheard for over a century and a half. In many cases nothing is known beyond the title. It would be going too far to claim them as lost masterpieces; yet many deserve a second hearing, Dörfeldt's own compositions in particular. The collection

Heinrich-August Neithardt (1793-1861), the bandmaster of the Kaiser Franz Grenadier Regiment from 1822 (Pen and ink sketch by Caroline Wood)

Georg Abraham Schneider (1770-1839) was from 1819 to 1838 Director of all the Bands and Choirs of the Prussian Guard and Grenadier Corps (Pen and ink sketch by Caroline Wood)

had been established, though, and was progressively added to over the next few years. (The first two 'new' marches, added in 1817, were the *Yorck'scher Marsch* and Johann Heinrich Walch's *Pariser Einzugsmarsch* of 1814). A third volume of cavalry marches was started in 1824. Meanwhile the slow march was falling out of favour, even at formal parades. For a short while after 1817, troops still marched past in slow, then in quick time (as still happens on the Queen's Birthday Parade in Britain), but the quick march was far more popular, and the Spanish *Matadura Marsch* (II/43) was one of the first to be added to accustom the troops to the new pace. It is significant that during the twenty years following the King's decree, only sixteen slow marches were added to the collection and seventy-seven quick ones. It was not enough to prescribe a repertoire; a central authority was needed to maintain standards. On 8th July 1819, the King appointed Georg Abraham Schneider as Director of Music for the 'Guards and Grenadier Corps' in Berlin. After 1820 the Berlin Grenadier Regiments were elevated to Guard status, and from 1860 carried the description 'Garde-Grenadier' in their regimental titles. Thereafter the Corps was simply known as the Guard Corps (Gardekorps) with the eventual eleven Guard infantry regiments styled either *Garde-Regiment zu Fuss* (Foot Guards), Garde-Grenadier (Grenadier Guards) or Garde-Füsilier (Fusilier Guards). Georg Abraham Schneider (1770-1839) was a court musician, the principal horn player at the Royal Opera and a composer and teacher with a fine reputation and many friends. One of them was Colonel von Witzleben, the future Minister of War, with whom Schneider played in a string quartet. Schneider was the man for the job, and over the next few years examined bandmasters, musicians, and new scores alike. Thanks to Schneider, Prussian military bands soon had a fine reputation. He was ably assisted by a generation of outstanding bandmasters, notably Heinrich-August Neithardt (1793-1861), the bandmaster of the Kaiser Franz Grenadier-Regiment from 1822 and a prolific composer and arranger of military and choral music. Military bands were becoming part of the cultural life of their garrison towns; this was particularly true of the Guards and Grenadiers in Berlin. It was in the 1820s that a new personality appeared; a man who was to dominate military music in Prussia.

The Wieprecht Revolution – 1825-1838

Wilhelm Wieprecht (1802-1872) was born in Aschersleben, the son of a musician. He studied at the Dresden Conservatoire, graduated in 1824 and took up a post at Berlin's Royal Opera as a trombonist. The Director of the Opera, Gasparo Spontini (1774-1851) was one of the best known composers of the time and his grand operas (*La Vestale, Olympia, Alcidor, Ferdinand Cortez*) enjoyed tremendous popularity. He was also vain and demanding; he conducted by wielding a massive ebony baton, more like a Field Marshal's staff than a conductor's baton, and standardised the placing of the members of an orchestra (he was short-sighted, too vain to wear spectacles and found this was the only way he could identify the players). Wieprecht's job was not an easy one. One day in May 1824 he took a break from rehearsals and was drawn by the sound of music to the daily guard changing on Unter den Linden, where the Kaiser Franz Grenadier-Regiment were being conducted by Neithardt. Their skill and their performance reduced Wieprecht (according to his own account) to tears and he resolved to devote his own efforts towards military music. In his own words "I felt myself called in this direction and saw at a glance that very soon I would achieve something in this field!" Wieprecht had been studying the orchestration of wind instruments, particularly the new valved brass instruments that were coming into use. In 1825 he produced his *Six Marches for Cavalry Band* which aroused immediate interest particularly with the Guard Dragoons who were soon playing his marches. Wieprecht had heard the mounted band of the Garde-Dragoner-Regiment at the Halle Gate, only a short distance from his office, which had inspired him to write these marches. The commanding officer of the Garde-Dragoner-Regiment paid 400 Thalers from his own pocket for new instruments. Wieprecht was in demand – regiments asked him to visit and teach the trumpeters. In 1829, the King requested that he train the Garde-Husaren-Regiment in Potsdam – the following year he was summoned to the 2nd Cavalry Brigade in Danzig. He was making useful contacts especially among the Royal Family, which would stand him in good stead. Meanwhile, the March collection continued to develop. One source of new marches was the visits of the Royal Family abroad. Princess Charlotte of Prussia had married Grand Duke Nicholas, the future Tsar Nicholas I, in 1817 and her brothers frequently visited St Petersburg, bringing back many Russian marches. In addition, the King and the Princes often visited Italy. Large numbers of Austrian troops were stationed there, and their marches, with those of the Neapolitan regiments, appeared in the collection often arranged by August Heinrich Neithardt. Some of these (*AM II, 73*; *AM II,75*) were popular – others (*AM II,51*; *AM II, 76*) soon fell out of favour or never caught the popular fancy. None were as popular as II,58, which the Crown Prince brought back from Munich and has been played ever since. Another march that has never left the repertoire is *AM II, 113*, the *Petersburger Marsch* which was the great hit of 1837, although its composer is unknown. The development of keyed instruments meant that cavalry bands could expand beyond a corps of trumpeters, while infantry bands gradually increased in size. By 1838 the official collection contained one-hundred-and-thirteen marches in Volume II, while the cavalry had twenty-one in Volume III. (Volume I, with its fifty-three marches, was virtually

Wilhelm Wieprecht (1802-1872), Director of Music for the Guard Corps and later unofficially the effective first overall chief of Prussian Army music. (Pen and ink sketch by Caroline Wood)

moribund – a group of 18th century marches would be added in 1841, but then no more were be added for fifty-four years.) This was the situation when, on 2nd February 1838, Wilhelm Wieprecht succeeded Schneider as Director of Music for the Prussian Guard Corps. This position he held for thirty-four years until his death in 1872.

Resentment and Reaction to Wieprecht's Reforms –1838-1872

No one doubted Wieprecht's ability, or the value of his work, but he had never served as a soldier. (Neither had Schneider, but a whole generation of talented military bandmasters had evolved in the previous twenty years.) The appointment was widely resented and the first sign of trouble came when Neithardt – who was responsible for Wieprecht's involvement in military music in the first place – resigned and devoted the rest of his life to choral music. Less obvious, but more significant, was the feud between Wieprecht and Johann Heinrich Rode, the Stabshornist of the Garde-Jäger-Bataillon, which lasted for nearly twenty years, and was continued by Rode's son after his father's death, and was of deep significance for Prussian military bands. In essence, this was a clash between two traditions – Rode wanted musicians to be soldiers first and to play music reflecting military traditions. Wieprecht, with his background in classical music, wished the military band to be a wind orchestra capable of the same style of performance. In addition, Wieprecht had a blind spot about the Jäger battalions' individual style – an all brass ensemble, centred around hunting horns and without percussion – and wished to introduce woodwind into their bands. He failed. While Wieprecht's dispute with some of his colleagues smouldered on, he was enjoying great success with the public who flocked to his concerts at the Circus Renz and the Victoria Theatre. His fellow classical musicians also admired him; Liszt and Meyerbeer approved of his arrangements, while Berlioz, who visited Berlin in 1843, speaks highly of him in his memoirs. He describes the Guards bandsmen as "....regiments of musicians", as opposed to just "regimental musicians", and was particularly impressed at a performance of his own *Francs-Juges Overture*. He claimed that no French orchestra could have played it as well as did the Prussian Guardsmen. One of Wieprecht's ambitions was to establish a standardised scoring – there were no printed scores until 1914 and the 'monster concerts' involving hundreds of musicians, for which Wieprecht became famous, involved copying on a vast scale. In 1844, for example, he conducted the massed bands of the Federal X Army Corps (Hanoverians, Brunswickers, Mecklenburgers, Oldenburgers and the Hanseatic Towns) – a total of 820 musicians and 300 drummers organised in seventeen bands. His wishes finally came true in 1860 with a decree from the Prussian War Ministry that only Wieprecht's arrangements were to be played in future.

New compositions and new personalities – 1840s

The 1840s saw new compositions and new personalities. Neithardt's successor, Wilhelm Christoph (1810-1859) made a name for himself through his introduction and arrangements of Austrian marches and the works of Johann Strauss the Elder, notably the *Oesterreicher Defiliermarsch* (*AM II, 141*) and the *Radetzkymarsch* (II, 145). He also arranged two themes from Strauss's quadrilles into one of the classic marches of the nineteenth century (*AM II, 126*). Meanwhile, the compositions of the Hungarian Josef Gung'l (*AM II, 127, 128, 129*) were widely popular. It was inevitable that the Guards in Berlin would have a dominant role, but there were also outstanding men working in the provinces. One returned from an eventful five years study in Berlin to take up his post as Bandmaster of the Infanterie-Regiment Nr. 8 in Frankfurt-an-der-Oder in 1843. On Friday, 24th May 1844, he announced a subscription concert for the following Friday, which would include works by Berlioz and Beethoven (an arrangement of the *Pathetique Sonata*). His name was Johann Gottfried Piefke. Not every work in the official collection was placed there on purely musical grounds. Politics played a role; when the new British Ambassador, Lord Westmoreland, arrived in Berlin an arrangement was made of a march from the opera *The Tournament* he had composed twenty years before (AM II, 140). Similarly in 1852, a march by the Turkish envoy Prince Caradja was added (AM I, 149) and sometimes King Friedrich Wilhelm IV, who preferred the arts to military affairs, asked for a march to be added. In 1844 Wieprecht had to arrange the piano piece *Gazelle* by Theodore Kullak (AM II, 133) and three years later Wilhelm Christoph arranged Joseph Labitzsky's *Jasminwalzer* (AM II, 142). There is no evidence that any of these marches were ever played. In an age without recordings, radio or television, and where few symphony orchestras existed, a garrison's military bands often provided the only means to hear an orchestral work in its original form. This fitted in with Wieprecht's views on the military band. Berlioz's experiences have already been described and we have the example of Gottfried Piefke in Frankfurt. Both Liszt and Wagner praised Piefke's arrangements, and in 1858 his arrangement of Beethoven's 7th Symphony was acclaimed by Hans von Bülow, the leading conductor of the day. Piefke's abiding passion was for Wagner, and he worked tirelessly introducing his music to the public. On one occasion, when Piefke's men had performed the overture to the *Mastersingers of Nuremberg*, a member of the public approached Piefke and congratulated him and his men for their performance " ... although I would rather hear a nice Polka than that dreadful thing." Piefke's reaction was immediate; incandescent with rage, and

Gottfried Piefke (1815-1884) was the most famous bandmaster in the history of the Prussian Army (Duncan Rogers)

grasping the hilt of his sword, he told the man in no uncertain terms that "Small children will always prefer a cheap coloured engraving to an old master drawing, and several people's musical taste is the same!" In 1876, the Bavarian government invited Piefke to the first Bayreuth Festival, a fitting reward for his labours. Opera and ballet were regarded as the 'pop' music of the mid-nineteenth century and marches on themes from them were popular. In the decades after Waterloo, Spontini's grand operas such as *La Vestale* and *Ferdinand Cortez* were all the rage and there are several marches based on them in the collection. In 1840, Hübner's march on themes from Meyerbeer's *The Huguenots* became AM II, 118 and has remained popular ever since. (It bears no resemblance to Dan Godfrey's slow march *The Huguenots,* which uses different themes from the same opera, and is played at every Trooping the Colour in Britain.) Often a march became and stayed popular when the opera was long-forgotten. Johann Carl Neumann's march on themes from Albrecht Adam's *The Brewer of Preston* (AM II, 116 of 1839) is an example, though it was helped when the newly-formed Prussian 3.Garde-Regiment zu Fuss adopted it as their regimental march in 1860. In contrast, the delightful (and anonymous) march on themes from *Rigoletto,* which Prince Albrecht of Prussia brought back from Brunswick in 1852, and which Wieprecht arranged (as AM II, 150) a year later never really became popular. It had to wait until its first recording – in the 1970s.

Berlin Bands and the Bock march competitions – 1850s

Throughout history there have been eras when a particular art reaches a high point in a particular city. For military bands, Berlin in the 1850s was such a place. The garrison's bands could be heard every day on parade and in concert, Changing the Guard at the Royal Palace or entertaining the crowds in parks and concert halls. Wieprecht was the undisputed ruler of this world now, and under his control were units such as the 2.Garde-Regiment zu Fuss under Johann Christian Meinberg, the Kaiser Alexander Grenadier-Regiment (Carl Liebig), the 2.Garde-Ulanen-Regiment (Albert Lorenz), the Garde-Schützen-Bataillon (Carl Neumann), and above all the Kaiser Franz Grenadier-Regiment under Wilhelm Christoph. In 1853 Frederick Wilhelm IV returned from Vienna with the score of what he considered the best new march he had heard for years, Leonhardt's *Alexander Caesarewich-Marsch*. Christoph arranged it and AM II, 161 has been played ever since. There was also a line regiment in the garrison; elements of the Infanterie-Regiment Nr. 8 from Frankfurt-an-der-Oder were on detachment in Berlin for Public Duties until 1860. The figure 8 of twisted cord on their shoulder straps earned them the nickname of 'The Pretzel Guard'. With them was their band under Gottfried Piefke.[2] One factor that made the bands so popular was the annual prize competition held between 1852 and 1861 and funded by the music publisher Gustav Bock (1813-1863), a partner in the well-known firm of Bote and Bock, the first competition open to Prussian bandmasters. The first judging ceremony was held on 19th February 1852 at the Royal theatre on the Gendarmenmarkt. There were twelve finalists, of whom five won prizes, and the whole affair was a great success. The following year, the judging took place in the Officers' Mess of the Potsdam garrison. The rules had been altered; the competition was now open to all military musicians, but to avoid any suggestion of favouritism the entries would be submitted under a pseudonym with the composer's identity in an attached sealed envelope. This time there were over fifty entries. Over the years, thirty-five compositions won prizes; Carl Neumann, Friedrich Zikoff of Infanterie-Regiment Nr. 18 and Heinrich Saro, Christoph's successor with the Kaiser Franz Grenadier-Regiment all won two prizes; Emil Winter of Grenadier-Regiment König Friedrich I (4.Ostpreussisches) Nr. 5 won four and Albert Lorenz won no less than seven. All of the prize-winning marches were published by Bote and Bock, fifteen became part of the Army March Collection. Many, such as Friedrich Lübbert's *Helenenmarsch* (AM II,173), Carl Faust's *Defiliermarsch* (AM II,168), Heinrich Saro's *Defiliermarsch* (AM II,176) and Emil Neumann's *Victoria Marsch* (AM II,174) (Princess Victoria, daughter of Queen Victoria, married Crown Prince Frederick of Prussia on 8th February 1858. Ed.) have been played ever since. The competition was a popular feature of Berlin's musical life until 1861, when Bock fell sick with what proved a fatal illness.

Prussian Army expansion – 3,000 military musicians – early 1860s

By then, the Army had undergone a fundamental reform and expansion; something Friedrich Wilhelm's brother (who had become Regent when the King suffered a debilitating stroke in 1857) had long felt was overdue. Prince Wilhelm, who would succeed to the throne in 1861, had been devoted to the army all his life and although he was often derided (notably by Friedrich Engels) as a parade-ground soldier, he recognised the new developments in weapons and tactics and the need for commanders who understood them. Ernst Roon became Minister of War and Helmuth von Moltke became Chief of the General Staff as the forces of the German confederation mobilised ready to intervene

2 Upon completion of their tour of Public Duties in Berlin, on 10th May 1860 this figure 8 was replaced by the FWR III royal cypher on their shoulder straps, when they were redesignated as Leib-grenadiere, 'Life Grenadiers'. But they nevertheless retained the 'Pretzel Guard' nickname until disbanded in 1919. Ed

August Kalkbrenner, the official biographer of Wilhelm Wieprecht. Incredibly, he is the only person to date to have written a biography of the real founder of the modern military band (see bibliography in Volume 4). He was a Royal Prussian Director of Music and led successively the bands of Infanterie-Regiment Landgraf Friedrich I von Hessen-Kassel (1.Kurhessisches) Nr. 81 in Franfurt/Main and then later Infanterie-Regiment Prinz Moritz von Anhalt-Dessau (5.Pommersches) Nr.42 in Stralsund. (Archive DGfMM eV)

if the war between Austria and France and Piedmont spread outside Italy. The crisis of 1859 soon ended in an Austrian defeat but serious weaknesses were revealed in the Prussian Army and a wholesale expansion took place; in 1860 thirty-six new infantry and sixteen cavalry regiments were raised. The Infanterie-Regiment Nr. 8, now back at Frankfurt-an-der-Oder, and re-titled Leib-Grenadier-Regiment König Friedrich Wilhelm III (1.Brandenburgisches) Nr. 8, found themselves brigaded with the new Infanterie-Regiment von Stülpnagel (5.Brandenburgisches) Nr. 48 stationed across the Oder in Küstrin. The new regiments needed bands and bandmasters to conduct them; the Infanterie-Regiment Nr. 48's bandmaster was Gottfried Piefke's twenty-five-year-old brother, Rudolf, who had previously served under Gottfried's command. By 1862 there were one-hundred-and-forty-eight military bands with over three thousand musicians. The new army was expensive and there was widespread opposition in Parliament. The King, frustrated, thought of abdicating; finally he resolved to appoint a new Minister President. He had his reservations about Otto von Bismarck, but no one else seemed capable of carrying out his policies. The team that would lead Prussia to the leadership of a united Germany was complete. On

2nd February 1863, Wilhelm Wieprecht celebrated his Silver Jubilee as Director of Music for the Guard Corps. That morning the massed bands of the Berlin garrison assembled outside No. 34 Unter den Linden, where Wieprecht lived above Schlesinger's Book and Music shop, and treated him to a serenade including several of his own compositions. That evening there was a banquet with music; Wieprecht was now the acknowledged master of his field. In the provinces, the newly-organised regiments were being put through their paces. The Commander of the III Corps, Prince Friedrich Karl (the King's nephew) organised a full corps manoeuvre around Lebus in Eastern Brandenburg in autumn 1863 and the 8th Leib-Grenadier Regiment played a prominent part. Gottfried Piefke composed a new march for the occasion, based on themes from Gounod's opera *Faust*, which is known in Germany as *Margarethe* (presumably to avoid confusion with Goethe's original). The *Margarethenmarsch* was an immediate success and became *AM II, 182* in 1864. By that time, Piefke and his regiment were on active service.

Schleswig-Holstein War 1863-64 – Piefke's band in action at Düppel

The war which broke out between Prussia and Austria and Denmark over the Duchies of Schleswig and Holstein was not the first to involve opposing nationalities living close together in the same area. Unlike its twentieth century successors, it was conducted with restraint and in many ways it can lay claim to be the most musical war in history. The tone was set in December 1863 when a force of Saxon and Hanoverian troops marched into Kiel led by their bands. (Friedrich Spohr's classic *Gruss an Kiel* (*HM, II 130*) dates from this occasion.) In the New Year the Prussians and Austrians advanced into Danish territory and they too brought their bands. Reinforcements arrived in March, including the Leib-Grenadiers and Gottfried Piefke. On 18th April 1864, the Prussians began a final bombardment of the fortifications at Düppel (Danish Dybbol). As the storming parties assembled, observers

Gottfried Piefke conducting the massed bands of III Corps in the trenches before Düppel in 1864 (Archive DGfMM eV)

might have seen a familiar figure in the second line of trenches, clambering awkwardly on to the firing step. Piefke had assembled the bands of his own regiment, those of Infanterie-Regiment Nr. 18 and Infanterie-Regiment Nr. 60 and Füsilier-Regiment Nr. 35, and was preparing to accompany the attack with music, conducting with a drawn sword to which he had attached a small Prussian flag. At 10 am, after six hours bombardment, a signal rocket went up and six assault columns went over the top, accompanied by the bands playing the *Yorck'scher Marsch*. The nearest redoubt to Piefke was Redoubt Number III, being attacked by his own regiment and other Brandenburg units; the bands continued with another familiar tune, the *Margarethenmarsch*, during which Piefke clearly heard a Danish bullet pass him. As the musicians began a third march, a shell burst on the parapet covering them with earth and stopping the music far better than any conductor could have done, according to Piefke; then they recovered their instruments, cleared the earth out of them and began to play again. As Prussian flags broke over the redoubts, they sounded a fanfare and the Prussian national anthem. By then, Piefke had acceeded to the pleas of the bandsmen and stepped down. Meanwhile, the company musicians – the drummers and buglers – were playing their part. Adalbert Rosenkötter, attacking Redoubt number IV with the 1st Company of Infanterie-Regiment Nr. 53 said "...the drummers and buglers were all beating and blowing like mad and we were all cheering as canister shot crackled away among the ranks and bullets whistled past our heads". The Prussians captured the first six redoubts in thirteen minutes and pressed on to take the second line. By early afternoon it was all over. Piefke's last act that day was to conduct the massed bands in that great hymn *Nun Danket ('Now Thank We All Our God')*. Some days later, King Wilhelm visited his troops; as he arrived at Flensburg Station, Piefke greeted him with a march he had composed before the 18th April and had now entitled *Düppeler Schanzen Sturmmarsch* (*AM II, 186*). It remains one of his best known compositions, though there is no evidence that it was played at the battle. The Official Collection acquired several compositions based on the war; Friedrich Zikoff of the 18th Regiment's *Düppeler Morgenroth* (*AM II,188*) and Carl Walther's *Lundby Marsch* (*AM II,199*) commemorating Infanterie-Regiment Nr. 50's baptism of fire. But Piefke dominated the selection. He produced a victory march (*Siegesmarsch* II, 189) featuring the Prussian national anthem as a counter melody and marches to commemorate the assault on Alsen (*AM II,190*), and the crossing of the Lym Fjord (*Lymfjordströmer AM II,191*). And he put his experiences on 18th April into his *Düppeler Marsch* (*AM II,185*) where a stroke on the bass drum silences all the instruments, except a solo fife, for several bars.[3] On 18th April, King Wilhelm had been reviewing troops in Magdeburg when news of the victory at Düppel arrived. The King immediately told the troops, "I know that you would have done the same if you had been chosen".

Bands in Battle! – The Austro-Prussian War 1866

Just over two years later, the Magdeburg regiments and the rest of the Prussian army had a chance to find out if they were capable, as the simmering hostility between Prussia and Austria boiled over into what was virtually a German civil war. In the campaign that followed, both sides took their bands into action but there is a frustrating lack of evidence as to what they played. At the climactic battle of Königgratz on 3rd July, for example, the advance of the 28th Brigade (Infanterie-Regiment Nr. 17 and Infanterie-Regiment Nr. 57) against the

3 Commemorating the shell which stopped the band music, but how the fifes and drums played on. Ed.

Wilhelm I (1797-1888) King of Prussia from 1861 and German Emperor from 1871 (Eagle & Lyre Picture Archive)

Austrian and Saxon positions near Problus was accompanied by music. The historian, Fritz Hoenig, present as an ensign with Infanterie-Regiment Nr. 57, tells us that the bands of both regiments played during the advance – no mean feat as the advance was made under artillery fire through fields of standing wet rye that left many men soaked from head to foot. The band of Infanterie-Regiment Nr. 57 under Bandmaster Northe continued to play as the regiment advanced up a slope towards the waiting enemy. The mounted officers who (naturally) could see further than the men ordered the band to stop playing, but Northe did not (apparently) hear the order. It took a peremptory "Northe, stop it!" from Colonel von der Osten, and a simultaneous opening volley from the Saxons two-hundred-and-fifty yards away to stop the music. Hönig also tells us that the last march played was the men's favourite one, with pauses in which they were accustomed to shout "*Oh Hannes, what a hat!*" – (or in low German "*O Hannes wat eyn Haut!*"). But he infuriatingly omits to identify the march.[4] There is no mystery, however, about the best known musical incident

4 Since Robert Mantle wrote this article Lt. Col. David Murray has discovered that the 'Oh Hannes wat eyn Haut!' story appears in the memoirs of an officer of the 73rd Hanoverian Fusiliers. The mystery is that the Hanoverians fought against Prussia as Austrian allies in 1866. He nevertheless claimed the story for his own regiment, and related that about the middle of the 19th century the people of Hanover were still nostalgic for the days when Hanover had belonged to the British Crown. Some still affected British fashions in dress. The 73rd were marching through the city one morning when one of the local gentlemen was seen wearing a traditional British morning-dress grey top hat. During a pause in the music one young soldier, seeing the grey top hat, called out 'Oh Hannes, wat en Haut', causing great mirth among the soldiers. It then became a regimental custom that when the band reached the pause in their regimental march, the *Alexandermarsch,* all the soldiers shouted at the top of their voices 'Oh Hannes, wat en Haut!' The author also claimed that the soldiers put it in with the Kaiser's authority, but that Hitler put an end

Heil dir im Siegerkranz: this tune, used today as the British national anthem, together with its German verses, became an unofficial national anthem of Imperial Germany from 1871-1918. Only from 1922 did today's *Deutschlandlied* officially replace it, the tune of which had previously been the Austrian Imperial anthem, *Gott erhalte uns're Kaiser*! – originally *Gott erhalte Franz den Kaiser*. Today, Austria uses a different anthem. There has been much swapping of national anthems over the past two hundred years!

of the day and the war, which involved Gottfried Piefke. Around 1 p.m. the increasingly desperate situation of the Prussian First Army led to the commitment of its final reserve, the Brandenburgers of the 5th and 6th Divisions. As the 5th Division advanced past King Wilhelm and the General Staff, they were led by Leib-Grenadier-Regiment Nr. 8 and their band; Piefke ordered his men to play Joseph Golde's *Preussenmarsch* (*AM II, 119*) based on the Prussian anthem *Heil dir in Siegeskranz* (the same tune as *God Save the Queen*) and August Heinrich Neithardt's patriotic song *Ich bin ein Preusse*. Later the King wrote to his wife "These were anxious times and I wasn't sure how things would turn out. Then Piefke and the Leib-Regiment came past and I suddenly heard our National Anthem, that was an inspiring moment." After all that it seems anticlimactic that the 5th division was hardly engaged, suffering far less than they had at Gitschin four days before, but by now the Prussian Second Army had begun a decisive attack on the Austrian flank. Piefke had time to compose (or more likely rehearse) a new composition which was played to the King that evening. Three encores were demanded and the King told Piefke "I will never forget what you did today". The *Königgratzer Marsch* (*AM II, 195*) immediately entered the Official Collection but it was forbidden to be played on large parades. This was because Piefke had

to it. Such frivolity on parade did not presumably suit Hitler's tastes! Back in 1866 perhaps the men of Prussian regiments which also used the *Alexandermarsch* unofficially copied this bit of Hanoverian fun? (Ed.)

Ich bin ein Preuße – this tune became the unofficial Prussian national anthem or 'Song of Prussia' – the *Preussenlied* by August Neithardt.

used the *Hohenfriedberg Marsch* as his trio, traditionally and wrongly ascribed to Frederick the Great. This commemoration of the battle of Hohenfriedberg in 1745 was by renaming the regimental march, already in use by that time, of the Bayreuth Dragoons, who by 1867 had evolved into the Prussian Kürassier-Regiment Königin (Pommersches) Nr. 2, one of the oldest and most aristocratic units of the army, and they objected to their march being played by anyone else. The musicians also showed that they could act as soldiers. On 28th June, during the battle of Nachod, an Austrian Jäger officer spotted Major General von Ollech, commanding the Prussian 17th Brigade, and directed his men's fire on him. As Ollech fell, hit by two bullets, Sergeant Drummer Braun of the 2nd Battalion of Infanterie-Regiment Nr. 58 snatched a rifle from a soldier and shot the Austrian from the saddle. (Ollech was badly wounded but recovered; Braun received the Military Honour Decoration 1st Class and the fate of the Austrian is unknown.)

The Prussian Victory Parade 1866 – "The Piefkes are coming!"

The Prussian Army never entered Vienna, but on 31st July there was a parade on the Marschfeld at Gänserdorf 25 kilometres north-west of Vienna, and with St Stephen's Cathedral clearly visible on the horizon. That day, King Wilhelm wore the uniform of Leib-Grenadier-Regiment Nr. 8, whose Colonel-in-Chief was always the reigning sovereign – and naturally the band of the regiment led the parade. Fifty thousand men of the First Army passed in review, led by Gottfried Piefke with his band of the Leib-Grenadier-Regiment Nr. 8; beside the Leib-Grenadiere was the band of Infanterie-Regiment Nr. 48 with Rudolf

Max Schneckenburger (1819-1849) author, and Karl Wilhelm (1815-1873) composer, created 19th and early 20th century Germany's most popular patriotic marching song *Die Wacht am Rhein* (Duncan Rogers)

Piefke, Gottfried's younger brother, at their head. Over the past few weeks both men had organised and conducted the music for serenades, concerts, parades, religious services and tattoos and it was fitting that they should be so honoured. Hundreds of people had come from Vienna to see the parade and were surprised to see that it was led by two rather unusual men, one stocky with bush eyebrows, a big moustache and mutton-chop whiskers that Franz Josef himself might have envied, and the other over six-foot tall (1.90m), broad-shouldered with a full beard. The soldiers on crowd duty recognised the two bandmasters, though, and the word spread – "Die Piefkes kommen". The Austrians picked it up; ever since, Prussians in general have been known in Austria and South Germany as 'Piefkes'. The Collection gained relatively few marches from the 1866 war; *AM II,194* and *197* have a direct connection, though Piefke's composition dominates the field. In 1867, however, one of the most popular marches of the past century-and-a-half was added. Ferdinand Radeck's *Fridericus-Rex-Grenadiermarsch* (*AM II, 198*), composed by the bandmaster of Grenadier-Regiment Nr. 6 in Posen and his only well-known composition. It is a march that has been almost impossible to avoid on record, or on the bandstand.

The Military Music competition at the Paris World Exhibition – 1867

One morning in May 1867, the band of the 2.Garde-Regiment zu Fuss were sitting in the back room of the Berlin pub, the 'Alte Dessauer' in the Artillerie Strasse, where they held their rehearsals. Music Director Meinberg was about to begin when the door opened and Wilhelm Wieprecht entered with surprising news – they were going to take part in

The German Kaiser Coronation of the King of Prussia in the Hall of Mirrors, Versailles, 18 January 1871.(Eagle & Lyre Prints Archive)

Waldhornistenkorps – Jäger Bataillon Nr. 5 at the Battle of Sedan – a sketch by Anton Werner (Archive DGfMM eV)

the Military Music competition at the Paris World Exhibition. Most of the other bands competing, Wieprecht told them, were larger than the forty-strong Foot Guards, so they would be combined with the band of the Kaiser Franz-Garde-Grenadier-Regiment under Heinrich Saro. Each competitor would play Weber's *Oberon* overture and a composition of their own choice, "but we'll discuss this later. Good morning, gentlemen". And Wieprecht left while the Guardsmen immediately celebrated. During the first rehearsals, Wieprecht revealed his composition; a fantasia on themes from Meyerbeer's *The Prophet* (once again revealing his vision of the band as a military symphony orchestra). After a two-day journey, the Guardsmen arrived in Paris to a rapturous reception. (They were not the first Prussian band to enter the city in peacetime; the sixty-two strong band of Füsilier-Regiment Nr. 34 under Albert Parlow had carried out a five-week engagement in November 1865.) Three days later, at a rehearsal in the Louvre, Hector Berlioz appeared and renewed his friendship with Wieprecht. Next day, Napoleon III and Empress Eugenie visited them, and finally on Sunday, 21st July came the concert itself in the exhibition hall. There were twenty thousand seats and room for ten-thousand people standing and the hall was sold out. The concert was to last from 1 p.m. to 7 p.m. and the competition included Austria's 73rd Infantry Regiment, the Dutch Guard Grenadiers and Jägers, the Russian Horse Guards under Anton Dörfeldt (junior), and the Paris National guard, plus bands from Baden, Bavaria, Belgium and Spain. The panel of judges was to be led by Rossini but he was ill and did not appear. The order of play was chosen by lot; the (1.Badisches) Leib-Grenadier-Regiment Nr. 109 led off followed by the Spanish 1st Engineer regiment. Then it was the Prussians' turn. When they finished playing Wieprecht's *Fantasia*, there was a brief silence, followed by thunderous applause. It was the same with the Oberon overture. Then it was a matter of waiting. Around 6.50 p.m. the last entry completed their programme and the jury deliberated. The final score was seventeen points to the Austrians, eighteen points to the Paris National Guards and twenty points to the Prussians, and then politics intervened and it was announced that there would be three first prizes! The French Press admired the Prussian Guardsmen's playing and their appearance..."Dieu! Les beaux hommes!". It was

'Iron Chancellor' Prince Otto von Bismarck declares King Wilhelm I of Prussia, 'German Emperor' (*Deutscher Kaiser*) on 18th January 1871 at Versailles. (Eagle & Lyre Picture Archive)

felt that the Austrians played with more delicacy but the Prussians played with more vigour and precision. One reviewer hoped to hear all the bands again – but he never wanted to hear the *Oberon* overture again – ever. Some weeks later, Wieprecht, now a Chevalier of the Legion of Honour, presented the Gold Medal he had won to the King, who immediately returned it: "You have earned this medal, my dear Wieprecht, not I." That day was probably the climax of Wilhelm Wieprecht's career.

The Franco-Prussian War 1870-1871

The final confrontation between France and the North German Confederation and its allies began just under three years later. It soon became clear that this war would be different from its two predecessors. Both sides possessed breech loaders (the French had better ones) and the battlefields were closer to those of 1914. Troops in close formations, (let alone with or without) bands playing them on, would be slaughtered and the Germans learnt this lesson the hard way in Alsace and around Metz. Only their superior artillery and their ability to learn quickly saved them from defeat – plus the complacency and incompetence of the French High Command. In this war we rarely catch a glimpse of the bandsmen and they are usually on the sidelines. On 6th August, Carl Walther conducted the band of the Infanterie-Regiment Nr. 50 in the village of Wörth, playing marches and patriotic airs as the men of the Third Army marched up to the firing line – but he didn't follow them. Even the company musicians had less to do; bugle calls had been discouraged on the battlefield (in 1866, signals intended for one unit were heard and acted on by others). When Trumpeter August Binkebank of Kürassier-Regiment von Seydlitz (Magdeburgisches) Nr.

Georg Goldschmidt was Stabshoboist (Bandmaster) of Grenadier-Regiment König Wilhelm I (2.Westpreussisches) Nr. 7 (Leignitz – raised 1797) from 1858 to 1899. He conducted the band at the Kaiser Coronation at Versailles in 1871 and was subject to the King's correction about the attribution of the Torgauer-Marsch. Uniquely at that time in the Prussian Army his band wore yellow rather than white collar Litzen, which meant that the Spielleute of their three battalions wore yellow rather than white lace on their swallowsnests. The only other Prussian regiment ever to wear yellow Litzen and thus yellow Spielleute lace was the later 1897 raised 5.Garde-Grenadier Regiment in Spandau. (Archive DGfMM eV)

7 sounded the '*Rally*' as the remnants of his regiment and the Ulanen-Regiment Hennigs von Treffenfeld (Altmärkisches) Nr. 16 regrouped after their charge at Vionville, the result was a blood-curdling shriek – a bullet had passed through the bell of the trumpet. It could almost be seen as an omen – and yet there was a last glimmer of the old tradition on 30th October, when the Second Prussian Guards Division moved out to recapture the village of Le Bourget. Two months before, the Guard Corps had stormed Saint Privat and been more than decimated as they advanced up the slope in close formation. This time, things would be different; the Guardsmen used fire and movement tactics, half a unit keeping the defenders' heads down while the other half advanced in short rushes. They gained the edge of the village without serious loss and were no longer outranged by the French. As a vicious house-to-house struggle began, the band of the Königin Elisabeth Garde-Grenadier-Regiment Nr. 3, led by Bandmaster Eduard Ruscheweyh, doubled forward over the fields, found a spot on the northern edge of the village that was sheltered from fire and began to play. (One of their marches was Johann Walch's *Pariser Einzugsmarsch* of 1814 (*AM II, 38*)). Soon afterwards, a group of French bandsmen, captured in the village, were marched

past; they cheered and took off their caps: "That's the way to make war!" one shouted. The authorities agreed – Ruscheweyh was awarded the Iron Cross Second Class. (On the same day, Drummer Friedrich Wilhelm Bümsen of No. 1 Company, Kaiser Alexander Garde-Grenadier Regiment Nr.1, won the Iron Cross leading his company to the attack whilst beating the *Sturmmarsch*. ('The Drummer of Le Bourget' became famous throughout Germany.)

Military Music at the 'Kaiser-Coronation' – Versailles 1871

The Kingdom of Prussia was founded on 18th January 1701. One hundred and seventy years later, the Second German Empire was proclaimed at Versailles. A grandiose ceremony had been organised – a military choir sang a setting of Psalm 66 ("Make a joyful noise unto God, all ye lands") while the bands of the Grenadier-Regiment König Wilhelm I (2.Westpreussisches) Nr. 7 and Infanterie-Regiment Nr. 47 and Infanterie-Regiment Nr. 58 provided music. The Crown Prince of Prussia had ordered that as the dignitaries left the ceremony, the massed bands were to play the Hohenfriedberg March (the Kürassier-Regiment Königin (Pommersches) Nr. 2, campaigning on the Loire, were in no position to object). The new Emperor, however, was in a bad mood. Unlike his son, he had no desire to be more than a King of Prussia, and the day before the ceremony he had burst into tears and told his chief minister: "Tomorrow will be the unhappiest day of my life. We are burying the Kingdom of Prussia and you, Prince Bismarck, are responsible." That evening, the Grenadier-Regiment König Wilhelm I (2.Westpreussisches) Nr. 7, directed by Georg Goldschmidt, played for their Colonel-in-Chief during dinner at the Prefecture of Versailles. Goldschmidt had included a march that was a personal favourite of the Royal Family (although it would not be included in the official collection until 1891). In the programme, Goldschmidt credited the *Torgauer Marsch* to Frederick the Great assuming a connection with the Battle of Torgau in 1760 and, after all, it was a dignified slow march of the style popular in the eighteenth century. Afterwards, the Emperor, programme in hand, walked over to him: "My dear Goldschmidt, you have said that the *Torgauer Marsch* was composed by His Majesty the Great King, but that's wrong. My beloved father brought the score back from Torgau in 1817 and it was composed by a teacher there, named Scholz. Please tell your colleagues!" Weeks later, France capitulated. The Germans occupied Paris for one day as the French desperately raised the money for the indemnity. Before the troops marched into the city there was a parade on Longchamp racecourse where Napoleon III's army had so often passed in review. As Emperor Wilhelm rode on to the field, the massed trumpeters of the 1st Guards Field Artillery Regiment played *Ich bin ein Preusse*. It is recorded that Wilhelm I smiled broadly.

The new German Empire – Prussia's Glory!

Gottfried Piefke had accompanied his regiment on campaign despite being over fifty-five. He fell ill during the siege of Metz and was evacuated back to their garrison in Frankfurt-an-der-Oder. None of his compositions from this period – the *Spicherer Siegesmarch*, the *Siegesmarsch von Metz* (which incorporates *Die Wacht am Rhein*), the *Neuer Pariser Einzugsmarsch* or the *Kaiser-Wilhelm Siegesmarch* – were included in the official collection, but he continued to compose, and as the troops returned home, he rehearsed a march that would welcome the Leib-Grenadiers back to an ecstatic Frankfurt, bedecked with the black-white-red horizontal tricolours of the new German Empire. The regiment would continue to play it after Piefke died – still on duty – in 1884, but it then fell into obscurity, until a former officer of the regiment, now commanding the 3.Garde-Regiment zu Fuss, sent for the score and had it played at the Guard Changing ceremony at the Palace in Berlin in 1912. For the moment this was all in the future, and in 1871 while his band and the other three battalion fife and drum corps of the regiment were still making their way home from France, Gottfried Piefke was rehearsing the march with the help of the small wind band created from the fifes and drums of the regiment's depôt training companies. He had decided to call it *Preussens Gloria...... Prussia's Glory!*

2

The Royal Prussian Army March Collection

The Original Quick Marches from Imperial Russia in 1817 (AM II, 1 to AM II, 36)

by Robert Mantle

The original 36 marches were selected from the Russian collection; in many cases, little or nothing is known about their composers or date of composition. As the vast majority fell out of use within a few years, these notes are brief. During the 1980s, Joachim Toeche-Mittler's researches revealed that several marches had been incorrectly attributed. Now that the Russian archives are (relatively) open to research, we may learn more.

AM II, 1 Marsch by Friedrich Sazenhofen
Now known to be Anton Dörfeldt's *Geschwindmarsch Nr 1* composed 1809/1810.

AM II, 2 Russischer Marsch (Pausenmarsch)
Now known to be by Dörfeldt – this was No. II, 6 in the Russian collection. There are eleven 'pauses'.

AM II, 3 Russischer Marsch
Another Dorfeldt composition, *Geschwindmarsch Nr 5* of 1809.

AM II, 4 Russischer Marsch

AM II, 5 Russischer Marsch
Number II, 12 in the Russian collection.

AM II, 6 Marsch by Klopow
Nothing is known of the composer, apart from his name on the score.

AM II, 7 Russischer Marsch

AM II, 8 Russischer Marsch
This attractive march was No. II,16 in the Russian collection and dates from before 1810. When it was first recorded in the 1970s it was incorrectly identified as the *Pausenmarsch.*

AM II, 9 Marsch by Francois Adrien Boieldieu (1775-1834)
The composer worked in St Petersburg between 1803 and 1810; this delightful march dates

from that time. In the Russian collection it was II, 17.

AM II, 10 Marsch by Charlotte Elisabeth Freiin von Stackelberg

Another incorrect attribution – this is Dörfeldt's *Ecossaise* from 1809-1910.

AM II, 11 Marsch aus der Ballett »Les Amours de Venus«, Andre Campara

Andre Campara (1660-1744) composed this ballet in 1712. It was successfully revived in St. Petersburg in 1813 and inspired several marches, three of which became part of the Russian and later Prussian collections.

AM II, 12 Marsch by Catterino Cavos, arranged by Anton Dörfeldt

Cavos (1775-1840) was a Venetian who arrived in St. Petersburg in 1798 and stayed. Among his achievements was the founding of the National Opera. This was II, 22 in the Russian collection.

AM II, 13 Marsch, by Catterino Cavos, arranged by Anton Dörfeldt

AM II, 14 Marsch des Sibirischen Grenadier Regiments

A Russian regimental march from the 18th century, which later became the regimental march of the Grenadier-Regiment Nr. 1 in Königsberg in East Prussia – one of the few marches from this period which was still being played a hundred and fifty years later. See AM II, 237 for a later arrangement.

AM II, 15 Marsch by Anton Dörfeldt

AM II, 16 Marsch aus dem Ballett »Les Amours de Venus« by Andre Campara arranged by Catterino Cavos

AM II, 17 Marsch nach Motiven der Oper »Der Wasserträger« by Luigi Cherubini.

Cherubini's opera *Les Deux Journées* (known on the German stage as *Der Wasserträger*) was premiered in Paris in 1800 and popular throughout Europe. This is the first march in the collection based on themes from an opera; it deserves a wider hearing.

AM II, 18 Marsch by Catterino Cavos arranged by Anton Dörfeldt

AM II, 19 Marsch des Russischen Grenadier Regiments König von Preussen by Anton Dörfeldt

King Friedrich Wilhelm III became Colonel-in-Chief of the St. Petersburg Grenadier Regiment on 7th October 1814. This march was number II, 35 in the Russian collection; the more familiar march of this regiment (AM II, 123) dates from 1840.

AM II, 20 Marsch by Anton Dörfeldt

AM II, 21 Marsch by Anton Dörfeldt

Number II/37 in the Russian collection, composed 1813-1814.

AM II, 22 Marsch by Anton Dörfeldt

AM II, 23 Marsch des Fanagorijski Grenadier Regiments

Two examples of a concert march, with changes of tempo guaranteed to throw any marching regiment out of step!

AM II, 24 Marsch aus der Oper »Aschenbrödel« by Nicolo Isouard

Isouard 1775-1818 was a popular French composer. His comic opera *Condrillon* was premiered in Paris in 1810 and Isouard arranged six marches on themes from it. They were published in 1815 and the Russian Army took copies back to St Petersburg where Dörfeldt added this one to the Russian collection as II, 48. And, *Aschenbrödel* is the German for *Cinderella.*

AM II, 25 Marsch des Russischen Grenadier Regiments König von Preussen by Catterino Cavos

Another march for the St Petersburg Grenadiers – in the Russian collection this was number II, 50.

AM II, 26 Marsch by Anton Dörfeldt

AM II, 27 Marsch by Anton Dörfeldt

AM II, 28 Pariser Einzugsmarsch (1815) arranged by Anton Dörfeldt

A Russian march which was II, 55 in their collection. The composer is unknown but the march includes themes from Gretry's opera *Lucille* which appeared in 1769. In 1869 Wilhelm Wieprecht made a new arrangement which suggests it was still in the repertoire alongside the better known AM II, 38.

AM II, 29 Marsch nach Motiven der Oper »Johann von Paris« by François Adrien Boieldieu, march by Anton Dörfeldt

Boieldieu's opera, a comedy based on disguises, was premiered in 1812 and inspired Dörfeldt to write one of his best marches.

AM II, 30 Marsch by Francois Devienne, arranged by Anton Dörfeldt

Devienne (1759-1803) was a flute virtuoso and later Professor at the Paris Conservatoire.

AM II, 31 Marsch by Daniel Steibelt arranged by Anton Dörfeldt

Steibelt was an excellent pianist with a chaotic personal life who moved to St. Petersburg in 1809 and became Director of the French Opera there two years later.

***AM II, 32 Marsch der Russischen Reserve-Artillerie (1815)* by Anton Dörfeldt**

***AM II, 33 Marsch* by Anton Dörfeldt**

***AM II, 34 Marsch* by Ferdinardo Paer arranged by Anton Dörfeldt**
Paer (1771-1839) was Director of the Paris Opera between 1812 and 1827.

***AM II, 35 Marsch* by Anton Dörfeldt**

***AM II, 36 Marsch nach Motiven der Oper* »Die Vestalin«, Opera by Gasparo Spontini, March by Anton Dörfeldt**
Spontini's grand operas dominated the first quarter of the nineteenth century *La Vestale* (*The Vestal Virgin*) was his first great success. It appeared in 1807 and inspired a large number of marches.

3

The Royal Prussian Army March Collection 1817-1918

Volume II Quick Marches (AM II, 37 to AM II, 244)

by Oberstleutnant der Luftwaffe Joachim Toeche-Mittler
Translation by Antony Dean

AM II, 37 Marsch des Yorckschen Korps (1813) by Ludwig van Beethoven

This march belongs to the most-used and most famous of all Prussian Army Marches. It comes from Vienna. It was written there by Ludwig van Beethoven (1717-1827) in the year 1809 with a dedication to Erzherzog Anton von Österreich (Grand Duke Antony of Austria). Later, above the score for the piece was written "...for the Bohemian Landwehr". It is one of the first marches ever to have been written in the new quick march pace (Geschwindschritt), which Beethoven indicates clearly on his original score. For this and his other marches Beethoven never used a publisher. It first became widely known with its use by the Prussian General von Yorck.[1] King Friedrich Wilhelm III took the piece in 1817 as the first march of his own choice (after the gift of the first thirty-six from the Tsar) in the Army March Collection with the number 37. It was the time when the Russians and Prussians were brothers in arms against Napoleon, and Alexander I, Tsar of 'All the Russias', was keen to help rebuild the plundered Kingdom of Prussia, and the March Books were but one of his many gifts. The publishing rights for this new 'Prussian' collection were given to Musikverlag Schlesinger (today Lienau) in Berlin. The added trio, Beethoven wrote much later, and it never officially became part of the Army March. Prussian Jäger battalions also played this piece as their Parademarsch (Parade March in Quick Time), for which it is especially beautifully arranged for their mellow French Horn-dominated ensembles.

AM II, 38 Pariser Einzugsmarsch (1814) by Johann Heinrich Walch

Johann Heinrich Walch (1776-1855) was head of chamber and choral music at the Court of the Dukes of Saxe-Gotha in Thuringia.This piece was already composed by 1813, but the following year was played in the old normal (slow) pace of 75 to the minute by bands of the Russian, Austrian and Prussian armies for their 'Entry into Paris' after the first total

---

1 Feldmarschall Yorck von Wartenburg was second in command of the Prussian Corps requisitioned for the campaign in Russia by Napoleon in 1812. He took his troops over to the side of the Tsar and began the War of Liberation against Napoleon. It ended with the joint Anglo-Prussian victory at Waterloo 1815. The march is the first of two marches in F Major by Ludwig van Beethoven (1770-1827) it was composed in 1809 as *Zapfenstreichmarsch Nr.1* and since 1813 has been known in Germany as the *Marsch des Yorck'schen Korps*. It is always played when German troops, with torches ablaze, join parade for Grand-Tattoo at night. Ed.

Joachim Toeche-Mittler

defeat of Bonaparte in 1814. It is still known in all three countries. In Prussia the tempo was increased first to 108 in 1817, then to 112 in 1867, and finally to 114 in 1888. This, in reality, transformed the march from quick time to virtually a trot. Played at breakneck speed, double the old time of 75, it became the General Salute (Präsentiermarsch) of the new Luftwaffe from 1935. Other than this, although the march remained in Volume II of Quick Marches for Infantry, in reality it became a trot march used by cavalry with fanfare trumpet parts added. Johann Heinrich Walch is famous in Swedish military music for his stunningly beautiful Swedish Long Reveille, *Svenska arméns revelj* and Swedish Grand Tattoo, *Svenska arméns tapto.*

AM II, 39 Marsch nach Motiven der Oper »Die Vestalin« by Gasparo Spontini

One of many marches made from *Die Vestalin*! Not the only thing the Prussians got from Spontini though! There are twelve Spontini marches in the Army March Collection, of which four are with themes from *Vestalin*. The wonderful music is from the Napoleonic War years, which gave rise to the most able musicians being in military service. The arranger of this march is unknown.

AM II, 40 Marsch nach Motiven der Oper »Ferdinand Cortez« – Opera by Gasparo Spontini – March by Anton Dörfeldt

The original manuscript of 1819 is marked that this quick march was played by the Imperial Russian Semenowski Guard Regiment as they entered Paris in 1814. That was after the heavy fighting against Napoleon since 1813 when the allied armies of Russia, Austria and

Prussia had finally triumphed and overthrown the French invader. The opera *Ferdinand Cortez* had had its premiere in 1809 in Paris. It was immediately famous throughout Europe and also in St Petersburg, where not only the French composer Boieldieu worked, but also many other foreigners. The themes from the opera are so clearly assembled here, and with its practical instrumentation, that the piece is certainly by Anton Dörfeldt who from 1809 was responsible for Russian march music, and who had already made three marches from the operas of Mozart. It was also a happy incidence when military bands abroad could play pieces honouring composers from the country they were then in. In this vein, it was possible to play Spontini in France, as one had a repertoire of compositions by him. From 1869 the Wieprecht arrangement is normal for enlarged band. The original was a gift to King Friedrich Wilhelm III from his son-in-law the Grand-Prince Nicholas of Russia in 1819.

AM II, 41 Wiener (Alexander) Marsch (1814) by Louis-sur Loiseau de Persius

After the defeat of Napoleon, the Princes and States of Europe met at the Congress of Vienna in 1814/15 to decide the future shape of Europe. Whilst there, the Russian Tsar Alexander (1777-1825), in conversation with other monarchs and princes, declared it to be his favourite 'most-beloved' march, indeed he called it his 'Favoritenmarsch' or 'Lieblingsmarsch'. At his particular request it was played and entered many march books and march score collections until this very day – as follows:

1816 in the Imperial Russian Army
1819 in the Royal Prussian Army Collection
1871 in a new arrangement by Wieprecht, listed as Nr 16 in his work
1901 in von Freymann's 'Russian March Collection' as Nr. 120
1914 in Prussia's first edition Marschheft (1. Folge)
1961 in Volume II of the Bundeswehr's march book as Nr. 105

As one of the very first available Geschwindmärsche (Quick marches) the piece was played frequently. Tsar Alexander visited his Prussian 'Kaiser Alexander Grenadier-Regiment' in Berlin, or his Hungarian 'Infanterie-Regiment Alexander, Kaiser von Russland' in Vienna, being Honorary Royal Colonel of both these foreign regiments, it was the royal diplomatic practice in Imperial Europe to parade with them and they performed concerts for him using this march.[2]

The composer is Louis-sur Loiseau de Persius (1769-1819), a French violonist, choir and opera director in Paris. The piece appeared in 1812 in his ballet *Der blöde Ritter* (*'The Imbecilic Knight'*). Tsar Alexander had seen it at the Paris Opera in 1814 and asked if he might take a copy of the score with him back to St Petersburg. It appeared later with an added trio. Until 1914 the march was in constant use. However, after 1921 (with the establishment of the Weimar Republican Reichswehr, the Bolshevik Red Army in Russia, and the collapse and fragmentation of the Austro-Hungarian Empire) the march was no longer pertinent to the age, and its use declined, but it did not disappear altogether.

2 It was commonplace for foreign royals to be made Honorary Colonels of Regiments in each other's armies. Seeing a foreign sovereign or Prince at a Royal Birthday Parade or equivalent event was quite normal, a tradition which can still be seen in modern times as Grand Duke Michael of Luxembourg paraded in full dress on horseback behind HM The Queen at Trooping the Colour each year in the 1990s, as honorary Royal Colonel of the Irish Guards. Ed.

AM II, 42 Marsch des Collardo by Hieronymus de Colloredo

The Colloredos hail from the countryside district of Friuli in northern Italy (formerly the Austrian district of Friaul). They were the very epitome of Austrian nobility of the 18th and 19th centuries; they were worthies in both the church and the military; an Archbishop of Salzburg, to whom Mozart dedicated his *Colloredo Serenade*, a Fieldmarshal, for whose regiment Joseph Haydn wrote a march. This march came into the Army March Collection in 1819. Such a light, moving melody could only be of Austrian 18th/19th century origin. It was never a widely-used piece.

AM II, 43 Marsch Matadura

A practical piece for drilling. It is not Russian but comes from Spain. It is very short – two sets of four bars repeated. So it can be repeated again, and remains clearly in the ears and the legs! It is exactly what was needed in 1819 for training men in the new Geschwindschritt (Quick pace) of the new Geschwindmarsch (Quick march) which was replacing the old slow time in practical use at this time. The certain and sure beat ensured the pace was kept when the band was helping in the training.

AM II, 44 Marsch nach Motiven des Balletts »Zephyr und Flora« – Opera by Catterino Cavos – March by Wilhelm Nolte

After the victory over Napoleon and his banishment to the Isle of Elba in 1814, the Prussian army was fundamentally re-organized. There were many who fought all through the wars who wanted to enjoy the peace. In the Guards in Berlin in October 1814, two new Grenadier regiments were created from the battle-proven Grenadier battalions of different provinces after the release of their reserves. The second of these new Grenadier regiments had the Austrian Emperor, Kaiser Franz, as its Royal Colonel and was named after him in his honour. The first thing to do was build a new regimental band, a job which the Commander of the Kaiser Franz Grenadier-Regiment gave to bandsman Wilhelm Nolte. Nolte was born in Lützensömmern (25km NNW of Erfurt) in 1772, and in 1803 became a bandsman (Hoboist) in the Prussian regiment of the Duke of Brunswick-Oels, with whom he fought in the War of Liberation. In 1814 he was called to be bandmaster of the newly-raised Kaiser Franz Grenadier-Regiment in Berlin, with a strength of three sergeants (Feldwebel) and 18 bandsmen (Hoboisten). Nolte composed and arranged much military music, amongst which was a topical suite *Die Schlacht bei Leipzig*, the Battle of Leipzig. The band he left his successor, Neithardt, in 1822, was outstanding.

AM II, 45 Marsch aus Warschau

In the year 1819, this nice piece came into our Army March collection from Congress Poland. Poland belonged at that time to Russia, and to the great joy of Tsar Alexander I he had inherited, in 1815, a complete Polish standing army. As Governor, Grand Prince Konstantin, the Tsar's brother, resided in Warsaw. With him he had Ferdinand Haase, a German from Prussian Silesia, who had become a prisoner of war of the Russians during the 1812 retreat from Moscow by Napoleon, his musical ability though being appreciated by the Grand Prince. (Prussia, anyway, had changed sides in 1813.) Grand Prince Konstantin (1779-1831) gave his prodigy, Haase, a solid musical further education by sending him to be trained in St Petersburg, and then appointed him as Chief Military Kapellmeister in Warsaw. Later, Haase became Dörfeldt's successor in St Petersburg as Chief Kapellmeister to the Imperial Russian Guard Corps. It is perhaps Haase who wrote this march and made it known in neighbouring Prussia. Marches at this time were mostly without a title. This was known at the time simply as *Polnischer Geschwindmarsch Warschau* or *Polnischer Marsch*.

AM II, 45a Sedan-Marsch by Carl Lange

The name of this march refers to the City of Sedan, but not from 1870 when Napoleon III capitulated there, but from the year 1818 when as part of the allied occupation of France after the fall of Napoleon I, the Prussian Grenadier-Regiment Nr. 7 was stationed there in occupation. The composer was the regiment's bandmaster. Carl Lange (1787-1857) had been a bandsman in the War of Liberation against Napoleon's dictatorship in 1813-15. In 1817 he became a bandmaster. The Headquarters of the Prussian 'Army Corps in France' was in Sedan. The Prussian king's second son was the Honorary Colonel of the regiment, and this march was dedicated to him. He later became Kaiser Wilhelm I. He rode at the head of the regiment when it came home in 1818 to Glogau in Silesia, entering the town to the strains of this march, the regiment gaining the title of the 'King's Grenadiers' (*Königsgrenadiere*) at the same time. In 1882 the Honorary Colonel, still the same Wilhelm, but now Kaiser and King of Prussia himself, backdated the entry of this march into the Collection – thus its number.

AM II, 46 Marsch nach Motiven der Oper »Ferdinand Cortez« – Opera by Gasparo Spontini – March by Carl Wagner

Carl Wagner was solo-cellist and French horn player at the Court of Landgrave Ludwig IX of Hesse from 1788. Upon Ludwig IX's death in 1790, his successor Grand Duke Ludwig I appointed Wagner to be Bandmaster (Stabshautboist) of the twenty-eight musicians and one Schellenbaum carrier who made up the band of the Hessian Leibgarde zu Fuss, Life-Regiment of Foot (later in Imperial Germany named the Leibgarde-Infanterie-Regiment Nr. 115) in Darmstadt. Wagner went to war with them first against Revolutionary France, and then allied with France under Napoleon. Carl Wagner (1771-1822), a native of Darmstadt, continued to provide Court music with his band, and after he left military service on 24th September 1811, he became Court Director of Music and Civilian Director of Army Music (Ober-Militär-Musik-Direktor). This march is from 1818, based on Spontini's Opera which had its premiere in 1809. In 1869, Wieprecht rearranged the march for use by modern band instrumentation.

AM II, 46a Marsch nach Motiven der Oper »Ferdinand Cortez« – Opera by Gasparo Spontini – March by Schaller

For twenty-five years after the end of the War of Liberation (1813-1815) we know that the Generalmusikdirektor in Berlin was Spontini, and that his music in Prussia was beyond praise. It was with this background that this march appeared. The long-famous themes from the 1809 appearing opera *Ferdinand Cortez* could always be used to come up with something new. Whether it be arrangements for piano or full orchestra. The personal details of the arranger of this march are unknown, but it was not composed after 1846 when it entered the Army March Collection, where there were already three marches with motifs from this opera.

AM II, 47 Marsch aus dem Ballet »Die vier Freier« by Constant Telle

The ballet *Die vier Freier* appeared in 1817. In the following seven years it was performed fifteen times in Berlin. The Burgers desired diversions through ballets and little operas after the hard years of French occupation. In military circles the new Quick Pace had been introduced, for which there were further marches needed. So, these friendly, popular ballet melodies had already provided one by 1819. Constant Telle (c. 1775-1846) worked as a ballet musician at the Berlin Opera and alongside his ballet composition arranged a related march composition.

AM II, 48 La Castiglione

The Italian title means 'A Little Castle'. We have here a good, true piece for use by the troops. Such a harmless, uncomplicated composition is just what is needed to hearten when on the march or when drilling, with its cheerful notes. In the trio, the soldiers found particular amusement. (and doubtless had doggerel words to it! Ed.) In 1819 the piece entered the AM collection. Who recommended it to the Prussian king? For official parades or as a Regimental Quick March it was not used!

AM II, 49 Marsch Brought back from St Petersburg by Prince Carl of Prussia (1801-1883) in June 1820.

When visiting his sister, Charlotte, who, since 1817 had been married to Grand Duke Nicholas of Russia, Prince Carl, from his bedroom window, heard the Mounted Band of the Imperial Russian Life Guard Hussars play this march. He was so struck by it that he wrote to Berlin mentioning it, found the score and later brought it back to Berlin. The same year it became a Prussian Army March. It is more of a concert piece than one in service use by troops. However, in Russia by 1900 it appears to have been forgotten as it does not appear in the 1900 book of Imperial Russian Regimental Marches.

AM II, 50 Marsch A gift from Troppau brought by Grand-Prince Nicholas of Russia in 1820

On 20 October 1820 there took place on the border between Austria and Prussian Silesia at Troppau a further Congress of Princes as part of the Holy Alliance organized by Prince Metternich of Austria. In December, the brother of the Tsar, Grand-Prince Nicholas of Russia, took part in the meeting. On the return journey, he stayed in Berlin with his father-in-law, the Prussian King Friedrich Wilhelm III, and brought this piece from Troppau for his March Collection. It became an Army March immediately. The rich melody is unmistakeably Bohemian.

AM II, 51 Marsch Brought back from Italy by Prince Carl of Prussia

Prince Carl of Prussia (1801-1883) the third son of the Prussian King Friedrich Wilhelm III and Queen Luise, at the behest of his father in 1822, attended the Princes' congress in Verona, and thereafter took a tour of Italy to Milan, Venice, Rome, Naples and finally Florence. With ever-open eyes and ears, the 'Prince of Art and Culture' had spotted this good march to take back for his own Prussian Grenadier-Regiment Nr. 12 in Frankfurt-on-Oder. It was actually an Austrian march, as at that time large parts of Italy were Austrian and Austrian regiments were stationed all over the country. His father immediately accepted the piece, along with four others brought back from his journey.

AM II, 52 Marsch des Hannoverschen Garde Grenadier Regiments (1821)

The short, stylish piece from the year 1821 is a Quick march with music from the earliest times. From 1820 on, there was a Grenadier Guard Regiment in Hanover, which from 1838 was known simply as the Garde-Regiment. The King of Hanover was then in personal union also King of Great Britain. Therefore this march is also known in England, where, as *The British Grenadiers*, it is often played today, although in a somewhat different arrangement. When in 1900 the regimental marches of the former Kingdom of Hanover were taken into the Prussian Army March Collection the piece, as one of eight, came in for a second time as AM II, 227. It was, however, not frequently played in Germany.

AM II, 53 Marsch aus Schweden

In 1822 King Friedrich Wilhelm III visited Sweden and perhaps heard this march then? We do not know for certain. In Sweden this march is long lost and totally forgotten. The composer is unknown.

AM II, 54 Marsch nach Motiven der Oper »Die Vestalin« – Opera by Gasparo Spontini – March by Wilhelm Nolte

We have two Army Marches from Nolte, AM II, 44 of 1819 and this one, the original version from 1822. Both pieces are of a great quality and can be used in both slow and quick time. Quick march-pasts were quickly over, and the old fundamental drill, the 'Erziehungs-Fundament' of slow time they did not want to lose, and so it became the custom to march past in both slow and quick time. This piece too had no change of key for the trio and therefore the then natural trumpets could play along with it. A Spontini theme is the basis of this march, the opera *Die Vestalin* having appeared much earlier in 1807. However, since 1820, Spontini was Generalmusikdirektor at the Court and in Berlin where the population held him in high regard. This march begins with four powerful introductory bars, the lively motif weaving its way through, in the second section reinforced in unison, and then a tuneful, swinging trio with a hard close tacked on the end.[3]

AM II, 55 Marsch des Österreichischen Infanterie Regiments 22 Prinz Leopold beider Sizilien

In 1822, two sons of the Prussian King Friedrich Wilhelm III, the Princes William and Carl journeyed to Verona for a congress of European monarchs. Graf Redern was the organiser and companion for the journey, which extended to visits to Venice, Rome and Naples. Graf Redern, famous as Berlin's 'musical Count' encouraged the Princes to collect marches and other pieces of music for their royal Father's collection in Berlin. Prince Carl heard this march played by the 22nd Austrian Infantry Regiment, who had marched to Verona from their garrison town of Mantua, 40km to the south. At that time, this part of Italy belonged to the Austrian Empire. In addition to this march, the Prussian king put three further Austrian regimental marches, heard by the Princes later in Naples, into his Army March Collection.

3 For Wilhelm Nolte's biography see *AM II, 44*

AM II, 56 Marsch des Österreichischen Infanterie Regiments 52 Erzherzog Franz Carl *&* *AM II, 57 Marsch des Österreichischen Infanterie Regiments 51 von Meczery*

In 1822 the Prussian king and his two sons Wilhelm and Carl toured Italy, collecting the scores for marches as they went. In Naples the King heard these two marches played by visiting bands from the Austro-Hungarian Empire. They were from the 52nd and 51st (Hungarian) Regiments respectively. In 1824 the pieces were arranged by G.A. Schneider in Berlin and placed in the AM collection. Wieprecht rearranged them in 1869. They remained in the march books of German Bandsmen until 1945. In Austria they can still be heard today, known as the *Erzherzog Carl-Marsch* and *Splényi-Marsch* respectively (the second named after Feldmarschall-Leutnant Gabriel Freiherr Splényi de Miháldy, Proprietor-Colonel of the 51st (Hungarian) Regiment from 1788-1822). In Austria the rather different arrangement is by Emil Kaiser (1853-1929) who was responsible for the Austro-Hungarian Imperial War Ministry's *Practical march book* of 1895, which contains forty-seven marches with parts scored for twenty-three different instruments.

AM II, 58 Marsch nach Motiven der Oper »Moses« by Gioacchino Rossini

The genial Italian opera composer Gioacchino Rossini (1792-1868) had his greatest era in the Twenties of the 19th century. His opera *William Tell* appeared in 1829, and already by the following year (1830) had had a trot march with motifs from it made into a Prussian Army March (*AM III, 19*). Rossini's opera *Moses* of 1818 had its German premiere in 1823 in Munich, and already in the same year the Infanterie-Leib-Regiment (The King of Bavaria's Household Infantry Regiment) paraded to it. It was possibly arranged by their Regimental Bandmaster Widder. The Prussian Crown Prince (later Friedrich Wilhelm IV) was there at the time, and fell for the piece. He asked if he might take the score with him, and in the next year (1824) it became an Army March in Prussia number *AM II, 58*. Good music travels fast. The easygoing melody, simple in construction, is in two sections plus a trio, all of sixteen bars with a further four bars for the trio. In the second section is the principal motif (the recitative and duet of Ossiride and Elcia) from the first act of the opera. The piece is especially suited to parades. The Haupt-Kadettenanstalt (the Central Cadet School) took it till 1919, the 1.Garde-Regiment zu Fuss (EGRzF: First Foot Guards) for parading in 'Regimentskolonne' and many others. It appeared in all piano albums. Wieprecht rewrote it for new instrumentation in 1871. The Hanoverian Jäger-Bataillon Nr. 10 in Goslar had the march bestowed on them as their Regimental Quick March. In 1900 it was the most played march, especially for marching past in 'Regimentskolonne'. In 1914 it came via Marschbuch 1.Folge to all military bands, and in 1961 in volume II to the Bundeswehr.

AM II 59 Marsch des Leib-Garde Wolynski Regiments by Ferdinand Haase arranged by Friedrich Weller

Of this wonderful piece there is so much to say it is difficult to know where to begin. We must notice first of all the construction, melody and instrumentation as it appears in the Army March Collection. And we must understand the age when such a sound came forth which despite being almost two hundred years ago still bewitches us today. Not only Oratorios, Symphonies or Lieder have their history and beauty, but also marches.

On 12th June 1817, the nineteen-year-old daughter of the Prussian king, Charlotte, began her journey from Berlin into strange Russia for her betrothal with the twenty-one-year-old Grand-Prince Nicholas in St Petersburg. The entire Prussian Royal Family accompanied her on the first part her journey, as far as Freienwalde, and the twenty-year-old Prince Wilhelm, the later Kaiser Wilhelm I, chose to accompany her the whole way to her new home. Once there he stayed for many months. It was not until January 1818, in the middle of the Russian winter, that the Prince made his way home via Smolensk. In Warsaw, he stayed with the elder brother of his new relations (by virtue of his sister's marriage), with the Grand-Prince Konstantin, who was Governor of the Kingdom of Poland (on behalf of the Tsar, who was also King of Poland by this time). It was here that the Russian Life Guard Wolynski Infantry Regiment had been raised two years before. It paraded from the start to this march. The composition originated from Ferdinand Haase, a young German from Silesia, who, based in Warsaw, was responsible for military music. Prince Wilhelm requested that he might take back the score for this beautiful piece with him, and just as he had brought back marches for the Prussian King from Italy in 1822 and 1824 so he wanted to do with this piece. The Berlin music publishers Adolph Martin Schlesinger published the score. It is an arrangement from the Bandmaster of the 2.Garde-Regiment zu Fuss in Berlin, Friedrich Weller (1790-1870), an outstanding personality, who had already been in charge of his band for ten years by this time. The arrangement is true to the original in that it retains the two-part flute melody which becomes three-part with the clarinet in a purposeful change, the trumpets with their natural tones overlay this intermittently or on the off beat. It is a full orchestral arrangement of around thirty musicians. The parts became available to all Prussian bands in 1824. In 1900, the piece was re-published in a four-volume set of conductors' scores of Russian Salute Marches. In Prussia in 1869, Wilhelm Wieprecht, at the command of his King who had brought back the piece almost fifty years before from Warsaw, wrote a new central conductors' score arranged for Infantry, Jäger and cavalry bands.

AM II, 60 Marsch aus dem Ballett »Das Schweizer Milchmädchen« by Adalbert Gyrowetz arranged by Carl Friedrich Seelicke

The Austrian piano virtuoso Gyrowetz (born 1763 Budweis in Bohemia – died 1850) in Vienna) was a much-loved and multi-talented composer. His forty-five ballets, alone, are a great achievement. This ballet, from 1821, we know elsewhere from Army March III, 9 (for cavalry). This, however, is a brisk 6/8 march for infantry. But in this arrangement, too, the stylish trumpet parts remind us of a gallop march in brass instrumentation, without which the character of the piece would be lost. Prussian King Friedrich Wilhelm III had heard this march in 1822 when on his Italian tour in Naples; he fell for the piece and asked to be able to take the music back with him. At home, bandmaster of the Grand Duchy of Mecklenburg's Grenadier-Garde-Bataillon, Friedrich Seelicke was made responsible for creating the instrumentation for infantry band. It was arranged anew by Wieprecht in 1869 for the expanded bands that had developed in the intervening years. The new scoring gave alternatives for infantry, Jäger and cavalry bands. Now it really could also be played by mounted troops as a gallop march.

This cover of a selection of patriotic Fatherland Songs and Army Marches arranged for pianoforte depicts the Bismarck tricolour of black-white-red and an Iron Cross of 1914. Other than the different date of issue the Iron Cross design remains identical to that awarded to Bocklet in 1813. (Eagle & Lyre Archive)

AM II, 61 Marsch nach Motiven der Oper »Alcidor« – Opera by Gasparo Spontini (1774-1851) – March by Johann Carl Bocklet (1791- c. 1860)

Spontini was Music Director of the Royal Opera House in Berlin from 1820-1842. During this time, thirteen marches appeared after themes in Spontini's works. *Alcidor* appeared in 1825. In the same year, Johan Carl Bocklet wrote his march, which became an official Army March in 1826. Bocklet was a wearer of the Iron Cross 2nd class for his actions at the Battles of Jüterbog and Dennewitz in 1813 during the War of Liberation against Napoleon. He became Bandmaster of the Kaiser Alexander Grenadier-Regiment in Berlin in 1818. He was much loved for his concerts in the school garden between the Brandenburg Gate and the Potsdam Gate. He also had a high reputation for good military music and often paraded his band before the visiting Tsar of Russia who was the regiment's Honorary Royal Colonel.

AM II, 62 Marsch des Leib-Garde Semenowski Regiments

In Tsarist Imperial Russia there were three original Life Guard Regiments, the Preobraschenski, the Semenowski and the Izmailowski, which had been established long before all the other later Russian Guard regiments. They were stationed in the capital, St Petersburg. At the behest of his father, the King of Prussia, Prince Wilhelm (later Kaiser Wilhelm I), early in 1826 had travelled there for the State Funeral of Tsar Alexander of Russia (Prussia's great ally in the war against Napoleon), and for the assumption of power by Tsar Nicholas and the Tsarina Alexandra, the sister of Prince Wilhelm. Here Prince Wilhelm heard the Regimental Quick March of the Semenowski Life Guards and wrote and asked for a copy of the score to take back to Berlin. Once he returned home, the Prussian king ordered that it be immediately included in the Army March Collection. It is the very epitome of a soldierly march, all four sections, which are each of eight bars with repeats, have a clearly precise rhythm. So the piece was used widely and for the greatest of parades in Prussia when the regiments paraded past in 'Regimentskolonne'. The 'Regimentskolonne' was the prescribed closely packed formation at the width of the entire company, and required for marching, a strong exact time beating in order to maintain dressing. The Grenadier-Regiment Nr. 2 in Stettin and Infanterie-Regiment Nr. 44 in Goldap (East Prussia) had the piece as their Regimental Quick March. In 1869 Wieprecht wrote a new arrangement. It was one of Prussia's most commonly played marches, and remains in the march books of today's Bundeswehr.

AM II, 63 Pratermarsch by Heinrich Hirtl (? – 1825)

The composer was a famous dance band leader and dance and march composer in Vienna in the age of Metternich. This piece was written in 1825 and was published by Diabelli & Co. Vienna. The Prussians took it in 1827 into their collection. It is no longer played.

AM II, 64 Marsch des Leib-Garde Izmailowski Regiments

In 1826 was the Coronation of Tsar Nicholas I of Russia, who was married to the daughter of Prussian King Friedrich Wilhelm III. Her brothers Wilhelm (later German Kaiser Wilhelm I) and Carl travelled to Moscow, and among the many and various ceremonies heard the regimental parade marches of the St Petersburg Life Guards, and those of the Semenowski and Izmailowski regiments they took back to Berlin. The Izmailowski bore the name in honour of the capture of the Turkish Port and City fortress, Izmail, at the mouth of the Danube, which, in 1790, was taken by Marshal Suvorov. The 'Present Arms' march of the Izmailowski Regiment is also in the Prussian Collection as AM I, 17. From 1827 this march was a Prussian Army March.

AM II, 65 Marsch aus dem Ballett »La Festa di Terpisichore« by Constant Telle, arranged by Johann Carl Bocklet

Here we have a Berlin march! On 16th December 1818, the ballet *La Festa di Terpisichore* opened in Berlin. It was a diversion, a little ballet to cheer up the burgers of Berlin who were then just getting over the difficult years of occupation and war years of the Napoleonic era. The composer, Telle (c.1775-1846) worked as a Ballet-Master at the Berlin Opera. The Berlin-based Bandmaster Bocklet (1791-?) took the well-known melodies and made them into a march with a heavy 6/8 rhythm in the first two sections, and both sections of the trio in a light 4/4, closing with a little Coda. Bocklet was, from 1818-1829, Bandmaster of the Kaiser Alexander Grenadier-Regiment in Berlin, and often performed in front of his Royal Colonel, the Tsar Alexander I of Russia. Bocklet had won the Iron Cross 2nd Class for his actions at the battles of Jüterbog and Dennewitz during the War of Liberation 1813-15, for a musician a very rare distinction.

AM II, 66 Marsch by Johann-Friedrich Naue

In the years 1824-1827 three marches by Naue came into the Army March Collection. It was a time at which the newly-mustered bands and trumpeter corps needed a further expansion of their rich march literature and good pieces were eagerly sought. Johann Friedrich Naue (1787-1858) was born the son of a manufacturer in Halle-on-the-Saale in a period of turbulent unrest. In 1789 the French Revolution broke out, and then followed the tribulations of war, and, finally, at the command of Napoleon, the campaign to Moscow. However, the highly musical Naue had good fortune. In his father's town, the position of Organist and Music Director at the University fell vacant, owing to the death of the incumbent, and the appointment of twenty-six-year-old Naue speaks much for his abilities. He then freely encouraged the population in its resistance to the French yoke. Central Europe was a war zone, soldiers everywhere, and Halle was in the thick of it. Naue wrote marches, hymns and pieces for harmoniemusik. However, his greatest skill lay in the area of his choir and church music. Already by 1818 King Friedrich Wilhelm III had accepted Naue's 'Proposals for a musical agenda' which four years later became law in Prussia. The liturgical songs stood under the influence of the Russian Lieder composer Bortnjanskij, which were adopted by the Prussian United Church and in constant use until 1945. Naue reformed and put in good order the Halle Concert Orchestra and founded an Academy of Song, which today is the Robert-Franz Singakademie.

AM II, 67 Marsch aus dem Ballett »Malle Cadella« by Friedrich August Belcke, arranged by August-Heinrich Neithardt

In 1828 the ballet *Malle Cadella* appeared. Ballet music was then very popular. They had memorable melodies which appeared in Literatur Whistling 2nd volume (1834) and cheered up the soldiers when played as Marschmusik when on their daily marching exercises on country roads. This piece became an Army March in the same year! Amongst other things, the composer and arranger were good friends, had already worked with one another for a long time, and both were respected musicians. Friedrich August Belcke (1795-

1874) came from Lucka in the Saxon-Thuringian countryside. His younger brother was a famous solo flautist. He, himself, enjoyed repute as a virtuoso trombonist. Already by 1815 he had performed in the famous Gewandhaus in Leipzig with his trombone. From 1816, as a member of the Royal Chamber Music Ensemble of the Berlin Opera House Orchestra, he went on concert tours, in addition on the bass trombone, and to universal astonishment he played mellow cantabiles of exquisite quality on the French Horn. In Rostock, Copenhagen, Kiel, Hamburg, Hanover, Prague and at the Saxon Court, he was fêted. Also on the tenor horn he gained a great knowledge. As a composer he wrote ballets, orchestral works, and concert pieces for trombone and piano pieces. It is from his piano pieces that this march appeared from Verlag Cosmar & Krause, Berlin, in 1828. The Army March from it was arranged for Prussian military band by August-Heinrich Neithardt (1793-1861), the talented Stabshoboist (Bandmaster) and later Director of Music of the Kaiser Franz Grenadier-Regiment of Berlin. He originated from Schleiz, also in the Saxon-Thuringian region. He was well-acquainted with Belcke, for whom he had already written trombone concert pieces. So it is of little surprise that this excellent 6/8 time march appeared for the troops in the year that it appeared. Also, forty years later, Wieprecht found further use for the piece and rearranged it for the expanded instrumentation of Prussian bands which had taken place since the piece first appeared.

AM II, 68 Marsch aus Warschau by Ferdinand Haase

Once upon a time, people were easy-going about titles for marches. One often saw simply 'Marcia' or 'Marsch', but we must be thankful in this case that Warsaw is noted. In 1828 the piece came into our Army March Collection as arranged by Ferdinand Haase (1788-1851). Naturally it is an arrangement by Haase, as he had been the foremost Bandmaster in the Kingdom of Poland (part then of the Russian Empire). He had arranged all his own compositions for band. This piece is, without doubt, his own work of composition. The quick-time pace and quick marches were at this time only about ten years old. If the composition had had another origin it would doubtless have been much more famous and more widely used. It is yet another good march from Haase, still only ever having been arranged in its original form. Haase was a first-rate creator.

AM II, 69 Marsch aus Posen

As agreed at the congress of Vienna in 1815, the area around Posen (today Poznan in Poland) became a Prussian Province. The similarly-named capital of the Province and formidable fortifications lay on the vital road between Russia and Prussia proper. The Statthalter (Governor) in Posen was Fürst Anton Heinrich Radziwill. He came from a long line of Lithuanian Princes and was married to a Prussian Princess, and their daughter was the youthful sweetheart of the later German Kaiser, Wilhelm I. The connection between the Prussians and Posen was close and many-sided, particularly later through the sons and grandsons of Prince Radziwill. So it is no wonder that we have a march from Posen. Whereby and wherefore we came by this score we do not know. In 1828 the piece came into the collection. The piece was not used much and never became a regimental march. For certain, military bands in Posen played an important role until 1914. Many highly-regarded and excellent Musikmeisters came from Posen, among whom was the Music Inspector, Prof. Hackenberger and later Deputy Inspector Prof. Berdien, and not forgetting our most beloved march '*der Fridericus*' (*AM II, 198*). Its composer Ferdinand Radeck was, from 1853 to 1867, Stabshoboist (Bandmaster) of the Grenadier-Regiment Nr. 6 in Posen.[4]

AM II, 70 Marsch Nach Motiven der Oper »Alcidor« – Opera by Gasparo Spontini – March by August-Heinrich Neithardt

The music director of the Kaiser Franz Grenadier-Regiment in Berlin, August-Heinrich Neithardt (1793-1861) created this march in 1825 from *Alcidor* by the composer Gasparo Spontini (1774-1851), not only General Music Director in Berlin but also, through his clever melodies, a favourite with the soldiers, so that we have ten marches with themes from his three operas *Vestalin, Cortez* and *Alcidor* in the Army March Collection. The full chords and long notes with a clear rhythm we hear in this march, so beloved by troops on parade when they have to keep step in quick time. We hear also the skill of the military Kapellmeister with his skillful harmonising of the instrumental parts for his whole band.

AM II, 71 Ungarischer Grenadier-Marsch arranged by Schneider

In 1828 Director of Music Schneider, of the Prussian Guard Corps arranged this then already old Hungarian march by an unknown composer, after the Prussian King Friedrich Wilhelm III had brought the score back from his 1827 trip to Teplitz, a cure resort in the Bohemian Erzgebirge (45 km south of Dresden).The King had heard an Austro-Hungarian band play it on the bandstand whilst promenading, and was so taken with it he asked for a copy of the score from the Bandmaster.

AM II, 72 Marsch nach Motiven der Oper »Die Weisse Dame« by Francois Adrien Boieldieu

The opera had its premiere in Paris in 1825 and by 1828 Berlin had its melody as a march. In 1871, Wieprecht rearranged it for the new system of military band instrumentation. In 1926, Professor Hackenberger put the piece in March Book '2nd series' and in 1961, Colonel Stephen put it in the Bundeswehr's Volume II. The melody has not readily coped with the increase in march tempo over the years. In 1830, in 106 to the minute it just about works, but at tempo 114 it is too fast. The cavalry also play it as a trot, but without the trio. The composer, Francois Adrien Boieldieu (1775-1834) was born in Rouen and died in Paris. He wrote thirty-eight comic operas. In 1803 he went to St Petersburg where for eight years he was an Imperial Russian Bandmaster. Alongside Anton Dörfeldt, the Austrian Bohemian, he had a French input into developing Russian military music. Dörfeldt took his pretty, indeed extremely pretty, Marche Militaire into the Imperial Russian March Collection as number 17, which the Prussians inherited as their AM II, 19.

AM II, 73 Marsch vom Kronprinzen aus Italien mitgebracht (1828) arranged by August-Heinrich Neithardt

The Crown Prince brought this back from his trip to Italy in 1828 and Bandmaster Neithardt of the Kaiser Franz Grenadier-Regiment arranged it for military band for King Friedrich Wilhelm III for the March Collection. Nine years later, Neithardt published a

4 Before 1914, the population of Posen was about sixty percent Polish and forty percent German speaking – it was granted to the newly-restored Poland by the Treaty of Versailles 1919, the German-speaking population virtually disappearing between 1919-1939, through emigration to Germany, a process completed after 1945. Today, Poznan is in west-central Poland and almost one hundred percent Polish-speaking. Ed.

version for piano. In 1869, Wieprecht's new arrangement appeared. Although stil played by the Bundeswehr since it went into their march book in 1961, it is no longer known in Italy.

AM II, 74 Marsch nach Motiven der Oper »Die Stumme von Portici« – Opera by Daniel Francois Esprit Auber (1782-1871) – March by Friedrich Schick (1794-1860)

Friedrich Schick was born in Berlin to his father Ernst Schick, a violinist of some repute, his mother, Margarete, was a wonderful singer, as was his elder sister, Julie. At the age of twenty-six, Friedrich Schick became Bandmaster of Füsiler-Regiment Nr. 34 in Stralsund in Prussian Pomerania for twelve years from 1820-1832. He obtained the same position in Berlin with the Kaiser Alexander Grenadier-Regiment from 1832-1846 when he really made a huge impression on the Berlin public, giving regular concerts in Teichmanns Flower Garden. The population flocked to hear his summer concerts with their arrangements of the latest operas, operettas, dances and other hits of the day. The French opera composer, Auber, brought out his *La Muette de Portici* in 1828 and Schick brought all the themes together in this wonderful march. It became an Army March in the same year 1828. In 1842, he became a Director of Music, but in 1846 left the service after the appointment of the eight-years-younger Wilhelm Wieprecht as the new Director of Music of the Guard Corps, who had never served in the army, had not seen action, and yet knew how everything could be done better! Schick cheerfully took to playing in the Royal Opera Orchestra in Berlin as an experienced clarinettist, and in chamber music as lst solo-clarinettist. Schick personally received from his King, on the 18 January 1847, the Order of the Red Eagle (4th class) (one of Prussia's highest decorations). Aged sixty-five he retired in 1859 and died the following year.

AM II, 75 Neapolitanischer Armeemarsch

This short piece in two sections was liked by the eldest son of King Friedrich Wilhelm III when he heard it in Naples on his 1828 Italian tour. He brought it home with him and in 1829 it became an Army March. The timing allows it to serve as either a slow or quick march, but it was not in long-lasting use by infantry troops. On the contrary, it was taken up by the Kürassier-Regiment Königin (Pommersches) Nr. 2 as their regimental trot march till 1919! In such guise it is played in an all brass cavalry arrangement. The Kürassier-Regiment Königin (Pommersches) Nr. 2 had a special place in the Prussian Army. Once the Dragoon Regiment Ansbach-Bayreuth, they were renowned for their famous attack at Hohenfriedberg in 1745, from when they always played the '*Hohenfriedberger*' at Kaiser Parades. In 1806, Queen Luise of Prussia became the first of a line of queens to be their Royal Colonel and thus they gained their new regimental title and designation.

AM II, 76 Marsch der Italienischen Garde-Cavalierie Brought back from Italy by the Crown Prince (later F.W. IV) arranged by Carl Engelhardt

The Crown Prince was fascinated by the history, culture, remains, architecture, churches and landscape of Italy. His position as Crown Prince prevented him from undertaking a tour until he was thirty-three years old. He travelled to Italy in October 1828, and was also much taken with the church music, street musicians, and military music, particularly in the capital of the Kingdom of the Two Sicilies, Naples, where he heard the Garde-Cavalry play this 2/4 march. He took the score back to Potsdam where Bandmaster Engelhardt arranged it for Prussian band. It entered the Army March Collection in 1829.

AM II, 77 Marsch des Italienischen 3. Regiments Svizzero Brought back from Italy 1828 by the Crown Prince (later F.W. IV) arranged by Carl Engelhardt

In Naples there were four Swiss regiments in Neapolitan service back in 1828, just as the Pope has his Swiss Guards today. Although the Crown Prince was not on an official visit the 3rd Swiss Regiment 'Svizzero' paraded and filed past to their Defiliermarsch for him. He took the score back to Berlin where Bandmaster Carl Engelhardt of the 1.Garde-Regiment zu Fuss in Potsdam arranged it for Prussian band. Engelhardt had just taken over the leadership of the Band of the 'Langen Kerls' in 1828, having previously since 1817 served as a bandsman with the Infanterie-Regiment Nr. 31 in Erfurt. Ten years after this march appeared in the collection in 1828, Verlag Schlesinger of Berlin brought out a Piano-forte score of this march for the public, arranged by Bandmaster August-Heinrich Neithardt of the Kaiser Franz Grenadier-Regiment in Berlin. It is a beautiful piece which still enchants to this day.

AM II, 78 Marsch Nr 1
&
AM II, 79 Marsch Nr 2 Both by Prince Frederick of Prussia (1794-1863)

The composer was the son of Prince Ludwig, the brother of King Friedrich Wilhelm III. He was soon parentless as his father died in 1796 and his mother remarried in 1798 and moved away. In the War of Liberation in 1813-1815, the Prince won the Iron Cross 2nd Class for bravery in 1815, commanding the lst Silesian Curassiers in Breslau. In 1817 he married Princess Louise of Anhalt-Bernburg. Both these good swinging marches were placed in the collection by the king in 1829. by this time, the Prince was Lt. General and Commander of the 14th Division in Düsseldorf. He later ended his military career as General of Cavalry and Governor of the Imperial Fortress in Luxembourg.

AM II, 80 Geschwindmarsch in F by Carl Merz (1807-1856)

Carl Merz lived in Berlin at Friedrichstrasse 236, in other words in central Berlin. He was well-known and much appreciated as a dance and march composer, as well as being a music teacher of some repute. Of his three quick marches, which were only ever written in his own hand, this one came into the collection in 1829. The local infantry regiments were always thankful for good 'street marches' (Strassenmärsche). It was proposed as an Army March by Georg Abraham Schneider, Director of all the Bands and Choirs of the Prussian Guard Corps. It was in this role, together with his other roles as an opera conductor and court musician that he came into personal contact with the musical life of Berlin and the likes of Carl Merz.

AM II, 81 Marsch nach Motiven der Oper »Die Belagerung von Corinth« – Opera by Gioacchino Rossini (1792-1868) – March by Johann Brandl (1760-1837)

Rossini's opera *The Siege of Corinth* appeared in 1826 in Paris. It no longer belongs to the best known of the works of this famous composer. Much more famous is his *Barber of Seville* (1816) and his *William Tell* (1829). This march, however, was that of the Grand Duchy of

Baden's Grenadiers and as such came into the Army March Collection in 1830. The troops of Baden had, at the beginning of the 19th century, taken the side of Napoleon and fought against Austria, Prussia and Russia. With the losses after the retreat from Moscow in 1812, the Badish Army had to be recruited and re-raised once again on the side of Napoleon, but after the 'Peoples' Battle' at Leipzig on 19 October 1813, this newly-raised Badish Army languished as Prussian prisoners of war. For the first time, Baden joined the allies against France in 1814-15. The Regimental Band of the old 3rd Baden Line Infantry Regiment was led by Johann Brandl. He was the first bandmaster of this regiment, with its garrison in Mannheim, the Grenadier companies in Karlsruhe. Brandl hailed from the district around Regensburg. Through assiduous hard work he gave high service to the Grand Duchy of Baden. He also gave tremendous and plentiful service in concert work for the Grand Ducal Court in Karlsruhe. From the Grenadiers of his Regiment was later created, after 1871, the 1.Badische Leib-Grenadier-Regiment Nr. 109 (until 1918), and in the Wehrmacht the Infanterieregiment 109 (until 1945). The 109th are to this very day a much-loved memory of the old days in Baden.

AM II, 82 Alpensängermarsch Based on Swiss National Melodies by Andreas Nemetz, arranged by August-Heinrich Neithardt

This is a March from the Austro-Hungarian Empire that gave so much pleasure in Prussia it was newly arranged no less than four times within a century; by Neithardt in 1830, Wieprecht in 1869, Rossberg in 1895 and Hackenberger in 1926. One cannot give a better recommendation to the composer than this. The composer Andreas Nemetz (1799-1846) hailed from Moravia. As a young man he was a music teacher in Ödenburg, Hungary and then a trombonist in the Opera Orchestra at the Viennese Court. In 1828 he took up the position of Bandmaster of the Austro-Hungarian 12th Infantry Regiment in Vienna. With his drive and enthusiasm he is remembered today particularly for his 1840, eight bar side drum introduction, which precedes marches, a style still in service use by the Austrian Army today. (Equivalent to the British two-three pace rolls on the drums, introducing a march.) Also, in his published works he shows talent and knowledge. In Verlag Diabelli & Co. Vienna in 1828, there appeared his 'Neueste Posaunen Schule' (New Trombone Tutor), Opus 16 and his 'Neueste Trompetenschule' Opus 17, and in 1844 his 'Algemeine Musikschule für Militärmusik'. Of his many marches, the Prussian Army March Collection took two practical pieces, the *Alpensängermarsch* (*AM II, 82*) and the *Pasta-Marsch* (*AM II, 83*). The *Alpensängermarsch* is based on Swiss national melodies. The Swiss motifs were popularly enjoyed. He retired on grounds of ill health in 1845 and died the following year. Before a piece could become an Army March it had to be arranged for the instrumentation of a Prussian military band. So we see that this was done by Bandmaster of the Kaiser Franz Grenadier-Regiment in Berlin, August-Heinrich Neithardt (1793-1861) in 1830, one of the most talented of military music arrangers.

AM II, 83 Pasta-Marsch by Andreas Nemetz arranged by August-Heinrich Neithardt

This march is dedicated to the Italian Opera singer Giuditta Pasta (1798-1865) whose heavenly two-and-a-half octave range voice entranced Andreas Nemetz (1799-1846), Bandmaster of the 19th Austrian Infantry Regiment in Vienna from 1828-1845. Bandmaster Neithardt of the Kaiser Franz Grenadier-Regiment in Berlin arranged it for

Prussian military band in 1830. In 1871, Wieprecht rearranged it for both Infantry and Cavalry band use.

AM II, 84 Marsch aus dem Haag (1829) by Francois Dunkler arranged by August-Heinrich Neithardt

From 1830 the piece is an Army March. Prussia's King Friedrich Wilhelm III was sent the piece by his daughter Luise, who lived in The Hague after her marriage to Prince Frederick of the Netherlands. The arrangement for Prussian band was undertaken by bandmaster Neithardt (1793-1861) of the Kaiser Franz Grenadier-Regiment in Berlin. The march would come to be much-played. So Wieprecht wrote his 1869 new arrangement for the then enlarged bands. In 1933 Professor Hermann Schmidt put the piece in his Marschbuch 4. Folge, and from 1961 the Bundeswehr have it in their volume II. However, until 1975 the name of the composer was no longer known in Germany. This research puts that right. Francois Dunkler (1779-1861) came from Rastatt (on the middle Rhine). His uncle, Francois Wöke, was 1st bassoonist in the Court band of the Margrave, later Grand Duke of Baden, and gave his nephew a good basic training on this instrument. Dunkler's father, a Bandmaster of a German regiment in France, took his son on as a bandsman. He obtained a further position as 2nd bassoonist with the 4. Bataillon Freiwillige von der Mosel (4th Moselle Volunteer Battalion) with which he served until its abolition. So Dunkler became a soldier and campaigned in the field and was wounded. He lived as a military musician further afield too. Eventually, he took up the position of Trumpet Major (bandmaster) in the French 2nd Carabiniers à cheval. In 1797 his regiment went to Egypt and Syria. Dunkler was again wounded. With them he went to Moscow (1812). It was an unsettled time! The French Revolution and Napoleon's Wars took men far and wide and a long way from their origins in life. In 1815 Dunkler entered Dutch service, at first as Trumpet-Major of the 5th Light Cavalry, and from 1816 as Bandmaster of the 11th Infantry Detachment in Namur, which then belonged to Holland. There, once more, his position was abolished. Dunkler took himself off to Russia. He was appointed as music instructor to the Russian 10th and 18th Regiments, which he much enjoyed, and to which he brought great benefits. It was as a trainer at military music school in this Russian Province that he came into contact with Anton Dörfeldt, his opposite number in St Petersburg with the Russian Life Guard Regiments. In 1819 he returned to Liege (then in Holland) and for ten years led the Band of the Dutch 11th Infantry Regiment, until at the request of Prince Frederick of the Netherlands, he was appointed as Bandmaster of the newly-raised Regiment of Grenadiers and Jägers in the Hague. Already in his first year there he composed a brisk *Grenadiermars* for his regiment. Prince and Princess Frederick were much taken with it, and the twenty-one-year-old Princess asked if she could send the score to her father in Berlin, which she proudly did as a present. The hunting motif in the trio relates to the Jäger part of the regiment. The Dutch publisher Molenaar in Wormerveer took up the copyright. Princess Luise engaged Dunkler often in conversation, as she so enjoyed his military music. Dunkler played frequently before the King of Holland. Dunkler was a virtuoso on flute, oboe, cor anglais, bassoon, horn and solo-trombone; he was truly gifted. In 1816 his son was born in Namur, a solo-clarinettist, who in 1847 took over from his father as Bandmaster of the Regiment of Grenadiers and Jägers in The Hague. In 1861, the year of his father's death, the son became a Director of Music, and in September 1867 went with this superb fifty-six strong Dutch band to compete in the Paris Fair against other European bands including

Wieprecht from Prussia. In 1876 he became Chief Inspector of the Military Music Service of the Netherlands and in 1877 of the Dutch Royal Navy too.

At the NATO music festival in 1976 in Mönchengladbach, I arranged for the entry-march of the Dutch to be their *Marsch aus dem Haag (1829)*, and before them two Schellenbaums engraved with the name of the Regiment of Grenadiers & Jägers, and the date 1829! The name of Dunkler, father and son, once forgotten, duly recognised properly once more.

AM II, 85 Marsch des Russischen Leib-Garde Jäger Regiments arranged by Carl Engelhardt

The friendship between Prussia and Russia, which grew at the beginning of the 19th century as a result of the war against Napoleon, remained strong for many decades. So came this pretty Russian regimental march to us in 1830. The Life Guard Yegerski Regiment belonged to the Imperial Russian Guard Corps and from 1813-14 had fought side by side with us against the French. The outstanding Musikdirektor Engelhardt (1796-1872), Bandmaster of the 1.Garde-Regiment zu Fuss in Potsdam, was responsible for preparing arrangements for pieces to be included in the collection and played by Prussian infantry Bands.

AM II, 86 Marsch des Russischen Leib-Garde Sapeur Bataillons arranged by Carl Engelhardt

During the War of Liberation 1813-15, the first pioneer units were raised as Sappers (for trench work), as Pontoneers (for crossing rivers), and as Miners (for laying mines and under mining work). To guard the positions these troops were stationed with the Infantry. They mounted Guard with their own band providing the 'Standort-Wache'. The requirements for the daily 'Standort-Wache' were considerable. Sentries and guard were required in Castles, Fortifications, for high dignatories, as well as rifle stores, munitions stores, supply depots, clothing stores, food stores, depots and hospitals – and, in addition to all these, at the Gates of the town. The Russian Life-Guard Sapper Battalion was raised in 1813 and had immediately a Band of ten musicians (two flutes, two clarinets, two bassoons, two French Horns, two trumpets). The Life-Guard Sapper Battalion belonged to the Guard Corps in St Petersburg and was in the same Brigade as the Pavlovski Life Guard Regiment. Still in 1880 the Battalion provided the Garrison Guard (Standort-Wache) in full Battalion strength. Each Sunday the Tsar attended the Guard Mounting Ceremony (Wachtparade), mounted upon his charger and dressed in the uniform of the Sapper Battalion, and then he attended the Drill Hall, the *Michaelsmanege*, where he watched them march past twice, in slow time and in quick time. For both paces the Battalion had beautiful inspiring marches. This one is the quick march. In 1830 it came into our Army March Collection in an arrangement by Engelhardt, the Bandmaster of the Prussian 1st Regiment of Foot Guards in Potsdam. So well known was the Guard Mounting Ceremony of the Life-Guard Sapper Battalion in Russia that on 13th March 1881, on his return ride to the Winter Palace, Tsar Alexander II, a great and true friend of Prussia, fell at the hands of an assassin.

AM II, 87 Marsch by Friedrich Weller

The Bandmaster Friedrich Weller (1791-1890) was a much-loved march and dance composer. This march is not his best, but his only one to make it into the Army March Collection. Unmistakeable is the strong and beautiful clarinet part, which tells us immediately that

Wilhelm Wieprecht conducts the Massed Bands at one of his "Monster Concerts" (*Illustrated London News* – Eagle & Lyre Prints Archive)

it is Weller, as he was a clarinettist himself. Weller came from Wörlitz (12 km East of Dessau) where to this day is the famous Wörlitzer Park. At the age of eighteen he joined the Band of the Leib-Infanterie Regiment in Berlin. The whole of Prussia was then under French occupation and Napoleon was organising his campaign against Russia. So Weller's regiment had to join in the campaign in Russia, but from 1813 it changed sides under Yorck and began the War of Liberation against Napoleon. After the battles of Gross Görschen and Bautzen in May, on the 12th June the Regiment released its Fusilier Battalion to act as a cadre for the creation of a new 2.Garde-Regiment zu Fuss, and the new Regimental Band was created by detaching some of the musicians with Weller appointed as the bandmaster of this new Guards Band. There were further battles: the 'Peoples' Battle at Leipzig, the 'Crossing of the Rhine', and the entry into Paris, and finally the Victory over Napoleon after his return from Elba at Waterloo-Belle Alliance. In the Berlin garrison after 1815 it was Weller's greatest era! With his capable Regimental Band underpinned by singularly excellent compositions, he began to gain a reputation for public concerts as well as the usual in and out of service commitments. On 1 December 1821, in the Jägerschen Saal in Unter den Linden, 'the great and the good' from Pritzwalk gathered to hear them for a special concert, which was being attended by the king and princes. In 1822 his Band played for the season in the School Garden between the Potsdam and Brandenburg Gates. In 1823 in the Flower Garden in the Potsdamer Chaussee no. 22, here he called upon the services of the Soldiers Choirs (Soldatenchöre) from a number of regiments, under the capable Choir-Master Leidel to join with his band to put on choral works. In 1824, in the summer season, his band played at Kempfers Lokal Tiergarten Nr. 46, and once again on 21st October, for the Birthday Celebrations of the Crown Prince, he gave a 'Great Vocal and Instrumental Concert' in the Adler-Saal, Unter den Linden 76. He played many well-known and popular arrangements for military band, but finally came the great symphonies of Haydn, Mozart and Beethoven, all arranged by Weller for military band, which were the highlights of the programme. With his summer concerts under blue skies, Weller set a standard for military musicians giving open-air concerts which in excellence and splendour and musicality set the standard for the next hundred years, both at home and abroad! Tireless and inexhaustibly Weller toiled. Together with Director of Music Neithardt from the Kaiser Franz Grenadier-Regiment, he brought out a complete book of music scores with the instrumental parts for eight marches (four from each of them).

The little, unsoldierly, Wieprecht as Director of Music of the Guard Corps, he never accepted. Together with the other two Berlin Guard Regiments' Directors of Music Neithardt and Schick, Weller resigned from the service. For thirty years he had been the Bandmaster of the 2.Garde-Regiment zu Fuss. Weller went off to his home town of Wörlitz. Wieprecht could only bear to do things his way. Immediately the enlarged French Horn section of Weller's ensemble was dispensed with, to Wieprecht they seemed inappropriate for military music with their mellow tones, and also because of their difficult blowing technique on the march. This did not immediately endear him to the Berliners, as Weller's concerts were held in high regard. As soon as possible, Weller's successor had engaged French Horn players once again, possibly furtively at first until it ceased to be an issue, when Wieprecht was busying himself with other things!

Weller belongs to the greatest! He was the first to delight the public with summer concerts in the park with a good military band, anywhere in the world. We must not forget him!

AM II, 88 Marsch

Since 1830 this piece has been in the Prussian Army March Collection. On every score is written only the title 'Marsch'. It appeared in the musical *Literatur Whistling* (second further Edition of 1834) as was the previous AM II, 87, and it was credited to Weller. That is, however, wrong and stated by Musikdirektor Neithardt who was a good friend of Musikdirektor Weller. We still do not know the composer or the basis for its inclusion in the collection. The piece is, nevertheless, clearly constructed, happy in conception, and has such a catchy, pretty trio that it engages in the pianoforte arrangements of 1840 by Musikdirektor Neithardt (*Pianoforte-Ausgabe der beliebsten Militair-märsche aus Preussen, Russland und Österreich).*

AM II, 89 Schweizermarsch by August-Heinrich Neithardt

In 1832 this composition appeared and instantly was named as an Army March. Prussia had then forty-five Infantry regiments, whose bands daily accompanied their troops for Guard Mount (Wachaufzug), Drill (Exerzieren) and Field Service (Felddienst) and played too on manoeuvres (Manöver). The demand for good Marschmusik was great, and the bandmaster of the Kaiser Franz Grenadier-Regiment, Neithardt (1793-1861), was just the man to come up with good pieces. From him alone are fourteen Army Marches with either his name as composer or arranger. His *Schweizermarsch* comes from a Swiss folk song. Switzerland, as the neighbouring land to the south, was the favourite country for touring on holiday. Its melodies ask to be used, and were for many an Army march.

AM II, 90 Marsch über den Chor der Emire Aus der Oper »Die Kreuzritter« – Opera by Giacomo Meyerbeer (1791-1824) – March by August-Heinrich Neithardt (1793-1861)

The Opera 'The Crusaders' (*Il Crociato in Egitto*) is from 1824, and had its premiere in Berlin in 1832. In the same year, Neithardt turned it into a march. Ten years later, in 1842, Meyerbeer succeeded Spontini as General Music Director of the Berlin Opera. Unlike the famous marches based on Meyerbeer's *Die Hugenotten*, this march has been lost in the mists of time.

AM II, 91 Marsch des Österreichischen Infanterie Regiments 42 Herzog von Wellington

The Theresienstadt garrisoned 42nd Austrian Infantry Regiment was given the title 'Duke of Wellington' in 1818, three years after Arthur Wellesley's triumph over Napoleon at Waterloo. Each year the Prussian king took the waters at the fashionable spa at Teplitz in Bohemia, where the band of the 42nd under their talented Bandmaster, Johann Schubert, serenaded the promenading visitors from the bandstand there. In 1832 the king obtained the score from Schubert and took this short, brisk and clean 6/8 march back to Berlin for his Army March collection. In 1838 the king obtained a further, much more famous, march from Schubert numbered AM II, 117 in the collection.

AM II, 92 Marsch des K.K. Ungarischen Infanterie Regiments 60 Prinz Wasa by Josef Reznicek, arranged by Carl Engelhardt

From 1825 until his death in 1848, Josef Reznicek was Bandmaster of the 60th Hungarian Regiment, named in honour of Prince Gustav of Wasa from 1831 onwards. Josef Reznicek was the nephew of Emil Nikolaus von Reznicek, the composer of the Overture *Donna Diana*. (The march was first published in Vienna by Verlag Diabelli.) Carl Engelhardt, Bandmaster of the l.Garde-Regiment zu Fuss, added a trio in his 1832 arrangement when it became *AM II, 92*. Five years later, in 1837, Bandmaster August-Heinrich Niethardt of the Kaiser Franz Grenadier-Regiment had his piano-forte arrangement published by Schlesinger Verlag.

AM II, 93 Marsch aus Petersburg arranged by Carl Engelhardt

This is another march from the Imperial Russian capital, St. Petersburg. Cleanly constructed and straight forward in structure, it plays happily along. It came into the Prussian collection in 1832-33. It was and remains arranged by Carl Engelhardt, Bandmaster of the 1.Garde-Regiment zu Fuss in Potsdam from 1828-1857. He served from 11th April 1817, joining first the Band of Infanterie-Regiment Nr. 31 in Erfurt, and retired on 11th April 1857 on the day of his 40th anniversary of service with the Colours in his 60th year. The original composer of the march is unknown.

AM II, 94 Marsch nach Steierischen Alpenliedern by August-Heinrich Neithardt (1793-1861)

Under 14 Army Marches, from a total of 89 which entered the Collection between 1824 and 1837, stands Neithardt's name. This indicates his contribution to military music and the regard in which he was held by his king. August-Heinrich Neithardt belongs to a particular era in the history of Berlin. He was Bandmaster and Director of Music there, leading the Band of the Kaiser Franz Grenadier-Regiment between 1822-1840, whose Royal Colonel was the Austrian Emperor. Neithardt spent his youth living under enemy occupation. When the 1813-15 War of Liberation began he was 20 years old and volunteered. Then in 1822, he took this leading position in the Prussian military music service in Berlin. He had an enormous musical talent and was extremely hard-working which is what led to this appointment. Before the war, he had had a solid education, being trained too as a clarinettist in the Court Music ensemble of the Elector of Reuss. During the War, he served as a Waldhornist (Horn player) in the Garde-Jäger-Bataillon, so that his Commanding Officer, later Prussian War Minister von Witzleben, spoke up for him when the vacancy arose for a Bandmaster to lead the band of the newly-raised Garde-Schützen-Bataillon (Guard Rifles) in Berlin in 1817. From there he finally took the thirty-three-man strong Regimental Band of the 'Franzers'. Neithardt was one of our greatest. So it is little wonder that he resigned his position when the younger and civilian Wieprecht was appointed a Music director over all the musicians of the Guard Corps. Furthermore, from then on Niethardt crowned his life's work with the creation and leadership of the Berlin Cathedral Choir. Neithardt's arrangements are a model example of the art. As a music teacher he had unrivalled knowledge and insight. His *Marsch nach Steirischen Alpenliedern* of 1833 brings us melodies that were much loved at that time. Switzerland and the Alps captivated people, so that there is also the *Alpensängermarsch AM II, 82* of 1830, and the *Schweizermarsch AM II, 89* of 1832, as a sign of this. On the original Army March score, the checker has noted briefly that it is "from Steyerische songs". We find that Neithardt calls it also by this friendly and understandable title in his second volume of Collected Works (Edition Whistling) in1834.

AM II, 95 Marsch aus Prag (1833)

All we know is that it is an old march from Prague, once capital of the Kingdom of Bohemia, one of a number of thrones on which the Austrian Hapsburgs sat until 1918. Prague was known as the 'Home of Instrumental Music' in the 19th and early 20th centuries, the home of Smetana until 1884, and Dvorak until his death in 1904.

AM II, 96 Marsch aus Turin (1833) by Henriette Sontag (once married, she became the Countess Rossi)

Henriette Sontag (1806-1854) was a solo soprano singer of great popularity, with a wide repertoire of over fifty operas. In 1824, she was engaged at the Royal City Theatre in Berlin and became the talk of the town. She later married the Sardinian Count Rossi and returned to Turin where she performed for the Prussian king on one of his Italian tours. She sang a special arrangement of songs for him, and the king asked Carl Engelhardt (1796-1872), Director of Music of the Prussian 1.Garde-Regiment zu Fuss, to arrange a march from these songs. It was placed in the collection in 1833.

AM II, 97 Marsch des Sardinischen Garde Jäger Regiments by J. Gouella arranged by August-Heinrich Neithardt

A march from the Kingdom of Sardinia, which in 1861 encompassed the regions of Piedmont, Savoy, Nizza, Genoa and the Island of Sardinia. In the capital, Turin, was stationed the *Cacciatori Guardi* (The Sardinian Guard Jäger Regiment) whose Regimental Quick March came to us in 1834 and immediately became an official Army March. The trio with melodies from Donizetti's opera *Der Liebestrank* (*'The Love Potion'*) made the piece instantly popular. The opera appeared in 1832 and belongs to the first masterworks by Gaetano Donizetti. August-Heinrich Neithardt (1793-1861) bandmaster of the Kaiser Franz Grenadier-Regiment, Berlin, wrote the arrangement for Prussian military band. The arrangement was printed by Musikverlag Schlesinger. The piece appeared from Verlag Bote & Bock, Berlin, a piano version from Verlag Richter, Magdeburg, where the march was popularly played. In 1869 Wieprecht wrote his new arrangement. About the composer, J.Gouelle, absolutely nothing is known.

AM II, 98 Marsch nach Motiven der Komischen Oper »Die Falschmünzer« – Opera by Daniel Francois Esprit Auber (1782-1871) – March by Christian Buschinsky (1797-1880)

The French Opera composer and Court Bandmaster in Paris, Auber, created much joy with his forty or so operas full of beautiful melodies and glittering instrumentation. The comic opera *Die Falschmünzer* ('The Coin Forger') appeared in 1832. Two years later, this march was published by Verlag Richter/Magdeburg and at the same time became an Army March (1834). Christian Buschinsky was Bandmaster of the Regimental Band of the Prussian Infanterie-Regiment Nr. 27 in Magdeburg from 1823-1847. He had previously also been a bandsman in this same regiment. He served under five successive Commanding Officers and contributed to making the garrison and fortress of Magdeburg renowned as a high point for military music concerts with his gift for composing dances, potpourris and marches.

AM II, 99 Marsch des Leib-Garde Preobaschenski Regiments arrangment Ferdinand Haase

Since Joachim Toeche Mittler wrote his notes on this march in the 1980s, major research work has been undertaken by Lt.Col. Werner Probst, who kindly gives permission for his recent findings to be published as follows:

> Here are my findings on the historic background on the marches of the PREOBRASHENSKI Life Guards Infantry Regiment (LGIR). I will discuss this issue from both a Russian and a German viewpoint.
>
> **Russia**
>
> The most valuable source on Russian (i.e. Tsarist) regimental marches and music is the collection of marches that was compiled and published by General von Freymann. (He was of Germano-Baltic descent, and a member of this family later served as director of music in the German Federal Armed Forces. His name is LTC Eberhard von Freymann).
>
> The Collection consists of four volumes and containes some 247 marches. They were published by the renowned publisher C.F. Peters in Leipzig during the first decade of the 20th century. The German Society for Military Music is in possession of copies of these volumes, and it truly was more than adventurous to obtain them during the Soviet period.
>
> The collection contains the well-known Preobrashenski march twice, in
>
> - Volume I, No. 1 March of the Preobrashenski LGIR. This is the German Army March (AM) I,30, and
> - Volume III, No. 178 March Peter the Great ('Petrovsky'). This also is AM I,30. Both entries do not show a composer.
>
> AM II,99 by Ferdinand Haase (to be discussed later on) is ***not*** contained in the Freymann-Collection.
>
> To avoid any misinterpretations I personally refer to AM I,30 (after having discussed the matter with my friend Bohumil Pešek of Prague, who is one of the pre-eminent authorities on Russian and Soviet military music) as 'March Peter the Great (i.e. Petrovsky) of the Preobrashenski LGIR'.
>
> Bohumil furthermore underlines several important viewpoints regarding the historic environment of this march:
>
> Russian sources generally link this march to the epoch of Peter the Great (1672-1725). Each victory of importance and other events of especial bearing (religious holidays, birthday of an heir to the throne, the burial ceremonies for the Tsar etc.) were celebrated with festive cantatas. These 'gimni' (i.e. hymns) were sung by large choirs as – at that time – there were not enough qualified musicians.
>
> The Russian text of the march suggests that the melody could have been (part of) such a cantata. Later on bands adopted it, when no choir was available.
>
> In addition the march as such is not really a 'modern' march and by its character dates back to the 18th century. It should best be described as 'the symbol' of the (Tsarist) army. After 1917 it was to become the national anthem of the republic, but due to lack of time this was never proclaimed officially. Bands of the White Army played it frequently. After 1941 it was also performed by Soviet bands on the occasion

of patriotic events in order to rehabilitate such Russian heroes like Nevsky, Suvorov, Kutuzov and others. From that time on it belonged to those marches carried in the Soviet Army's march books.

Today the march again more or less may well be referred to as 'symbol of the Russian forces'.

The name Donajevsky that shows up for the first time when the Royal Marines adopted this march as their official slow march does not appear anywhere in connection with the march. This pertains to both Russian and Soviet sources.

Germany

Let us first have a look at the Army March Collection. The 1914 edition compiled by Theodor Grawert says:

AM I,30: Russian March

AM II,99: March of the LG Preobraschensky Regiment from St. Petersburg; arr. Haase

In the second volume of his works on German military music, the German musicologist Joachim Toeche Mittler states:

AM I,30: Identical to II,99, army march in 1817

AM II,99: March of the LG Preobraschenski Regiment by Ferdinand Haase – the trio contains the *Lemberger Lied* ('Lemberg Song') – composed in 1816 – a slow march (Präsentiermarsch) (also see AM I,30), army march in 1834

Discussion of Toeche-Mittler's findings:

It is somewhat astonishing that Toeche Mittler evidently mixes up factual information and creates associations of his own.

a) He states that AM I,30 and II,99 are identical. This is definitely wrong, as AM II,99 is a different composition as we shall see later on.
b) AM I,30 and II, 99 – if identical – were not composed by Ferdinand Haase.
c) It is true that AM I,30 belonged to the first lot of 'Prussian' army marches that all came from the Russian collection compiled by Dörfeldt and others in St. Petersburg. Consequently the entry is correct that it was accepted into the Prussian collection in 1817.
d) It is not known, where he got the information that the march was composed in 1816. Today the Russian position is generally accepted according to which the march dates back to the 18th century without a precise year of composition being shown.
e) AM I,30 / II,99 do not contain the 'Lemberg Song' in the trio. This statement reflects a major confusion indeed. (The city of) Lemberg in Polish is Lwow and Lviv in Ukranian. We were not able to identify a so-called 'Lemberg Song' in Russian sources. However, Lvov also is the name of the composer of the Tsarist anthem. We shall return to this issue down below.

Army March II,99 by Ferdinand Haase

a) The research on this march carried out by the German Society for Military Music finally produced the results that AM II,99 is a completely different march – composed by Ferdinand Haase.

b) Thanks to the efforts of the International Society for the Promotion and Research of Wind Music a so-called 'Luxury Edition of Army Marches' comprising AM II,1 to AM II,113 that was published in the 1840s was eventually re-issued.

Items c) and d) of Werner Probst's research quote from copyrighted sources. We are therefore unable to reproduce them here. However, to summarise:

c) Proves that entry II,99 was originally listed (in 1817) as No.99 a Quick March from St. Petersburg of the (Life Guard) Preobrashensk Regt. In 1834 composed by (Ferdinand) Haas(e).
d) The footnotes state that No.68 also comes from Haase, but the march is not identical with the similarly titled AM I/Nr.30. The writer Findeisen in 1914 emphasizes in his biographical notes about No.68 (page 2) that Haase's importance for German military music is on the basis of No. 99: "Some of Haase's composed marches have even become part of German military music, such as the Quick March Preobrazhenski Garde Regiment (with the anthem of L'vov in the trio of the march)." The following translation from the Russian original is "Although occasionally denied, it is the anthem of the Russian composer Aleksei Fëdorovič L'vov (1798-1870), which is in fact in the trio of No. 99, but easily 'hidden away', particularly in the voices of the oboes, bassoons and valve trumpets, and always just as dominant is the "filigree encirclement" by the remaining woodwind register." Haase was therefore extremely topical, because after the research by Gaub in 2004 we know that L'vov composed the anthem in 1833, the march itself was already in use by 1834 and finally in 1835 became No.99 of the Prussian Army March Collection.
e) It is important to note on the basis of these footnotes that AM II,99 is not identical to AM I,30 and that II,99 really incorporates the Tsarist anthem by Alexei Lvov in the trio. It is kind of 'hidden' there particularly in the woodwinds. Toeche Mittler consequently was wrong regarding the 'Lemberg Song', as it is the music by Lvov which cannot be translated into German, as it is a proper name.
f) It is true that the real II,99 became an Army March in 1834.
g) It can no longer be traced down when and why the confusion regarding II,99 and I,30 came about as the march collections of the 19th century carried two distinctly different marches.
h) Nowhere in German sources does the name Donajewsky show up as composer or arranger.

Since Werner Probst supplied this article it has also come to light that the current British attribution of the Preobajenski March to Ernest Donajowski (born Calais 1845, died London 1922) is certainly an error. The British version bestowed upon the Royal Marines and The Life Guards by the late Earl Mountbatten was taken from a score printed by Donajowski's music publishing company which traded in Britain from 1872-1917, and was from this source arranged for band by Lt.Col. Sir Vivian Dunn with the erroneous Donajowski attribution as composer added, although in this he was only copying an earlier error of naming Donajowski as the composer, and was not the first to make this error in Britain. Presumably when originally published in the UK Donajowski confusingly forgot to state that he was only the arranger, not the composer? Ed.)

AM II, 100 Marsch aus Wien (1834)

Georg Abraham Schneider, Musikdirektor of the Garde-Corps, arranged this Viennese piece for Prussian band. Ninety-one bars long, it was published by Neithardt, the Bandmaster of the Kaiser Franz Grenadier-Regiment in his book of best-loved marches for piano-forte in 1837, but the composer remained unknown. It is simply described as a *March from Vienna (1834)*. It ceased to be used after the middle of the 19th century.

AM II, 101 Marsch nach Motiven der Oper »Lestocq« by Daniel Francois Esprit Auber (1782-1871)

A third march after melodies from this Opera. There is also a fourth listed as *HM II, 129*. The march appeared in 1834.

AM II, 102 Marsch auf einen spanischen Nationaltanz Erinnerung an Kalisch (1835) by Princess William of Prussia (1811-1890, later Empress Augusta)

Before photographs and recordings, great festival occasions were often celebrated by works of music being composed. This is one such. For ten days in September 1835, there was a great European folk festival hosted jointly by the Tsar and his wife, the Tsarina, who was the King of Prussia's daughter, with the Prussian King Friedrich Wilhelm III and all the Princes and Princesses of the Prussian Royal House of Hohenzollern as guests. This included Prince and Princess William, the composer of this march. The festival was the 20th Anniversary Celebration of the defeat of Napoleon, and folk groups from all the allied nations attended. This festival at Kalisch (100 km north-west of Breslau, on the then border between Prussian Silesia and Russian Poland – today in central modern Poland) involved Long Reveille and Tattoos by the armed forces and numerous theatrical, orchestral and folk dance events, along with spectacular firework displays etc. The Princess was entranced and wrote this march after seeing a Spanish national folk dance performance. Director of Music Schneider of the Guard Corps arranged it for her and it became an Army March in the same year. In 1869, Wieprecht re-arranged it for the new instrumentation. This composition by his wife was much loved by the old Kaiser Wilhelm I, who required it be performed often at military reviews. It was reprinted in 1926 and used extensively by the German Army until 1945.

AM II, 103 Marsch des Österreichischen Infanterie Regiments 25 Von Trapp by Johann Prochaska

In March 1835, a young prince Wilhelm (later Kaiser Wilhelm I) was sent on a diplomatic visit to Kaiser Franz I of Austria by his father. En route to Vienna, in Prague, he heard the Austrian 25th Regiment play this march and brought the score back to Berlin, having obtained a copy from the composer Johann Prochaska (1802-1860), Bandmaster of the 25th Regiment named after Freiherr von Trapp between 1823 and 1842. Prochaska was famous for his dance compositions in mid 19th century Vienna. The march was rearranged by Wieprecht in 1869 and again in 1933 by Schmidt, published in his Marschbuch '4th series' (1933).

AM II, 104 Marsch aus dem Ballett »Der gestiefelte Kater« and *AM II, 112 Marsch aus der Schauspielmusik* »Der Militärbefehl« Both by Hermann Schmidt (1810-1845)

Hermann Schmidt was a flautist and Royal Chamber musician in the Royal Orchestra in Berlin. He also wrote musical for ballets and small musical show pieces which had their heyday in the short thirty-five years of his lifetime. The King named him as Court Composer, and he went on to compose *Der Polterabend, Undine* and others. His classical works were published by Verlag Moritz Westphal/Berlin who were bought out by Bote & Bock in 1840. However, his marches were published by Verlag Schlesinger, now Lienau/Berlin. A year after these marches appeared in 1836, Bandmaster Neithardt of the Kaiser Franz Grenadier-Regiment in 1837 had published, by Bote & Bock, a collection of Quick Marches arranged for Pianoforte in which these two marches appeared, as well as an arrangement by Neithardt of a march of themes from Schmidt's 1845 ballet *Der Schutzgeist*, which, although it did not become an Army March, is still played by Riding Associations after 150 years. The Bundeswehr also have this march in their books but without knowing that it was originally a ballet by Hermann Schmidt.

The two marches listed here, popular once, are rarely heard today.

AM II, 105 Marsch des 26 Infanterie Regiments by Wilhelm Körner

Wilhelm Körner had a number of melodic pieces published between 1834 and 1839 by music publishers Richter in Magdeburg, the home garrison city of the Infanterie-Regiment Nr. 26. It appeared in piano-forte arrangement in Neithardt's 1836 *Sammlung der beliebtesten Militairmärsche der Königl. Preuss. Armee,* used infrequently after the 1850s prize march competitions as better marches were available.

AM II, 106 Marsch über die Romanze »Der Reiter und sein Liebchen« – Romanze by Gustav Reichardt (1797-1884) – March by Johann Carl Neumann (1797-?)

Gustav Reichardt was a famous and much-loved song composer. His Opus 7 of 1825 *Was ist des Deutschen Vaterland* by words by Ernst Moritz Arndt was on everyone's lips in the 19th century. Later, Director of Music Carl Walther of the Prussian Infanterie-Regiment Nr. 50 in Posen incorporated it as the trio in his march *Der Sedaner* (Opus 41) which the Band of the Infanterie-Regiment Nr. 59, playing in support of their Colour Company, turned out for the Kaiser's Coronation on 18th January 1871 at the Palace of Versailles. Reichardt was also a much sought- after song teacher and voice coach. He had, himself, a wonderful bass voice which he used at oratorios, concerts and festivals. Prince and Princess Wilhelm engaged him to tutor their sons in music. Reichardt's romanze 'The Rider and his Beloved' (*Der Reiter und sein Liebchen*) appeared in 1831. Johann Carl Neumann, Bandmaster of the Kaiser Alexander Grenadier-Regiment in Berlin, turned it into a march for his band to play. King Friedrich Wilhelm III liked it and made it an Army March in 1836. Neumann worked happily with many Princes, Singers, Directors of Music etc., for the benefit of promoting music in the Fatherland. Neumann served with the 'Alexander' Regiment from 1818-1847.

AM II, 107 Marsch des Österreichischen Infanterie Regiments 12 Graf Rothkirch by Johann Proksch

Proksch was the Bandmaster of the 12th Austrian Infantry Regiment from 1833-1844. The Proprietor of the Regiment from 1834-1842 was Fieldmarshal-Lieutenant Leonhard Duke of Rothkirk and Panthen after whom this march is named. The march came to Prussia in 1836.

AM II, 108 Marsch des Russischen Infanterie-Regiments Prinz Carl von Preussen by Job von Witzleben, arranged by August-Heinrich Neithardt

Job von Witzleben (1783-1837) was a Prussian Lieutenant General and from 1833 War Minister. Himself an able musician, he had played chamber music with Georg Abraham Schneider, the Director of the Bands of Music and Choirs of the Gardekorps and responsible for Court Music. The War Minister also composed marches such as this one from 1836, which through the friendship with the Imperial Russian Army he dedicated to the Lithuanian Infantry Regiment. From 1829, this Regiment had been given the designation as the 9th Regiment and from October 23rd 1823 bore the name of Prince Carl of Prussia, named in honour of the son of the Prussian King. August-Heinrich Neithardt was asked to write an arrangement for Prussian military band instrumentation which, as usual, he did ably.

AM II, 109 Marsch by Crown Prince Oskar of Sweden

The Prussian Army Collection got this attractive piece in 1836 from Sweden. It was created by the then Crown Prince Oskar (1799, Paris – 1859, Stockholm), son of Napoleon's Marshal, Bernadotte who, from 1818 as King Karl XIV Johann, reigned over both Sweden and Norway. The young Oskar was taken to Sweden aged eleven, from 1818 Crown Prince, and was well known as a composer of Operas, Lieder etc. He succeeded his father in 1844 as King Oskar I. Musikdirektor Neithardt brought out a pianoforte arrangement of this pretty piece, which is number 10 in his 'collection of military marches for pianoforte' *(Sammlung beliebter Militärmärsche für Pianoforte)* published by Schlesinger'schen Buch- und Musikhandlung/Berlin.

AM II, 110 Marsch der Frau Prinzessin Wilhelm von Preussen gewidmet by Job von Witzleben (1783-1837)

When this march appeared in 1836, the composer was a Prussian Lieutenant-General and the War Minister in Berlin. He had campaigned in the War of Liberation against Napoleon, had served on the General Staff, and in 1818 became the King's Adjutant-General. He was appointed Minister of War in 1833. The area which was his seat at the southern end of the Charlottenburg area of West Berlin is today called the Witzleben District after him. He was a passionate musician, and in evenings during the War of Liberation had entertained his fellow officers by playing with Georg Abraham Schneider and others in a string quartet. In 1819 Schneider went on to become the first-ever Director of all the Bands and Choirs of the Guard Corps. Witzleben professionally concentrated on his military and political career but maintained a close friendship with Schneider, so that when he composed this march it was proposed with alacrity by Schneider to the King, who made it an Army March. Witzleben dedicated it to the Princess Wilhelm of Prussia, who the previous year had had her march (*AM II, 102* – a march based on Spanish national dances, memories of Kalisch) included as an Army March, with which he was much taken. It was a dedication to an admired fellow composer as much as to a member of the Royal House he so faithfully served until his death in 1837.

AM II, 111 Marsch des Leib-Garde Pawlowski Regiments by Heinrich Soussmann (1796-1848)

The composer was a Berliner. At the beginning of the War of Liberation in 1813 he joined up as a volunteer in the Reich'schen Jägern (Imperial Jaegers). Soon after, he became a bandsman (Hoboist) with the Colberg Infantry Regiment and took part in the Battles of Gross-Görschen, Dennewitz, and Leipzig, and campaigned in France with them, also at the 1815 Battle of Ligny and Belle Alliance (Waterloo) during the one hundred days campaign by the returning Napoleon. In one battle he was severely wounded. At the close of hostilities it was difficult in plundered and ruined Prussia to find a position as a civilian musician. Even the Royal Orchestra in Berlin could not offer him a position. So Soussmann undertook occasional work and responded to an advertisement for a position, being lucky in Russia! In the Imperial Orchestra at St Petersburg he was a flautist from 1822-1837. Soussmann composed much, amongst which is this march dedicated to the Pavlovski Life Guard Regiment which the Prussian king took into his Army March Collection in 1836.[5]

AM II, 112 (See AM II, 104)

AM II, 113 Marsch aus Petersburg (1837) (anon.)

Every German before 1914 was able to say 'Army March 113' whenever they heard this march, it was so famous. The Berliners always sang "Denkste denn, denkste denn, du Berliner Pflanze", as they still do today whenever they hear it. Played in Prussia too from 1832 it was taken into the Prussian Army March Collection as *Marsch aus Petersburg* in 1837. It became the regimental quick march of the 7. Württembergischen Infanterie-Regiments König Friedrich von Preussen Nr. 125 until 1919. It was also reputed to have been a onetime favourite march of the last Kaiser, Wilhelm II, and was played often at Birthday Parades in Imperial Berlin. Immediately after 1900 the parts were available from Freymann in the original Russian arrangement. Wieprecht wrote a new arrangement in 1871. The Bundeswehr have it today and play it frequently. The melody and rhythm is easily adapted to 2/4 dance, a 'Russian' or 'Rutschern' , also a 'Bade-Galopps', so that in the soldier-unfriendly atmosphere of 1948 it was still frequently heard in Berlin but as a dance, played loudly by a dance wind-band!

(Since Toeche Mittler's notes on this march were written in the 1980s there has been considerable debate about the origins of this march. Just over ten years ago the well respected contemporary Finnish military music researcher, Jan T. Päkki discovered that the march was claimed to have been composed by Sergeant Eric Ericsson (or Erik Eriksson). The story goes as follows: Eric Ericsson was born in Uusimaa in 1806 and aged thirteen in 1819 he joined the band of the Imperial Russian Life-Guard Grenadier Battalion ('The Finnish Guard Rifles') in Helsinki. On 24 January 1834 he was promoted to Sergeant Musician 1st

5 Pavlovsk is a district 30 km south of St Petersburg, from which this famous Russian Regiment was raised. Like two of the Prussian Guard Regiments, they wore tall metal-fronted mitres, in the 18th century style, on parade until 1914. Indeed, the Kaiser Alexander Grenadier Guards of Berlin were modelled on them, only wearing Prussian blue tunics instead of the Pavlovskis' Russian green. Ed.

Class. He retired from the service on 12 December 1838 and died about two years later. At Krasnaya Selo (near St. Petersburg) on the 5 July 1837 Tsar Nicholas I presented him with a gold watch in recognition of his circa 1830 composition *Parade March of the Guard* which was the favourite march of his wife the Tsaritsa.

Once this information was published in *Piipari* (The Journal of the Finnish Military Music Society) in 2000 (volume II, page 11), for a short while Ericsson was thus thought to have been definitely identified as the composer of the march. However since, in the IGEB publication of *Reprints und Manuskripte – Materialien zur Blasmusikforschung – Reprints Band 5*, Dr. Hofer comments on the march II, 113 that several composers of that period come into view and claim it as their own composition, but under different titles not associated with St. Petersburg – all of whom seem in truth to be arrangers of an earlier 'Hopser', the pre-cursor of the 'Galopp', the tune of which appeared in Germany sometime around 1800 in a handwritten manuscript book for pianoforte begun in 1792 for Anna Margretha Ebio (1778-1840). Interestingly, although a collection ostensibly for piano, it is clearly arranged from either six or seven parts for two oboes, (one clarinet?) one piccolo/flute, two horns and bass (the latter part is missing but identified as one of the parts). The original manuscript is in the private collection of Hartmut Friedel. The composer is anonymous. It seems therefore that Ericsson's arrangement of it into a march, and thus the link with St.Petersburg, is probably the source of the march in the Prussian Army March Collection. Ed)

AM II, 114 Marsch by Johann Kelch

This was written by a bandmaster in Cologne who composed carnival music that every band once marched to on *Rosenmontag* (the last Monday before Lent). So it comes from Johann Kelch (born 1814 – died?) who hailed from far off East Prussia, not the Rhineland. As an able bandsman in 1839 he was appointed Bandmaster of Infanterie-Regiment Nr. 28, the I and II Battalions stationed in Cologne, the Fusilier (III) Battalion in Ehrenbreitstein. The Honorary Colonel of the Regiment was, from 1826, the Duke of Wellington, who as a personal gift presented the Band with its Schellenbaum. Already in his first year in this position Kelch wrote this march, which in 1839 immediately became an Army March. There followed Overtures, Waltzes and other pieces. Kelch was extremely busy with his band making music. For the Cologne Deaf and Dumb Institute he held yearly fund-raising concerts, further concerts for the victims of Fire and Flood and for other fundraising events for old comrades etc. Charitable work was the life of his band. His ability to direct, conduct and his own virtuosity one can still read of in the archive newspapers in Cologne. Kelch's band was greatly loved. After the suppression of the unrest in Baden, the Regiment was stationed from 1851 in Aachen, this city being the garrison for its HQ staff. Kelch did not enjoy good fortune whilst there. His wife Pauline died in 1852. He then bought himself out and went with his children to the home city of his late wife, Berlin. His march was later no longer played by other regiments and was heard no more.

AM II, 115 Marsch arranged by Ferdinand Haase

Another brisk march from Russia! It was a gift in 1838/9 from Grand-Prince Michael. Grand-Prince Michael Pavlovitch was the younger brother of Tsar Nicholas, and from 1823 was the Royal Honorary Colonel of the Prussian Kürassier-Regiment Nr. 7 in Halberstadt (Harz Mountains). He knew that the King of Prussia, his brother's father-in-law, had an extensive Army March Collection largely from Russia and had been instrumental in enhancing it further with such marches. The arrangement is unmistakeably by Ferdinand Haase, who from 1830 onwards was the Director of the Bands and Choirs of the Russian Imperial Guard Corps in St Petersburg and responsible for many good marches.

AM II, 116 Marsch nach Motiven der Oper »Der Brauer von Preston« – Opera by Adolphe Charles Adam (1803-1856) – March by Johann Carl Neumann (1797-?)

This is a quick march of the 3.Garde-Regiment zu Fuss who were stationed from 1878 in Berlin-Kreuzberg, Wrangelstrasse in a new imposing barracks. It was frequently heard on the Tempelhoferfeld when they marched past at the twice-yearly Trooping of the Colours. General-Feldmarschall von Hindenburg could produce the melody of the trio of this march on the rim of his wine glass as a party trick! The opera 'The Brewer from Preston' appeared in 1838. Neumann was a Band Sergeant in the Band of the Kaiser Alexander Grenadier-Regiment in Berlin from 1818-1847. It is still played by the Bundeswehr.

AM II, 117 Marsch des Österreichischen Infanterie Regiments 42 Herzog von Wellington by Johann Schubert

Johann Schubert (1807-1859), a virtuoso on the violin and mandolin, qualified at the Prague Conservatory. For twenty-three years (1828-51) he led the band of the 42nd Austrian Infantry Regiment in the little fortress town of Theresienstadt in Bohemia. At a concert at the cure resort of Teplitz in 1838, King Friedrich Wilhelm III of Prussia heard it performed and asked Schubert for the score. It was first put in the Prussian Collection in 1839 with Schubert's own arrangement, but Wieprecht rearranged it in 1869. Grawert published it in his 'Folge I' March book in 1914, and it is again available in the Bundeswehr's volume II since 1961. A very popular march.

AM II, 118 Marsch nach Motiven der Oper »Die Hugenotten« Opera by Giacomo Meyerbeer – March by Hübner

The Opera appeared in 1836 and in Berlin for the first time in 1842. Already in 1839 King Friedrich Wilhelm III had put this march in the Prussian Army March Collection, the parts being published and distributed to all bandsmen by the music publishers Adolph Martin Schlesinger. Since then it has been universally played. Even Army Music Inspector Professor Schmidt put the parts in the 1933 March Book, despite the fact that Meyerbeer was a forbidden Jewish composer!" Everyone laughed – who was going to need it? Well, the Breslau battalions continued to use it, and I remember how even a band of the SA (Nazi Party Brown Shirts, the Storm Troops. Ed.) gave a sparkling performance of it whilst on the march through Tangermünde! The march was easy, everyone had the parts, and nothing was going to stop it. And so it came to today's Bundeswehr.

AM II, 119 Preussenmarsch by Joseph Golde (1802-1886)

Golde was Bandmaster of Infanterie-Regiment Nr. 32 in Erfurt from 1827-1862 and well-regarded in his city for his concert work with the Regimental Band. The march is one of the most significant in German history. It originally appeared as *Marsch über National-Melodien* in 1840, being based on both the Haydn national anthem *Heil dir im Siegerkranz* (the tune known in the UK as *God Save the Queen*. Ed.) and *Ich bin ein Preusse* ('I am a

Prussian') by Guards Bandmaster Neithardt with words by Bernhard Thiersch from 1830. On 3 July 1866 the Leib-Grenadier-Regiment Nr. 8 band under Gottfried Piefke's baton provided this march out during the Prussian advance at Königgrätz, so strengthening and steadying the Prussian King's nerve that he never forgot Piefke's service that day. It remained in this triumphalist form until the Great War. It is the most exciting arrangement of *Heil dir im Siegerkranz* ('God Save the Queen') ever composed. In 1922 it was rearranged by Theodor Grawert during the Weimar Republic, the old Haydn national anthem being replaced by *Deutschland über Alles* instead, after the fall of the German monarchy, Germany and Britain no longer sharing the same tune for their national anthems. This march was frequently used by the bands of the various Prussian Guard infantry regiments when Guard Mounting in Unter den Linden.

AM II, 120 Ungarischer Marsch by Alexander Radowski, arranged by Franz Liszt

On 4th October 1841, the score for this march was published by Adolph Martin Schlesinger Verlag, Berlin. A long work of sixteen pages, it was recorded then as being *'componiert von Radoosky'*. The piece was in four sections 16, 12, 8 and 16 bars with repeats. In 1895, Dr Thouret discovered during his research in the Berlin Schloss that the original score for Infantry band and also one for piano-forte had been arranged by Franz Liszt (1811-86) from an original by Alexander Radowski, a Hungarian composer.

AM II, 121 Marsch nach Motiven der Oper »Sappho« and *AM II, 122 Marsch nach Motiven des Balletts* »Die Eroberung von Constantin« *und der Oper* »Sappho«, both by Giovanni Pacini (1796-1867)

The composer was an Italian born in Syracuse. He lived and worked in Venice, writing much church music. His opera *Sappho* appeared in 1840, followed by his ballet *Die Eroberung von Constantin* in 1841. Of his sixty comic operas, *Sappho* is his best and gained wide popularity at the time. His style is very similar to that of Rossini. The AM II, 121 is in 2/4 time and *AM II, 122* in 6/8 time. These pretty marches were heard in Naples by Graf von Redern and brought back to Prussia by the Royal Princes after their Italian tour with the 'Musical Count' von Redern.

AM II, 123 Marsch des Russischen Grenadier Regiments König Friedrich Wilhelm III

Just as there was in Berlin a Guard Regiment from 25 December 1814, named after the allied Russian Tsar, the 'Kaiser Alexander Grenadier-Regiment', so in St Petersburg at the same time a Russian regiment was named 'Grenadier Regiment König Friedrich Wilhelm III'. Its marches are of much interest. Already by 1817 the Prussians had it with the title of Armeemarsch II, 19, one of Anton Dörfeldt's dedicated compositions. Then in 1843 came another march similarly titled as a march from Petersburg, and became *AM II, 123*. It is a breathtakingly good piece, and is also known in the Kingdom of Sweden and was known in the old Kingdom of Hanover, being played very often. In Hanover it was played by the 1st Hanoverian Leib-Regiment. When the Prussians took up the traditions of the former Hanoverian troops it became the Regimental Quick March of Infanterie-Regiment Nr. 79

in Hildesheim on 27th January 1900. The un-haltingly long piece has, after six introductory bars, two sections of sixteen bars and a trio, but the second section with sixteen bars, and all subsequent sections are repeated. Already, by 1871, Wieprecht had published a new arrangement. In 1926 it appeared in an arrangement by Professor Oskar Hackenberger in Marschbuch (second series), from which it entered the Bundeswehr Volume II in 1961.

AM II, 124 Marsch nach Motiven der Oper »Die Regimentstochter« by Gaetano Donizetti

One finds it difficult to imagine in our technically overladen age of cars, computers and television, what an impact a good composer once had with a new composition. That applies to Gaetano Donizetti, born in Bergamo, North Italy in 1797, and who died there in 1848. He was a restless soul. Tirelessly busy, often changing his home address, Naples, Paris, Vienna, and staying with his contemporary Italian comrades Rossini and Bellini. He wrote Lieder, songs, quartets, church music, symphonies, and especially the seventy operas, whose enchanting themes bring such joy. His greatest work *Die Regimentstochter* (Daughter of the Regiment) appeared in 1840 in Paris. The pretty melodies were the basis for the creation of this march, and in 1843/44 it was taken into the Army March Collection. Since then, for a further one hundred and fifty years, it has continued to be played, more at concerts than in service use. Since 1933 it is in Marschbuch '4th series', since 1961 in Volume II of Bundeswehr marches. Always and for evermore will Donizetti's sounds bring joy. In his youth he had served as a Bandmaster of an Austrian Regiment serving in the Italian provinces of the Austrian Empire. His younger brother, Giuseppe Donizetti, led the whole of the Turkish military music service from his office in Constantinople from 1831 onwards.

AM II, 125 Marsch by Ferdinand Dregert

It was not only military bandmasters who led the way by being called to write good marches. It was also the work of their musicians, bandsmen and trumpeters, which shows the value of a good grounding in composition during basic training. Two of the most famous and frequently played pieces are by bandsmen, namely the *Victoriamarsch* (*AM II, 174*) and *Soldatenklänge* (*AM II, 175*). The *Victoriamarsch* after one-hundred-and-twenty-five years remains in the march books of the Bundeswehr in volume II.

The composer of this piece is Ferdinand Dregert (1814-1852). He was, from 1840 to 1850, a bandsman in the Kaiser Alexander Grenadier-Regiment in Berlin, and seved for his entire period under the outstanding Director of Music, Schick. The march originated in 1844 and was immediately named as an Army March by King Friedrich Wilhelm IV. On 20th July 1844, the score was published by Musikverlag Schlesinger, Berlin. Almost ninety years later in 1933 the piece went to all German Musik-und Trompeterkorps with its publication in the 4th Series (4.Folge) Marschbuch by Professor Hermann Schmidt.

AM II, 126 Geschwindmarsch nach Motiven aus Quadrillen by Johann Strauss, father

The march standard! In Prussia this has an unbroken service use of more than one hundred years, and as such is a piece of military history. In Bavaria it was not played, nor Saxony, and not by Jägers, Pioneers, the Navy, nor Mounted Troops. It was only ever used by the Infantry. The piece was created from two Strauss quadrilles by a Garde-Kapellmeister in Berlin. These beautiful and famous melodies, bade him craft a march of them. There is no

Johann Strauss (Father) (1804-1849) (Duncan Rogers)

finer piece for parades and troop movement on the streets than this. The march is note for note a true construction of the themes of two Quadrilles by father Strauss (1804-1849), namely from the Jubel quadrille (Opus130), which in 1841 appeared for the jubilee of the Austrian Empress Maria Anna, and from the Ferdinandquadrille (Opus 151) which is for the 1843 (jubilee?) of Emperor Ferdinand I. The two first sections are from the Jubelquadrille and were the first section from 'Tour 2 (été)', the second section from 'Tour 1 (Pantalon)'. The trio of the march has as its first section from Ferdinandquadrille 'Tour 6 (finale)' and the second section once again from the Jubelquadrille, 'Tour 5 (Pastourelle)'. And as already said, true note for note, only with a change of tone and coupled together. So the arranger found no need to do anything other than this. It appeared we know in 1844 from Wilhelm Christoph (1810-1859), who for nineteen years from 1st July 1840 until his death on 25 February 1859 was the Bandmaster (Stabshoboist) of the Kaiser Franz Grenadier-Regiment. Austria's Kaiser Franz had been the ally of King Friedrich Wilhelm III in the War of Liberation against Napoleon, and on 18 October 1814 had been made Honorary Royal Colonel of this Regiment, and until its abolition in 1919 carried the name of his title, 'Kaiser Franz'. The Austrian Kaiser often visited the Regiment for parades and exercises, and the Regimental Band travelled frequently to Vienna from Berlin to play concerts for him. The association was close. In May 1853, Prussian King Frederick Wilhelm IV took Bandmaster Christoph on his State Visit to Vienna in his own entourage, as he much enjoyed his company and learned a great deal about music from him. Never had a military Kapellmeister ever been an official part of a Court entourage on a State Visit before. The march was most popularly played in Prussia and Baden, between Gumbinnen (in East Prussia) and Aachen (on the Belgian border) and between Cologne (on the Rhine) and Freiburg (in Breisgau/Black Forest) it was played as a regimental quick march. In 1871, Wieprecht brought out a new arrangement. In 1898, in the particular form required for marching past in 'Regimentskolonne', Rossberg wrote an arrangement and in 1914 it appeared in the first edition of the Marschbuch (first series), and since 1961 the Bundeswehr have it in their Volume II.

In 1849, the Kaiser Franz Grenadier-Regiment took gladly to their new Regimental Quick March the 'Radetzky' which was bestowed on them by Royal Decree. So this *Marsch nach Strausschen Quadrillen* was taken up by the Königin Elisabeth Garde-Grenadier-Regiment Nr. 3, newly raised in Breslau in 1860, who finally moved into their Charlottenburg barracks as part of the Berlin garrison in 1896.

I have myself seen the old comrades of the 'Elisabethers' march past to the strains of this march.

One of our best Prussian Infantry marches![6]

AM II, 127 Kriegers Lust and *AM II, 128 Steyrers Heimweh* and *AM II, 129 Potsdamer Casinomarsch.* all three marches by Josef Gung'l (1810-1889)

Gung'l joined the Band of the Austro-Hungarian 5th Artillery Regiment in Budapest in 1828, transferring to the 4th Artillery Regiment in Graz he soon became their Bandmaster. In 1836 he took his band on a tour of neighbouring Germany and unusually for an Austro-Hungarian had his first composition, a 'Hungarian March', published by the Berlin publishers Bote & Bock, and all his subsequent marches thereafter. He was heavily influenced by the work of Leonhardt, Bandmaster of the Austrian 27th Infantry Regiment also stationed in Graz. In 1843 he left military service and was employed by Bote & Bock, in 1844 publishing a collection of his Military marches dedicated to the King of Prussia, Friedrich Wilhelm IV. In 1848-49 he had an eleven-month tour of the United States of America, and led his own band on six-month- long summer concert tours of St Petersburg and Powlowsk (30 km to the south) each year from 1850-1855.

AM II, 127 Kriegers Lust, his Opus 26, was composed as *Festmarsch* in 1843 and dedicated to Graf von Redern.

AM II, 128 Steyrers Heimweh, his Opus 38, an army march from 1843, has a stunning F trumpet part in the trio.

AM II, 129 Potsdamer Casinomarsch, his Opus 45, appeared as *Potsdamer-Casino-Polka* and was dedicated to the Premier-Leutnant of the Prussian Garde-Husaren-Regiment, Job von Witzleben, who was the eldest son of the famous Prussian War Minister.

On 31 December 1849, Gung'l was awarded the honorary title of Royal Prussian Music Director, an unusual honour for an Austro-Hungarian. Aged 46, Gung'l returned to Austrian service as Military Kapellmeister of the 23rd Infantry Regiment in Brünn, a position he held from 1856-1864. In retirement he moved to Weimar, where his daughter was a successful singer, but ever-restless he made a further conducting tour to London in 1873, where he received high acclaim.

6 In the 1970s I twice saw the Guard Regiment of the East German Nationale Volksarmee goose-step past to this march, one of their favourites too. Ed.

Friedrich Wilhelm, Graf von Redern (1802-1883) the 'Musical Count of Berlin' who accompanied the young Prussian princes on their grand tours, and later was Chairman of Judges for the Bock March Competitions in the 1850s. He is shown here as a younger man. (Duncan Rogers)

AM II, 130 Soldatengruss by August M. Canthal (1804-1881), arranged by Carl Engelhardt

The composer was born and lived and died in Hamburg. He was solo and first flautist with the Hamburg Theatre Orchestra and then their Director of Music from 1853 to 1855. In later life he directed a private orchestra. This march appeared in 1846, and was arranged by Bandmaster Engelhardt of the 1.Garde-Regiment zu Fuss in Potsdam for wind band. As a composer, Canthal is known to have written two operas and much popular dance music. In retirement he gave singing lessons and died at the age of seventy-seven years.

AM II, 131 Geschwindmarsch
and
AM II, 163 Marsch
and
AM II, 165 Geschwindmarsch all by Wilhelm Friedrich Graf von Redern

During the reign of King Friedrich Wilhelm IV, indeed from 1840 to 1861, Wilhelm Friedrich Count von Redern was responsible for the music of the Prussian Court. The people nicknamed him the 'Musik-Graf'. To his position belonged the responsibility too for overseeing the work of all Prussian military music choirs and orchestras. The King had thus a rare and uniquely talented individual in this position. A by-product of this is the composition of these three marches, written by Count Redern who also published the score. At the time nobody sought a new arrangement or use for them. Even Wieprecht himself, when he rearranged all military music in use, left it as it was. Also then for the Reichswehr's music books, Army Music Inspector Professor Hackenberger put all three marches unaltered from their original in his '2nd Series' of 1926. The Bundeswehr copied them in their book (1961) again as they were. So the original arrangements can still be heard today.

AM II, 131 appeared in 1846. It is a charmingly light, springy, wonderful piece,which carries the listener along with it. After the obligatory 1st and 2nd section are thirty-seven powerful bars, followed by the trio with 2 x 8 bars.

AM II, 163 is from the year 1855. It is heavier and famously used by the Prussian Guards as a Parademarsch. The Bundeswehr continues to use this march often as a street march.

AM II, 165 is from 1856. Again, very different from the others. There are six introductory bars; the march then follows in three distinct sections before the trio begins. Within the last bars of the trios, these typically German marches powerfully and loudly reinforce the trio theme, whereas Austrian marches at this point reach their highpoint of the tune itself.

AM II, 132 Militär-Festklänge by Ferdinand Kreinecker

Written in 1846 by a young oboist, Sergeant Kreinecker went on to serve for over twenty-five years in the Band of the 1.Garde-Regiment zu Fuss in Potsdam. He was a gifted pupil of the outstanding Carl Engelhardt (1796-1872), Bandmaster of the 1.Garde-Regiment zu Fuss from 1828-1857. The march never became a Regimental or Divisional march but was often a parade showpiece. Kreinecker played in the band at the Battle of Königgrätz in 1866.

AM II, 133 Marsch nach der »Gazelle« – Piano piece by Dr Theodor Kullak (1818-1882) – March by Wilhelm Wieprecht

Theodor Kullak and his younger brother Adolph hailed from the Province of Posen. Both gifted pianists, they were sponsored by Count Radzwill, the Prussian-Polish landowner who was an excellent composer himself. From 1842 they went to the Viennese Court to study under the famous pianist Czerny, and Nicolai (composer of *The Merry Wives of Windsor*) the Court Kapellmeister. In 1843 Theodor Kullak was appointed as piano teacher to the daughter of Prince Carl of Prussia, and from 1846 became the Court Pianist. In the same year, his Opus 22 *La Gazelle* appeared a salon piece for piano-forte. Entranced by it, the Prussian King Friedrich Wilhelm IV asked Wieprecht, Director of Music of the Guard Corps, to make a march out of it. Although heard on parade, the fifty-nine bar long piece is not really for marching movements but for interludes during parades.

AM II, 134 Corsomarsch by Maximilien Graziani

Both the march and the composer have been entirely forgotten. The march remained arranged for piano only, the score being found again by Dr Thouret after 1889. It was taken into the collection by King Friedrich Wilhelm IV in 1846, and is apparently the composer's Opus 35. It is really a concert piece and it is not known ever to have been used by a military band on parade.

Wilhelm Wieprecht (1802-1872) Director of Music for the Guard Corps and later unofficially the effective first overall chief of Prussian Army music, here photographed in old age. (Archive DGfMM eV)

AM II, 135 Marsch nach Motiven der Oper »Stadella« – Opera by Friedrich Freiherr von Flotow – March by Albert Leutner

Albert Leutner (1815-1871) was, by the age of 23, Bandmaster of the Prussian Grenadier-Regiment Nr. 12 in Frankfurt-an-der-Oder. The years during which he was their Bandmaster (1838-1854) were very busy and unsettled for the Regiment. To begin with, the band had to travel to provide musical support for Battalions stationed in three separate garrisons, the HQ Staff and 1st Battalion in Frankfurt-on-Oder, the 2nd Battalion in Krossen (60 km away) and the 3rd (Fusilier) Battalion in Sorau (100 km away). In 1847, the HQ Staff and 1st Battalion moved to Guben, then in 1848 was sent to Berlin to quell the pro-democracy insurrection. In 1849 all three Battalions were sent to the north to fight in the war against Denmark. However, from 1850 the HQ Staff, 1st and 3rd Battalions were garrisoned in Frankfurt-on-Oder. Only the 2nd Battalion was in Sorau. The Regiment's Colonel-in-Chief (Chef) was, from 1823, Prince Carl, the brother of the King, who often required 'his' band to travel to perform for him. Altogether, Leutner's job as Bandmaster was frenetic, the band always on the move! Despite this, Leutner gained a reputation as the 'Polka King'. By 1835 he had already composed many dances, marches, quadrilles, occasional music for events, and local ensemble pieces. But above all, Polkas, for which he was much loved. He also was well known to Bote & Bock, the Berlin music publishers who list his first sixty-four compositions. In 1852 he won 2nd Prize with his *Bellona-Marsch* in their march competition. Unfortunately it did not become an Army March, unlike his six years' previous (1846) *Stradelle* we have listed here. The Opera composer, Friedrich Freiherr von

Flotow (1812-1883) gained great acclaim in 1844 when this opera appeared, a reputation he consolidated with his 1853 opera *Martha*. In addition to themes from *Stradelle*, Leutner also includes other strange themes from an unknown source, perhaps his own composition. Altogether it is a fine march. The trio alone from this march was used in 6/8 as a Parade march in Gallop by the Saxon 5.Feld-Artillerie-Regiment Nr. 64 in Pirna until the end of the Great War.

AM II, 136 Marsch nach Motiven der Oper »Die Zigeunerin« by Michael William Balfe (1808-1870)

The composer was a London Opera Director and composer. When Kaiser Wilhelm I was a young prince he had heard this march played by the Austrian 2nd Feldhaubitzen Regiment Graf von Geldern-Egmond, when visiting Vienna. He sent it to his brother, King Friedrich Wilhelm IV, who in turn made it an Army March. From 1860-1919 it was the Quick March of the Prussian Königin Augusta Garde-Grenadier-Regiment Nr. 4. Wieprecht wrote a new arrangement in 1871.

AM II, 137 Pochhammer-Marsch by Gottfried Piefke

Gottfried Piefke (1815-1884) was the most famous and most significant Militärkapellmeister in the Prussian army. His creative work began on 1st October 1843 when he took over the leadership of the Regimental Band of the Prussian Leib-Infanterie-Regiment Nr. 8 in Frankfurt-on-Oder, and he held this position for 40 years until his death. There could be no greater recommendation of his abilities than that 13 successive Regimental Commanding Officers expressed unreserved praise and delight at his work. Piefke also had a good deal of luck in finding a good patron. Following a re-organisation the regiment belonged to the 5th Division whose proprietor, on dynastic grounds that today we would not understand, was Prince Albrecht of Prussia (the King's brother) who moved Divisional HQ away from Berlin. With him on 1st January 1844 came the Division Staff to their old garrison of Frankfurt-on-Oder, and with them Major-General Wilhelm von Pochhammer (1785-1856) as the new Divisional Commander. He was an officer with a wide range of abilities, on top of which he was highly musical. So he encouraged and promoted Piefke and made the King very aware of this talented Stabshoboist. Piefke, for his part in 1845, dedicated his first march to the Divisional Commander, the *Pochhammer-Marsch* which became an Army March in 1846. The piece is absolutely typical in style for the instrumental composition of infantry bands in the early 19th century. It is in F Major key with an attacking style like the *Sedan-Marsch (AM II, 45a)* and *die deutsche Kaisergarde (AM II, 208)*, in this key which infantry bandmasters liked to use at that time. However, later, Wieprecht re-arranged it in the key of Eb, so that at large concerts cavalry bands with their natural fanfare trumpets could play along with it. From Piefke came many more marches including the famous *Königgrätzer* and *Preussens Gloria*. Piefke worked his way to become a Director of Music and eventually Director of all bands of the III. Korps (all the Brandenburg regiments, whilst simultaneously keeping his regimental position with the 8th Leib-regiment band). On 18th January 1869 Piefke received personally from the King the Order of the House of Hohenzollern at an investiture in the Berlin Schloss attended by all the Princes of the realm, including the Chancellor, Prince Bismarck. In 1848 Generalmajor von Pochhammer retired from the service. His grandson, Generalmajor Erich von Pochhammer was killed in action in 1914 at Argonne in front of his brigade. He was my paternal uncle (married to my father's sister).

Gottfried Piefke (1815-1884) (Archive DGfMM eV)

AM II, 138 Grande Marche Militaire by Philipp Musard (1793-1859)

What Johann Strauss (father) was to Vienna; Philipp Musard was to Paris at the same time. At the head of a leading, wonderful orchestra he played light music for the population so that he became lovingly known as 'The French Strauss', much fêted and admired. He wrote himself valuable dances, marches and incidental music, including much for the military. But, just as Franz Schubert wrote his military marches for two pianos, so the march is unknown in music for strings. It came into the Army March Collection in 1846, but because Quick-time tempo at that time in Volume II was at 108 to the minute (raised later to 114), it is played much quicker and more lightly. The French Infantry march to it at a much quicker tempo.

AM II, 139 Marsch des Österreichischen Infanterie Regiments 18 Baron Reisinger

Prince Carl of Prussia (1801-1883) journeyed to Lombardy in Upper Italy in July 1841. In the then Austrian- Italian Province he heard the 18th Bohemian Infantry Regiment play this attractive, typically Austrian march full of melodies. So he sent the parts back to his royal brother in Berlin for the Army March Collection. Earlier that year, King Friedrich Wilhelm IV had just taken over the reins of power. So he tucked it away – and forgot all about it! Some years later, it was unearthed and Wilhelm Christoph (1810-1859), Stabshoboist of the Kaiser Franz Regiment in Berlin, arranged it for Prussian military band. The King heard it and decreed it should be an Army March in the collection. This all took place in 1846-7 when the march was numbered. Twenty-five years later, in 1871, it was arranged again by Wieprecht as he, too, found this pretty piece most enchanting. The Austro-Hungarian (K.U.K.) Imperial and Royal War Ministry in Vienna declared the march to be simply the *Reisinger-Marsch* in their *Prachtalbum* (Service Manual) entitled the *Historische Armeemärsche und sonstige Kompositionen für das Kaiserliche und Königliche Heer* in 1895, (Historic Army Marches and other diverse compositions for the Imperial and Royal Army) in a modernised and somewhat altered arrangement by Emil Kaiser (1853-1929). Finally, the march was rearranged by Armeemusikinspizient Professor Oskar Hackenberger (1872-1929) in 1926 in his '2nd series' to all German military musicians. There is no more beautiful march surviving one-hundred-and-fifty years!

AM II, 140 Marsch nach Motiven der Oper »Il Torneo« by John Jane Duke of Westmorland

The Englishman, John Jane, Duke of Westmorland (1784-1859), was in the first half of the 19th century a famous personality. As a thirty-year-old, he fought in Portugal, Spain and in 1815 at Waterloo/Belle Alliance as Adjutant to the British Commander-in-Chief, the Duke of Wellington. In the same year, 1815, the Duke of Westmorland began his diplomatic career as the British Ambassador to Florence and from 1841 in the same position at the Prussian Court in Berlin. He was decorated with the Order of the Red Eagle 1st Class (Prussia's highest decoration) by the Prussian King. The Opera *Il Torneo* was written by the Duke of Westmorland in Italy in 1829. The melodies were turned into a march by him later when he was Ambassador in Berlin, and in 1847 it was made an Army March by the King. Prussian troops, however, never used the piece in service. (It was probably included in the Royal Collection of Army Marches as a diplomatic compliment.)

AM II, 141 Österreichischer Defiliermarsch by Johann Strauss (father) (1804-1849), arranged by Wilhelm Christoph (1810-1859)

It was written in August 1847 as Opus 209 and went with him on his band tour to Berlin. In Charlottenburg Castle it was performed before the Prussian Court. In the same year, the King, Frederick Wilhelm IV, had it arranged by Christoph for the march collection and bestowed it upon the 2.Garde-Regiment zu Fuss as their Regimental Quick march. The last Bandmaster of the Regiment, Max Graf, used to render it in a particularly hard syncopated rhythm for parades on the Tempelhoferfeld in the early years of the 20th century. Wieprecht had rearranged it in 1871. It appeared in 1926 in Hackenberger's '2nd series' and in 1961 Colonel Stephan put it in the Bundeswehr's Volume II.

AM II, 142 Marsch nach dem »Jasminwalzer« – Waltz by Joseph Labitzky (1802-1881) – March by Wilhelm Christoph (1810-1859)

The Jasmine Waltz by Labitzky was his Opus 74. He was known in the Austro-Hungarian Empire as the 'Bohemian Waltz King' at the same period as 'Father' Strauss had the same accolade but as the Viennese King of waltzes. Labitzky had his own band from 1825 and went on concert tour to Warsaw from 1829 to 1830. After he took over the Karlsbad Kur orchestra in 1835, he went on tour to London and St Petersburg. In 1847, Wilhelm Christoph of the Kaiser Franz Grenadier-Regiment in Berlin, keen on Austrian music, turned this waltz into a march for his band with wonderful clarinet parts. Christoph, before he became Bandmaster in 1840, had been a virtuoso clarinettist himself! Twenty years later, two other waltzes were made into marches. In 1867, Director of Music Saro marched past

Napoleon III at the Paris Exhibition to his arrangement of *Les Roses* by Metra, and in 1864 Gottfried Piefke arranged the *Faust-Waltz* by Gounod as his *Margarethenmarsch.*

AM II, 143 Prinz Eugen-Geschwindmarsch by Carl Neumann (1822 – ?)

Prince Eugene of Savoy (1663-1736), the great Austrian Commander-in-Chief, and the folksong of him, the 'edlen ritter', has been used in the trio of two marches, the Belgrad-marsch (*HM II, 142*) by Schifferl, and this one by the Bugle-Major/Bandmaster from 1848 to 1859 of the Guard Rifles Battalion in Berlin. In 1859 Neumann transferred to Düsseldorf to the newly-raised Westphalian Jäger-Bataillon Nr. 7, creating the Battalion's first band in time for the march to their new garrison of Cleves in 1860.

AM II, 144 Defiliermarsch by Princess Charlotte of Prussia (1831-1855)

The composer was the niece of King Wilhelm III and Queen Louise. Trained as a pianist by Taubert and then Kullak, her talent as a composer is revealed in this, her first work. Wieprecht, the Director of Music of the Guard Corps, had an excellent working relationship with her, arranging her further two Defilier marches and two cavalry marches for military band use. They even continued to work together when she left Berlin to marry the Crown Prince George of Saxe-Meiningen, and it was only her untimely death in childbirth that brought an abrupt end to this fruitful musical partnership. Prussian regiments frequently and keenly played all her compositions for over a century.

AM II, 145 Radetzkymarsch by Johann Strauss, father, arranged by Wilhelm Christoph

Everyone today knows the opening bars of this piece. And when they ring out, and you drum the rhythm on the table top, it brings a smile to the face; naturally famous, how nice, how pretty, the Radetzky. Today's appreciation is not in keeping with its origins though! It was a march for marching soldiers in a war situation. It is also not quite right to call it a 'military' march as such. (It is a piece of propaganda on the home front.) Johann Strauss (father 1804-1849) wrote the piece for use in wartime, further, for the benefit of the military. He wrote this Opus 228 on 29 September 1848 for his salon-orchestra which he conducted himself, and gave it the tone and rendition he wanted. And he named it 'To Honour the Great Field Commander'. Austria had every reason to thank this great man. The piece was jubilantly taken on and spread far and wide. Today it is the most famous march of all! The composer died on 25th September 1849. His Radetzky march was one of his last works before his death. Almost immediately, in the middle of October, the Prussian King ordered the publication of it in the Army March Collection, and for his Kaiser Franz Grenadier-Regiment to play it at all their parades. Their Regimental Kapellmeister, Wilhelm Christoph (1810-1859), had to arrange it. In Austria the march was banned in 1851 for fear of demonstrations, but was later popularly re-habilitated when its associations with anti-reform forces of the old regime had subsided. In 1871 it appeared in a new arrangement by Wieprecht, which was in the 1914 March Book '1st Series'. In 1921 the 3rd Battalion of the 8. (Preussisches) Infanterie Regiment, stationed in Görlitz, took over the traditions of the old Kaiser Franz Garde-Grenadier-Regiment Nr. 2. Since 1961 it is in the Bundeswehr's Volume II.

Which parade marches did the Prussian Guard Corps play? The 1.Garde-Regiment zu Fuss and the 2.Garde-Regiment zu Fuss played Beethoven's *Yorckscher* and Daddy Strauss's Austrian *Defiliermarsch*, and the 'Alexanders' and 'Franzers' had Leonhardt's

Field Marshal Johann Josef Wenzel Anton Franz Karl, Graf Radetzky von Radetz (1766-1858) who led the Austrians to victory against Piedmontese and Italian rebel forces at the battles of Custoza (1848) and Novara (1849) during the First Italian War of Independence from Austria. In 1849 he also re-captured Venice for the Austrian Empire. (Duncan Rogers)

Alexandermarsch and the *Radetzky* respectively – Ja! music certainly comes out of Vienna!

AM II, 146 Wrangelmarsch mit dem Wrangellied by Carl Hering

'Papa Wrangel', as the Berliners called him, was a famous 'one off' by the time this march appeared in 1849. A larger than life character, he was a General of Cavalry, and by this time, at sixty-five years of age, Commander in Chief of the II Army Corps in Stettin. Famous for anecdotes, he had a service career stretching back further than anyone could remember. He wore the Order of the Red Eagle, Iron Cross 1st and 2nd Class with swords and diamonds, the Blue Max (Pour le Merité), all won way back during the Wars against Napoleon. He loved 'military buffooning', and everyone laughed when he claimed that the 1848 insurrection would melt away if he could only appear in Berlin and "have a word" with the crowd. He once said jokingly that "Military parades are not only about pristine uniforms, the whiteness of leatherwork and polished weapons, but also about my appearance at them!" Laughter and good humour followed Wrangel around. Naturally enough there were therefore Wrangel-Lieder (songs) and Wrangel-Märsche (marches) and Carl Hering's Opus 10 of the 9 December 1849 had the luck to become a recognised Army March. Hering (1819-1889) was a famous touring concert violinist. From 1846 he was the first Concert Manager of the Royal Orchestra in Berlin. Later he led his own music school and published Elementary School music books. The Wrangellied was his most famous work.

Friedrich Heinrich Ernst Graf von Wrangel (1784-1877) at the time of the First Schleswig-Holstein War 1848. (Duncan Rogers)

AM II, 147 Wiener Kreuzer-Polka by Johann Strauss, father

This march appeared on 26 April 1848 from the publishers Haslinger of Vienna as Opus 220 from this famous composer. In 1851 it was arranged by Wieprecht for Prussian military band and published by Bote & Bock of Berlin. At the same time, it became AM II, 147 in the Prussian Collection. It was superseded by Prize marches from the Gustav Bock competitions, which began in 1852, and was rarely used on parade. Despite this, Professor Hackenberger included it in his March book '2nd Series' of 1926.

AM II, 148 Geschwindmarsch by Crown Princess Charlotte of Saxe-Meiningen

This is the third of five of her marches in the Army March Collection and appeared in 1851. It was published by Gustav Bock, Berlin.

AM II, 149 Marsch by John, Count of Caradja

This march from 1852 is no parade march, nor a route march, but a little bit of diplomatic politics! The composer was the Prime Legation Secretary of the Turkish Ottoman Mission to the Prussian Court in Berlin at the outbreak of the Crimean War. The Prussian King was very keen to keep out of the conflict, especially with East Prussia so vulnerable to Russian attack and his sister being the Tsarina! He managed to do so despite considerable pressure from Britain and France and not least Turkey. The official adoption of this march was a piece of diplomatic flattery. Prussian Army bands were never known to have actually played it on parade!

AM II, 150 Defiliermarsch nach Motiven der Oper »Rigoletto« – Opera by Giuseppe Verdi (1813-1901) – Arranged by Wilhelm Wieprecht

Rigoletto appeared in 1851 from this world famous composer. Prince Albrecht of Prussia first heard the Opera in Brunswick and suggested to Wieprecht that it would make a good march. In 1852 Wieprecht obliged and the King named the piece as Army March II, 150 in 1853. Briefly very popular, the march was soon superseded by better ones from the prize march competitions held by Bock Music Publishers in the same decade.

AM II, 151 Marsch nach Motiven des Ballets »Catarina« by Cesare Pugni (1802-1870), arranged by Wilhelm Wieprecht

Cesare Pugni's ballet appeared in Russia in 1846. Prince Carl of Prussia visited his sister the Tsarina in September 1851 to celebrate the Silver Jubilee of the Russian Royal Couple's coronation. Whilst in Moscow he heard the Opera and took the score back to Berlin for his brother the King who asked Wieprecht to make a march out of themes from the opera. In 1853 Musikverlag Schlesinger published the parts for this new Army March. Sixteen years later, in 1869, Wieprecht rearranged his own work as the technical advances in musical instruments and enlargement of bands made this necessary.

AM II, 152 Marsch über den Musketiertanz aus der Ballettmusik »Satanella« – Ballet by Peter Ludwig Hertel (1817-1899) – March by Wilhelm Wieprecht (1802-1872)

Hertel was a court composer in 19th century Berlin. A number of his pretty melodies have been turned into marches, most notably from his ballet *Fantaska* of 1889, from which the Bundeswehr's Volume III, No 214 *Amazonenmarsch* is derived. There are a number of other trot and gallop marches, one used by the Bavarian 3.Cheveau-Legers from his ballet *Flick and Flock,* his Opus 200 of 1866. This march from his 1852 ballet *Satanella*, his Opus 40, was made into an Army March by Wieprecht in 1853 when he used Hertel's melodies for a potpourri at one of his monster concerts performed by the massed bands and cavalry trumpeter corps of the Guard Corps in Berlin.

AM II, 153 Marsch by Anton von Kontsky (1817-1899), arranged by Wilhelm Wieprecht

Kontsky was a famous virtuoso on the pianoforte in the middle of the 19th century. He hailed from Cracow in Galicia, then part of the Austrian Empire, today in Poland. He became Court Pianist at the Court of the Prussian King, Friedrich Wilhelm IV, between 1851 and 1854. It is at this time that Wieprecht arranged his march for Army bands. In 1853 it was published by Musikverlag Schlesinger, Berlin as a conductor's score and became an Army March by Royal command. The composer later went to the Court at St Petersburg and later to London. He finally took a position in New York, his most famous composition being his heroic piece *The Waking of Lions* (Opus 115).

AM II, 154 Franz Joseph-Marsch by Giovanni Oldrini, arranged by Wilhelm Christoph

Austrian, no doubt, as Franz Joseph ruled Austria for sixty-eight years until his death in 1916. Oldrini was Bandmaster of the 28th Austrian Infantry Regiment in Milan between 1847 and 1858. He also composed the *Bellano-marsch*, *Varenna-marsch*, *Corsa sul lario-*

Emperor Franz Joseph of Austria, c.1866. (Duncan Rogers)

marsch, *Garibaldi-marsch*, *Marcia trionfale* dedicated to King Victor Emmanuel II. He presumably transferred his allegiance from Austria to Italy when his native provinces gained their independence from Austrian rule. This 'Franz Joseph' march appeared in 1852 published by Publishers G. Ricordi u.Co/Milan. Bote & Bock issued the march score for Prussian bands in March 1853, when it became an Army March arranged by Wilhelm Christoph of the Kaiser Franz Grenadier-Regiment.

AM II, 155 Marsch nach Motiven der Oper »Indra« – Opera by Friedrich Freiherr von Flotow – March by Carl Neumann

From our Opera composer from Mecklenburg, Friedrich Freiherr von Flotow (1812-1883) there appeared in 1853 the Opera *Indra*. Similarly to his other later operas *Stradella* and *Martha*, much loved. The swinging, effective, memorable and sing-along melodies Carl Neumann (born 1822) brought together in this march at the same time. Neumann was from 1848 to 1859 Stabshornist of the Garde-Schützen-Bataillon in Berlin. In the same year, 1853, it became an Army March and has since been endlessly played. The memory of the Opera has long been surpassed by the fame of the march. It appears in the first published March Book '1st Series ' of 1914, and continues in use since 1961 in Volume II of the Bundeswehr. A popular and frequently played parade march and street march of the Infantry.

AM II, 156 Marsch nach Melodies des Königs von Hannover by William Christoph

A light Viennese-style march with full-blown clarinets gives us the melodies of the Kings of Hanover in fortuitous colours. King George V of Hanover (1819-1878) reigned from 1851 to 1866. Trained as a pianist, he studied composition with Greulich and Kücken in Berlin. His works are competent, mostly piano pieces, songs, male voice choir songs, and church music. Special compositions appeared for festivals. The excellent melodies were, and still are, eagerly played. This is true particularly in Hanover. Wilhelm Christoph (1810-1859) was from 1840 to 1859 Stabshoboist of the Kaiser Franz Garde-Grenadier-Regiment Nr. 2 in Berlin. From 1828 this regiment had the Austrian Kaiser as its Royal Colonel, who on journeys to visit them had been serenaded by them and, in turn, he had bestowed much Viennese music on them, the style of which comes out in the arrangement of this march although it is Hanoverian. By this method as arranger and composer for his King, this pretty march became an Army March in 1853. There was a new arrangement in 1926 by Army Musik Inspector Professor Oskar Hackenberger. It came to the Bundeswehr in 1961.

AM II, 157 Kolonnenmarsch
AM II, 169 Manövriermarsch both by Emil Winter

Emil Winter (died c. 1870) was bandmaster of one of the oldest regiments of the Prussian Army, namely the 4.Ostpreussisches Infanterie-Regiment Nr. 5 (after 1860 titled Grenadier-Regiment Nr. 5) in Danzig. During his period of service as bandmaster 1844 to 1866, Winter worked under a succession of eight different Regimental Commanding Officers, and the name of this regiment was altered as a result of the reorganisation of the Prussian Army, which came into effect on 4 July 1860. The regiment's new full title was 4. Ostpreussisches Grenadier-Regiment Nr. 5. The garrison was, at this time and until the abolition of the regiment as a result of the 'Diktat' of Versailles in 1919, in the Hanseatic City of Danzig. On 18 January 1855 Winter was awarded the Allgemeine Ehrenzeichen and on 2 February 1863 he took part in Wilhelm Wieprecht's twenty-five year Jubilee (celebrating Wieprecht's service to military music) in Berlin. Emil Winter was a gifted composer, whose works enjoyed considerable success in the Court Music Publisher Gustav Bock's 'Royal Prussian Army Prize March' competitions held between 1852 and 1861. Through this we have to this day four beautiful swing-along *Strassenmärsche* ('Street marches') from this composer.

The *Kolonnenmarsch* gained 3rd Prize in the 1853 competition, and that October became a recognised Army March. The *Manövriermarsch* gained 2nd Prize, and in March of the next year became an Army March. There are two further marches by Winter in the archives of Music Publishers Bote & Bock, Berlin. These are the *Elisabethmarsch* from the 1854 competition, awarded 2nd Prize, and the *Friedrich Wilhelm-Marsch* from the 1855 competition, which was in the shortlist for prizes drawn-up by the examining committee under Count Redern's chairmanship. In all four years 1853 to 1857 Winter's entries were prize winners, and all four entries were scored as Infantry marches. The two which became official Army Marches belong, in my opinion, to the most beautiful of our *Strassenmärsche* (Street marches or route marches)! Thus they appeared in the first published Marschbuch 1. Folge (1st series) in 1914 and remained available to all military musicians until 1945 and were frequently played.

AM II, 158 Marsch nach Motiven der Oper »Grossfürstin Sophia Catharina« – Opera by Friedrich Freiherr von Flotow – March by Gottfried Meinberg

The 2.Garde-Regiment zu Fuss in Berlin had three Bandmasters with the name Meinberg, all one after another, for fifty years from 1844 to 1894. This march hails from the middle one, Gottfried Christian Meinberg (1816-1894). He led the band from 1849 to 1873. As Stabshoboist of the foremost regiment in the capital, he was well known and much valued by his Kings, Chancellor Bismarck and the Berliners. With his regiment he went to war for the campaign in Bohemia in 1866 and in France in 1870 to 1871. A leading event, however, was on 21 July 1867 when the competition of European military bands took place at the World Fair in Paris. The Prussians took part under the leadership of Wieprecht with a combined band of the 2.Garde-Regiment zu Fuss and the Kaiser Franz Garde-Grenadier-Regiment Nr. 2 and took 1st Prize. Emperor Napoleon III congratulated Meinberg personally. In Meinberg's time of service the prize march competitions by Gustav Bock, the Berlin music publishers, were run to which competition, in 1852, Meinberg sent this march and gained 3rd Prize. The opera *Grossfürstin Sophia Catharina* by Friedrich Freiherr von Flotow (1812-1883) appeared in 1850, the combined melodies of which are in the march which became an Army March in 1853. In 1926, Army Music Inspector Oskar Hackenberger brought out a new arrangement for all German military musicians in March Book '2nd series'.

AM II, 159 Marsch des Ungarnschen Infanterie Regiments Prinz von Preussen Nr 34 by Philipp Salvator Basilius Laino

Here we have the march of an old Hungarian Regiment from the year 1853. Officially the regiment was called simply the K.K. Infantry Regiment Nr. 34, but by tradition and in use it was known as 'Hungarian'. The march is by Philipp Laino (or Lanino, 1805-1860), born an Italian, who was from 1847 to 1860 Bandmaster of the Regiment. The Prince of Prussia (later Kaiser Wilhelm I) was, from 1841 onwards, Inhaber of the Regiment. At a Princely get-together in Ölmütz in Moravia in 1853, the Prussian King, Friedrich Wilhelm IV, met his brother Prince William. The Hungarian Regiment was garrisoned at Ölmütz and after being visited by the King and Prince William, this march dedicated by their Bandmaster was taken back to Berlin. So the Prussian Army March Collection got hold of the score for this piece. Eleven years later, this Hungarian regiment marched through Berlin (see *AM II, 193*) and in the afternoon, at 2 pm, gave a gala concern in the White Hall of the Berlin Stadtschloss conducted by Laino's successor, Levengly. At the end of the Great War in 1918, this splendid Regiment found its dissolution with the collapse of the Austro-Hungarian Empire.

AM II, 160 Pepitamarsch by Friedrich Pfeifke

Before me lies the original handwritten letter of Prince Albert of Prussia to Wieprecht, it reads:

> His Majesty expressed a wish today at dinner, at which Count Redern was present, that the *Pepita-Marsch* should be raised to the status of an Army March. Let me know, my dear Wieprecht, so that I can inform Graf Redern at the earliest opportunity.
>
> Berlin, 5 February 1854 Signed: Albrecht Prinz von Preussen

With this, the Pepitamarsch became an Army March at the direct command of King Friedrich Wilhelm IV in the year 1854. The piece has been composed more than thirty years before (c. 1820) by the bandsman (Hoboist) Friedrich Pfeifke (born 1790-?), who later served as Bandmaster of the Swedish Värmland-Regiment. The theme comes from a Spanish folk dance, the title after a ballerina. Stabshornist (Bugle Major, de facto Light Infantry Bandmaster) Carl Neumann (Born 1822-?) of the Garde-Schützen-Bataillon in Berlin quickly wrote an arrangement. The resulting piece quickly became a much-played and widely-loved march which, over one hundred and thirty years later, is still in constant use by the bands of the Bundeswehr.

AM II, 161 Alexandermarsch by Andreas Leonhardt, arranged by Wilhelm Christoph

Andreas Leonhardt (1800-1866) came from Bohemia, from Asch (20 km NW of Eger on the border with Upper Franconia). He had already gained a reputation over many decades as an Austrian bandleader and excellent composer. However, he had yet more to do. He took up a new position as Military Kapellmeister in chief to the K.K. (Austrian Imperial and Royal Hungarian) Armed Forces. He became the Austro-Hungarian equivalent to Wieprecht in Prussia. The sudden growth of military music in European countries at that time put him in a high-profile position. His work was an example to all. However, in 1862 his position was abolished (by a parsimonious exchequer). From the year 1853 appears Leonhardt's beautiful 6/8 march. Entitled by him *Alexander Cesarewitsch-Marsch,* it was dedicated to the thirty-five- year-old Russian heir to the throne, later Tsar Alexander II. When the Prussian King Frederick Wilhelm IV heard it on 20th May 1853 at a grand parade on the Glacis (the Vienna equivalent to Horse Guards Parade) he declared it to be the best march he had heard in a long while. His brother, the Prince of Prussia, took part in the parade (as Honorary Royal Colonel of one of the Austrian Regiments). Bandmaster Wilhelm Christoph (1810-1859) from the Prussian Kaiser Franz Regiment, who had accompanied the King on his visit to Austria, asked if he might take the score back to Berlin. Once home, he arranged it for the instrumentation of a Prussian Band. In 1854 it became an Army March as *Alexandermarsch* and was bestowed upon the Kaiser Alexander Grenadier-Regiment in Berlin as their Regimental Quick March (Parademarsch). In 1871 Wieprecht wrote a new arrangement. In 1914 it appeared in Marschbuch 1. Folge, and since 1961 the Bundeswehr has it. The march (with words from the 'Cat and the Idiot') was understandably popular and often played. It also remains well known in Russia to this day, but no longer in Austria whence it came.

AM II, 162 Marsch by Crown Princess Charlotte von Sachsen-Meiningen

In the Army March Collection there are five marches by this very interesting composer. *AM II, 144* and *AM III,* 50 were written before she was married when she was a Princess of Prussia. The others, *AM II, 148, AM III, 55* and this one were written after her marriage when she became the Crown Princess of Saxe-Meiningen. The Princess (1831-1855) was the daughter of Prince Albert, and thereby niece of the King of Prussia, Friedrich Wilhelm III and Queen Louise. Her father, Albert, was a soldier and very interested in march music. Her mother was a Princess of Holland who had composed *AM, 21* in 1836. This quick march was the last of Crown Princess Charlotte's compositions before her early death at the age of twenty-four. It appeared in September/October 1854. The King who appreciated the march immediately put it into the Collection. Wieprecht arranged the military band parts for the Princess. It was published by Adolph Martin Schlesinger/Berlin (today, Lienau-Verlag).

AM II, 163 (see *AM II, 131*)

AM II, 164 Gitana-Marsch by Gottfried Piefke

Gitana is Spanish for a gypsy dance. The background to the reason for this march is no longer known. It is certain, however, that the Prussian King Friedrich Wilhelm IV experienced a Spanish gypsy dance in 1855 and wished for a memento of it in march form. So Gottfried Piefke (1815-1884), bandmaster of the Leib-Grenadier-Regiment Nr. 8 (then in Berlin on Ceremonial Public Duties), wrote the piece. It found favour coming from this royal favourite of all bandmasters, entering the Army March Collection immediately, being published by Verlag Schlesinger of Berlin. It was not the first occasion on which the King had put out a request for a march as a desired memento. Already in 1846 he had been much taken with the salon piece *La Gazella* by the court pianist, Theodor Kullak. The then in place Musikdirektor of the Guard Corps, Wieprecht, had to arrange a march from it. It became *AM II, 133*. Likewise, there was a famous composition by Court pianist, Anton von Kontsky, which the King liked in 1853. Wieprecht again obliged. It became *AM II 153*.

AM II, 165 (see *AM II, 131*)

AM II, 166 Geschwindmarsch über das Kölner Dombaulied by Heinrich Laudenbach

In the middle of the 19th century it was decided to complete the building of Cologne Cathedral, which had begun in 1248 but never been finished. To celebrate its completion, a great rededication ceremony took place on 25 July 1856, and from 5.30 p.m. Wieprecht conducted a great concert and grand tattoo in front of the Cathedral with the bands of Infanterie-Regiment Nr. 16, Infanterie-Regiment Nr. 30 and Infanterie-Regiment Nr. 33 and the Trompeterkorps of Kürassier-Regiment Nr. 8. Busso von Hagen (1809-1842), a lieutenant in the Infanterie-Regiment Nr. 28, wrote verses which were set to music by Cologne music teacher Franz Derckum (1812-1872). Then followed this march composed especially for the event by Heinrich Laudenbach, bandmaster of the 33rd Infantry Regimental Band, which led into Beethoven's *Battle of Vittoria* as the highlight of the programme before the formal Grosse Zapfenstreich (Grand Tattoo). Laudenbach's march was such a success that Wieprecht used it in further concerts throughout Prussia, and so popular was it that in 1926 Professor Oskar Hackenberger wrote a new arrangement of it for modern military band instrumentation appearing in Marschbuch 2. Folge. The composer of the march, Heinrich Laudenbach (1827-1907) originated from Holstein. He took over the leadership of this band in 1855, his regimental commander being the later famous War Minister, von Roon. He wrote a lot of marches and many for the Cologne Carnival, which made him a popular figure in the City. A further march is by him *Marsch von Problus und Prim am 3. Juli 1866* (*AM II, 194*). He led his band into battle at Königgrätz, and in the campaign in 1870/71 he was awarded the Iron Cross 2nd Class for bravery (an unusual distinction for an Infantry Bandmaster). He wrote the march *Auf dem Schlachtfeld von Gravelotte* in memory of these exploits ('On the Battlefield of Gravelotte'). The Regiment was sent to a new garrison in Danzig in 1871 and he went with them. In Danzig as well as Cologne his band had an enviable reputation for excellence at public concerts. In 1881 the Regiment was again re-garrisoned in Königsberg, East Prussia. However Laudenbach decided he would rather retire, and after twenty-six years service as bandmaster to the Infanterie-Regiment Nr. 33, he went to become Leader of the Town Band and Music Society in Kevela. He was married but had no children. The people of Cologne never forgot him. On his eightieth birthday, on 7 June 1907, he was fêted at a special celebration in the City, to which all his old comrades had been invited. Two months later he died after a fall. Laudenbach was a gifted personality, full of youthful vigour, admired everywhere, and as a composer and bandmaster singularly blessed.

AM II, 167 Defiliermarsch by Friedrich Orlin (1813- ?)

Orlin was Bandmaster of the Infanterie-Regiment König Friedrich Wilhelm IV (1.Pommersches) Nr. 2 in Stettin from 1852 to 1880. After 1860 it became titled Grenadier-Regiment Nr. 2, when the 12 senior Prussian Line Infanterie-Regiments were re-named as Grenadier-Regiments. On 20 July 1855, this was one of twelve marches entered for the Bock march competition and was played by the 1.Garde-Regiment zu Fuss Band before Graf von Redern, Meyerbee, Neithardt and Leutner, who, as judges, gave this 5th prize. The four better marches disappeared into Bock's archives, but by some accident this one surfaced and was played by the 2.Garde-Regiment zu Fuss Band in front of the king in March 1856. He liked it and made it an official Army March. Perhaps Orlin's luck had something to do with the fact that the King was also his own Regiment's Honorary Colonel and thus familiar with the name of the Bandmaster of the Infänterie-Regiment König Friedrich Wilhelm IV (1.Pommersches) Nr. 2!

AM II, 168 Defiliermarsch by Carl Faust

The composer Carl Faust was a man who really made his mark. With over four hundred agreeable works of dance and church music, he has given mankind much joy and still does one hundred years after his death! Carl Faust was a Silesian, born in 1825 in Neisse, he died in 1892 in Bad Kudowa. In his youth he obtained a first-rate training at the Military-Boys-Preparatory Institute in Annaburg (20 km north of Torgau) from Musikdirektor Herrling. At the end of which he became a musician in the Prussian Army, spending his entire life as a conductor and composer. Next, as military bandmaster, he led the Regimental Band of Infanterie-Regiment Nr.36 (After 1860 named as Füsilier-Regiment Nr. 36) in the German Federal Fortress in Luxembourg from 1853 to 1859, then the Grenadier-Regiment Nr. 11 Band in Breslau from 1859 to 1865, the last couple of years in Flensburg with the occupation forces against Denmark. Finally, he changed to the Königin Elisabeth Garde-Grenadier-Regiment Nr. 3, again back in Breslau from 1866 to 1869. From here he took over the Waldenburg Miners Band in Silesia as their Director of Music. From 1880 he was in Görlitz, Breslau and Beuthen often a welcome sight in his capacity as their Bandmaster. Finally, he led the Cure Band in Bad Kudowa, where, at sixty-seven years old, he died. Faust was a much loved dance and march composer. His compositions always betrayed a freshness, catchy melodies and lively rhythms. Of his marches, this *Defiliermarsch* became his most famous. Written in 1855, he sent the piece from his garrison in Luxembourg to Berlin for the march competition held by the music publisher Gustav Bock, where in 1856 he won the first prize with it, and from 1857 the king named it as an official 'Army March'.

Professor Gustav Rossberg (1838-1910), Prussian Army Inspector of Music, 1890 to 1908. (Archive DGfMM eV)

Later regiments also took it on as their regimental Parade March; for example the 4.Garde-Regiment zu Fuss on the day they were raised in 1860. The fresh and progressive Stabshoboist Gustav Rossberg had got to know it when Bandmaster of the 2.Garde-Regiment zu Fuss in Berlin. Now, after fifty years use (1860-1914) by the Guards Regiments it was known by everyone. In the Reichswehr from 1921, the Berlin Wachtruppe (Guard Troops) and the Band of the Kommandantur Berlin in the Moabit Barracks, once the home of the old 4.Garde-Regiment zu Fuss, was led by Musikmeister Ahlers, who continued the tradition. So between the two world wars (1919-1939) there was no parade or festivity, or Guard of Honour, when this was not heard. As an officer of the Colour Company, I marched past Reich's President Hindenburg and Field Marshal Mackensen to the sounds of this march. Now the march is in the March Book of the Bundeswehr. It is worth remembering that two further marches by Faust are also in use. Saxon Grenadier-Regiment Nr. 101 in Dresden has played, since 1867, the very beautiful *Glück auf!* (Opus 127 of 1865) and Mecklenburg's Füsilier-Regiment Nr. 90 in Rostock from 1871 their dedicated *Loigny Marsch* (Opus 177 of 1870). All Dresden and Rostock know these pieces. Then the Reichswehr battalions there from 1921 continued the tradition. The wonderful gallop march *Wo lustig die Hörner erschallen* (Opus 257 of 1876) and, similarly wonderful trot march, *Die Marketenderin* (Opus 303 of 1879) were made HM marches in 1933 as numbers III B, 29 and 36. The last of these the Bundeswehr have in Volume III. Still today we hear these pretty pieces without realizing that they emanate from Faust.

Prinz Friedrich Wilhelm (later Kaiser Friedrich III) (Duncan Rogers)

AM II, 169 (see *AM II, 157*)

AM II, 170 Marsch by Friedrich Löhrcke

This beautiful march of 1857 with the Trio from Beethoven's A major sonata is not Löhrcke's famous Bock competition prize march of five years previously in 1852 which never became an Army March. The parts for that are held by Bote & Bock/Berlin.

Of this march: Friedrich Löhrcke (1813 – c.1900) was a bandsman, and from 1842 Bandmaster of the Infanterie-Regiment Nr. 10 in Breslau (After 1860 styled the Grenadier-Regiment Nr. 10). In 1850 he changed to be Bandmaster of the Garde-Artillerie-Regiment in Berlin, who had an infantry-style band. It was whilst in this position that he wrote the two above-mentioned marches. On 18th January 1854, he gained the Allgemeine Ehrenzeichen medal. In 1860 he left the service. It was at this time that the Artillery Regiments were brigaded and their bands transformed into mounted trumpeter corps.

AM II, 171 Rekrutenmarsch by Ludwig Jeschko

After the expulsion of Napoleon from central Europe in 1815, the Deutsche Bund (German Federation) created five Federal Fortresses, in which federation troops were stationed. In the Federal Fortress in Mainz lay, amongst others, the Austrian Infantry Regiment Baron Wernhardt Nr 16, their Bandmaster Ludwig Jeschko (1830-1863) wrote there in 1857 this melodic piece, published by Verlag B. Schotts & Söhne/Mainz. Immediately it was taken into the Prussian Army March Collection and since then popularly played. In 1914 it appeared in March Book '1st series' distributed to all Prussian military musicians. When one compares the theme in the trio by Jeschko from 1857 in Mainz and the trio in

Heinrich Saro (1827-1891) Bandmaster of the elite Kaiser Franz Garde-Grenadier Regiment in Berlin from 1859 to 1887. He was a prolific and gifted arranger. Very popular was his Kriegs-Errinnerung 1870-71 potpourri of Franco-Prussian War battle music which was used extensively at concerts and Son et Lumière shows until 1914. (Archive DGfMM eV Sammlung Meißner)

the *Douzy-Marsch* (*HM III A, 61*) by Saxon Lancer Stabstrompeter Franz from the year 1870 before Sedan, one must remember that it is not plagiarism but, on the contrary, a compliment to the sound of a rhythmic melody in the air.

AM II, 172 Prinz Friedrich Wilhelm-Marsch and*AM II, 176 Defiliermarsch* by Heinrich Saro

On New Year's Day 1860, the Prince Regent (later Kaiser Wilhelm I) commanded that at the family dinner table in his Berlin Palace, Unter den Linden No. 9, the marches that in the years 1856-1859 had won a prize in the competitions of the music publishers Bock of Berlin should be played. The Infantry and Jäger marches were played by the Bands of the Kaiser Alexander Grenadier-Regiment under their (Infantry Bandmaster) Stabshoboist Liebig, the cavalry marches by the Trumpeterkorps of the Guard Dragoons under their Stabstrompeter (Cavalry Bandmaster) Wollenhaupt. Both were Berlin-based Regiments. All nine pieces were named by the Prince Regent three weeks later as official Army Marches. Thereby both the above stated marches entered the Collection, the first a Jägermarsch from the 1856 competition which had gained 3rd prize, the other from the 1859 competition which had won 1st prize. The prize-winner and composer was Heinrich Saro (1827-1891), Stabshoboist of the Infanterie-Regiment Nr. 11 in Breslau since 1856. the title *Prinz*

This illustration is taken from the cover of a pianoforte arrangement of Grosser Zapfenstreich arranged by Heinrich Saro published in 1882. This is how Prussian bands in full dress looked until 1914. (Eagle & Lyre Archive)

Friedrich Wilhelm-Marsch he named after the son of the Prince Regent who later became Kaiser Friedrich III, husband to Victoria, Princess Royal of England. In the year 1856/57, he had undertaken his induction training to qualify as a Regimental Commander with the Infanterie-Regiment Nr. 11, and the Stabshoboist Saro knew him. So well-known was Saro by Prince Friedrich Wilhelm, as Saro was such a capable and huge personality, that he went on to be Stabshoboist of the elite Kaiser Franz Grenadier-Regiment in Berlin, when the highly respected Wilhelm Christoph suddenly dropped dead in 1859. The vacant position was secured by the Prince for Saro. In addition, the Commander of the Kaiser Franz Grenadier-Regiment, Oberst von Plessen (father of the later faithful General-Adjutant to Kaiser Wilhelm II) was overjoyed about the appointment. So, Saro became for almost thirty years (1859-1887) a Regimental Bandmaster in Berlin. Saro benefited from his association from then on with General Musikdirektor Wieprecht, twenty-five years his senior. Saro took part in Wieprecht's festival jubilee in Berlin on 2 February 1863. He was also with Wieprecht at the Paris World Fair, where Wieprecht with Saro's Band combined with the Band of the 2.Garde-Regiment zu Fuss won the competition of European military musicians on 21 July 1867. The Emperor, Napoleon III, heaped special praise on Saro for a march with his favourite melodies from Metra's *Les Roses Walzer* which Saro had hastily finished in order to perform it at the march past in front of the Emperor of the French in Paris that year. In September 1872, Saro conducted and led the Grand-Concert for the Berlin meeting of the Three Emperors (Russia, Austria and Germany) as

Bronsart von Schellendorf, whose beautiful wife Helene gave rise to the Helenen-Marsch. (Duncan Rogers)

Wieprecht had died the previous month. However, Wieprecht's position was never filled again. In 1887 there appeared the new position of Armeemusik-inspizient, in between Saro fulfilled this role unofficially. In 1873 he conducted, in the Opera House in Stuttgart, all the military musicians of Wurttemberg in front of the King of Wurttemberg. On 11 June 1879 he conducted a Grand-Concert in the Dönnhoffsplatz in Berlin for the Golden Wedding Anniversary of Kaiser Wilhelm and Kaiserin Augusta. Militärmusikdirektor Saro was, above all, hard-working and knowledgeable. He composed above one hundred compositions. In 1872, his book *Instrumentations-Lehre für Militärmusik* appeared, two-hundred-and-eight large format pages with a wealth of score examples and guidance, a valuable work to this day. His greatest service is his singular dedication and initiative in the field of designing training for Military Bandmaster courses, in which his influence is still felt today. Military music has much to thank Musikdirektor Saro for. The two prize marches by Saro went into the 1926 Marschbuch '2nd series'. Saro's *Defiliermarsch* is in the Volume II of the Bundeswehr since 1961. This piece is the very image of a parade march and street march for infantry. Saro remarked about the original that the march, which is in concert C, would sound better played in G major!

AM II, 173 Helenenmarsch by Friedrich Lübbert

This belongs to our best of marches! For one hundred years always being played, widely loved and still in service use. With its festive and happy rhythmic melody, it is ideal as a Parade march, a street march, a concert march, and for exercises. The foremost troops took the piece as their regimental march. So cleanly is it constructed with 8 bar sections, after 4 bars introduction, the 1st section with 2 x 8 bars (without repeat) the 2nd section with 3 x 8 bars (with repeat) and the trio in the 1st section with 2 x 8 bars and in the 2nd section with 8 bars, the two trio sections and repeats. Wieprecht played the piece as soon as it appeared in 1857 in all his great concerts. Where did the piece come from? It came from Luxembourg! After Kapellmeister Faust of Infanterie-Regiment Nr. 36, stationed in Luxembourg, won the Bock march competition with 1st Prize in 1856 with his later-numbered *AM II, 168*, Kapellmeister Lübbert from Infanterie-Regiment Nr. 35 (both regiments were styled 'Füsilier-Regiment' after 1860) won in the following year 1857, he also was garrisoned in Luxembourg. Faust and Lübbert were Stabshoboisten in the same garrison town and knew each other well; through their children they became related by marriage. And who was Helene? She was the wife of the Regimental Commander, Colonel Bronsart von Schellendorff, whose regimental band Lübbert led, and with whom he achieved the very best results. They all had a very good working relationship.

Friedrich Lübbert (1818-1892), seven years older than his colleague Faust of the IR36, was Stabshoboist of the IR35 (later the famous Prussian Füsilier-Regiment Nr. 35) in the Federal fortress of Luxembourg since 1854, and went with the regiment when it relocated to a new garrison in Brandenburg/Havel. After twenty-seven years service as a Kapellmeister, he left the service in 1881 as a Director of Music. Lübbert composed further marches which are in the archives of the music publishers, Bote & Bock. The *Helenenmarsch* was first deemed an Army March in 1860 because of the illness of the Prussian King. In 1914 it appeared as a piece in March Book 'series 1' for all Prussian military musicians; from 1961 the Bundeswehr has it in their Volume II.

AM II, 174 Victoriamarsch by Emil Neumann
&
AM II, 175 Soldatenklänge by Eduard Buchholtz

These are two Prize marches from the march competition held by Gustav Bock in Berlin in the years 1852 to 1861. Entry was open to all active Prussian service musicians. At the same time, in 1858, two able Sergeant-Hoboisten from the Kaiser Alexander Grenadier-Regiment in Berlin, entered their compositions. Their Stabshoboist, the able Carl Liebig, wanted to help and guide his musicians, and their scores were written out sitting next to him. Out of thirty-five entries, Sergeant Emil Neumann's (1834-1922) march won 1st Prize, and Sergeant Eduard Buchholtz the 2nd prize. The examination commission consisted of the former military Directors of Music, August-Heinrich Neithardt, Albert Leutner, Wilhelm Grimm , and the old Opera-Ballet conductor Wenzel Gährich who chose twelve pieces which, on the 26th March 1858, were festively premiered at the Berlin Opera House before various Princes, the Countess Liegnitz, Field Marshal von Wrangel, the 'Musical Count' von Redern, and many officers. No pieces could be passed to be approved as Army Marches as the King was ill. On New Year's Day 1860, all prize-winning marches (from 1856 to 1859 already in use by the Alexanders and Guard Dragoons) were laid on the dining table of the then Prince Regent (later Kaiser Wilhelm I) in his Berlin Palace on the Unter den Linden Avenue, he being the Royal Colonel of these two Regiments. Three weeks later they were all made Army Marches, including these two. Over fifty years later, in 1914, the two marches appeared in March Book 'Ist series' for all Prussian military musicians. Both pieces are much played, the first the Bundeswehr has in their Volume II.

Field Marshal Friedrich, Graf von Wrangel (1784-1877) when an old man. This is how he would have appeared at the time he was on the panel of judges for the Bock March Competitions in the 1850s. (Eagle & Lyre Prints Collection)

AM II, 176 (see *AM II, 172*)

AM II, 177 Kavalleriemarsch by Friedrich Speer

One must remember about this march that it was composed by a long-serving Infantry Bandmaster, used to marching from dawn to dusk on foot but writing a 'cavalry ' march. From his position on high, Wieprecht, responsible for keeping the Royal Army March Collection in good order, saw the piece was by an Infantry Bandmaster and wrongly placed it in volume II for Infantry Quick marches, where it has remained for over a century since 1860. Army Music Inspector Professor Grawert published a new arrangement for Infantry bands in his 1926 Music Book '2nd series', which was used by all Reichswehr bands. The piece begins with eight beautifully expressive bars, and in the trio there is an unusual double counter melody until the very last bar. The composer Friedrich Speer (1817-1903) was, from 1853 to 1878, for twenty-five long years, Bandmaster of the 28th Infantry Regiment in Aachen. It was a 'Bergish' regiment (raised in the little state of Cleves-Berg), with its Battle Honour of 'Belle Alliance' (the name the Prussians gave to the Battle of Waterloo 1815) it was long associated with the Duke of Wellington who was its Honorary Colonel ('Chef') for many years. Speer served under a succession of nine Commanding Officers, went to war in 1866 and 1870-71 with the Regiment, and was decorated in 1865 with the Allgemeine Ehrenzeichen and in 1877 with the Cross of the Order of the House of Hohenzollern. Speer gave high quality concerts in Aachen and also composed many works which he had published by Verlag Naus of Aachen. When the Regiment re-located to a new garrison in Koblenz in 1877, Speer left the service the following year. He took a house in Burtscheid (today part of Aachen) together with his daughter, Kätchen, a music teacher.

AM II, 178 Fahnenweihmarsch by Gustav Loewenthal

About this beautiful march and its composer there is a story to tell. Gustav Loewenthal (1833 – circa 1903) hailed from Sonnenburg in the Brandenburg Neumark (east of the Oder, today in Poland) (11 1/2 km east of Küstrin). At twenty-five-years-old he took the position of Stabshornist with Jäger-Bataillon Nr. 5 in Görlitz. When, in 1860, the Prussian Army was reorganised and expanded and in Breslau the Garde-Grenadier-Regiment Nr. 3 was raised, he went to join them. So Loewenthal was the first Stabshoboist of this high-profile regiment, whose Band he assembled and built up. He was a great superb revelation. On 18 January 1861 he travelled with the representatives of his regiment to Berlin for the Presentation of Colours Ceremony (Fahnenweihe) to all the new regiments. It was one of the most colourful events of that era and was a once-in-a-lifetime sight. One-hundred-and-forty-two fluttering Colours and Standards were carried in three ranks, forty-six men wide, in parade step to the sound of the *Yorck'sher Marsch* in front of the Berlin Stadtschloss down the Unter den Linden Avenue, specially cleared of deep snow for the occasion, to the great memorial statue to Frederick the Great (which, having been restored to its original position, stands again in Berlin today – a large bronze statue of 'Old Fritz' on horseback). In front of this great procession marched the massed fife and drum corps and Regimental Band of the Prussian 1.Garde-Regiment zu Fuss, in greatcoat order but with their Full Dress red horsehair plumes on their Pickelhauben. Either side of the Avenue, the Berlin regiments provided route liners shoulder to shoulder, while the local Berlin population crammed into the surrounding streets shouting heir heads off "Hurra! Hurra!" Under such an influence, Loewenthal was inspired to write his *Fahnenweihmarsch*. It was to become an Army March in 1862, being published by Bote & Bock/Berlin. In 1926 Armeemusikinspizient Professor Hackenberger arranged the piece anew and took it into his Marschbuch '2 Folge' for all German bandsmen. However, his successor, Heeresmusikinspizient Professor Schmidt, laid it aside in 1935 – the composer was Jewish!? That was not so, and not the responsibility of a Music Inspector, especially without proof! The Military Garrison Chapel Register entries numbers 1721 and 1505 make it clear that Gustav Loewenthal and his wife, Bianka Kuhl, shortly after his birth registered him as Evangelical, he was confirmed in Glogau as an Evangelical in 1859, and both parents were indisputably Evangelical. So anyway, at least we can still find today the notes of this beautiful march in Marschbuch '2 Folge' of 1926.

When the Garde-Grenadier-Regiment Nr. 3 Commanding Officer returned to Breslau on 24 January 1861, he gave the Colours received in Berlin to their respective Battalions, and for the first time Stabshoboist Loewenthal and his Band played the Regimental Präsentiermarsch as a salute to the Colours, and for the subsequent regimental march past their Regimentsmarsch. In the same year, on 18 October 1861, the Dowager Queen Mother, Elisabeth (1801-1873) took the Honorary Colonelcy of the now re-styled Königin Elisabeth Garde-Grenadier-Regiment Nr. 3, the name the regiment kept until disbanded in 1919. The 'Elisabether' had much to thank their first Honorary Colonel for. The Music Fund each year from 1 January 1862 received yearly 150 Thalers, an enormous help for buying music scores and additional instruments for such a young Regimental Band. And their Regimental Quick March we all know as *den Elisabether*, as shorthand for the

Geschwindmarsch nach Motiven aus Quadrillen (AM II, 126). Barely ready, the regiment was sent to the Danish campaign in 1864 to liberate Schleswig-Holstein. The winter months on the narrow strip of land between the North Sea and the Baltic, with snow, storms, freezing cold and rain needed the strength and fortitude offered by marches, but Marschmusik was impossible there. However, it was available in quarters, on rest days, and by arrangement. At the storming of the Düppel Redoubts on 18 April 1864, Musikdirektor Piefke conducted and led the Regimental Bands of the Leib-GR8, IR18, FR35 and IR60 regiments, but Loewenthal's Band, although available there, was not included in the attack. However, it was visited and heard by the King, Crown Prince, and Field Marshals von Wrangel, Prince Albert the Elder, Prince Friedrich Carl, and other dignitaries too heard the Band play frequently. In 1866, Loewenthal left the service. Later he led the Kurmusik in Bad Reinerz-Grafschaft Glatz.

AM II, 179 Triumphmarsch by Georg Goldschmidt

A march, which one cannot march to! Whether at the slow march, quick march, even mounted troops! It is all but impossible because the piece changes tempo, and is also rather too long with 136 bars (51 pages, the conductor's score). It is a concert piece, not really a concert march. With an opening of fanfare bars, it festively follows the style of our cavalry marches. The 61st bar begins the trio, but that is not the end of it, for after 21 bars its tonality is changed all over again. The end is a powerful and mighty long coda. How did this become an Army March? The answer that follows is tied up with the fact that the composer was an Infantry Bandmaster, and a bureaucratic blunder that put everything into the 'Parademärsche' for Infantry (II Sammlung). The composer, Georg Goldschmidt (1823-1904), was a well-known personality, he was namely the Bandmaster of the 'King's Grenadiers', The Grenadier-Regiment Nr. 7 in Liegnitz, Silesia, whose Colonel-in-Chief was the 'old Kaiser' from 1817, when he had been Prince William of Prussia, until his death seventy years later as Kaiser Wilhelm I did he remain so. Goldschmidt could also reckon up his service in decades; he was Bandmaster of the Regiment from 1st February 1858 until 31st December 1898, a total of forty-one years. When his predecessor, Carl Lange (from whom the Sedan-Marsch), died on 12th December 1857, Goldschmidt got the position on the recommendation of the Regiment's Colonel-in-Chief. He was thirty-four years old, and had a Kapellmeister's certificate and came from Piefke's schooling. That guaranteed ability and certain reliability. The Regimental Commander, Colonel von Sommerfeld, was lucky to be able to fill his vacant Bandmaster position so well. Three years later, in 1861, the Regiment's Colonel-in-Chief and Prince Regent became the Prussian King. Thence, in 1862, came Goldschmidt's *Triumpmarsch* into the collection. Indeed, one must not forget the reputation of the Regiment which, for so long, had always stood in the front line. It fought in 1866 at Königgrätz, and in 1870 at Wörth and Sedan. It gave concerts to the King at Headquarters, and the band was placed in the Hall of Mirrors in the Palace of Versailles in 1871 for the Kaiser Proclamation. At all these events Goldschmidt was in charge. Goldschmidt demanded of himself dedication to the service and personable qualities. Twelve different Regimental Commanders had the good fortune to serve with this Bandmaster over a period of forty years without concern. In 1869, Goldschmidt became a Director of Music and in 1893 he celebrated his fifty years of service. Liegnitz and the 'Königsgrenadiere' were unthinkable without Goldschmidt. The young Kaiser Wilhelm II, who reigned from 1888, honoured Goldschmidt in writing when he had visited the Regiment. Goldschmidt was, by this time, wearing a long snow-white full set of whiskers and beard. At seventy-five, Goldschmidt retired on 31st December 1898. He had received eleven Orders and medals, including the Iron Cross 2nd Class of 1870, the Order of the Red Eagle, the Order of the Crown 4th Class,and the Cross of the Head of the House Order of the Hohenzollerns. As a special farewell he was honoured with an honorary commission as Leutnant, which the Press, in congratulating him, described him as the 'Regiment's youngest Lieutenant'!!

AM II, 180 Angriffskolonnen-Marsch by Friedrich WilhelmVoigt

Friedrich Wilhelm Voigt (1833-1894) was a great musician, and from 12 September 1857 Bandmaster of the 1.Garde-Regiment zu Fuss in Potsdam. His band, as the first in the Prussian Army, provided Court Music. With the illness of the King and the necessary regency of the Crown Prince, leading to the eventual death of the King in 1861, the first five years for Voigt were unsettled and difficult. In the Army March collection are eight pieces by him, this his Opus 32, the first. It appeared in 1862 in Verlag Adolph Martin Schlesinger of Berlin, where from this time all Army Marches were available in print.

AM II, 181 Hohenzollern-Marsch with the *Hohenzollern Lied* by Ernst Mahler

Ernst Mahler was, from 1850, the Bandmaster of Infanterie-Regiment Nr. 40 (then Reserve-Infanterie-Regiment Nr. 8) in Saarloreis, which from 1860 had the new title of Hohenzollernisches Füsilier-Regiment Nr. 40 and was then re-garrisoned in Trier from 1861, to Cologne in 1871 (after returning from fighting in the Franco-Prussian War), and finally from 1895 in Aachen (Aix La Chapelle) on the Belgian frontier. From 1877 onwards, until the fall of the German monarchies in 1918, the Count von Hohenzollern was always the Honorary Colonel-in-Chief (Chef), and an elite company drawn from the Regiment always mounted Guard at the Burg Hohenzollern 100 kms to the south of the Regiment's garrison town. (Burg Hohenzollern was the seat of the Catholic southern branch of the family who in the 16th century dynastically split from the Protestant northern branch who later became Kings of Prussia and German Emperors after 1871.) This march is peculiar in that it is really three verses of the Hohenzollern Lied, a poem *Vom Felsen bis zum Meere* (between the alps and the North and Baltic Seas), the so-called *Preussenlied*. The first two verses were written unaccompanied and this march was a stand-alone trio for the final verse. It was not widely used, despite being the Regimental March of the Infanterie-Regiment Nr. 40 . It was attempted by the Infanterie-Regiment Nr. 40 to have their column of soldiers sing the poem, with the Regimental Band striking up with this march for the trio, but it was difficult to execute on the march and fell from use as a route march, from then on being played only at formal parades of the regiment.

AM II, 182 Margarethenmarsch nach den Motiven der Oper »Margarethe« – Opera by Charles Gounod – March by Gottfried Piefke

It is impossible to believe but the Bundeswehr does not have this piece in their March Book! Especially when one considers that here is a beautiful, well-known waltz (by Charles Gounod 1818-1893 for his opera *Margarethe*) created into such a lovely and well-known march. Which, just about three years after it appeared in 1864, Musikdirektor Saro played along with the much loved *Les Roses-Walzer* by Metra as he marched past the Emperor

Napoleon III in Paris, shortly before his triumph at the World Fair international Band competition in 1867. At all events, the *Margarethenmarsch* belonged to one of the most played Army Marches for seventy-five years and was a real piece of Prussiandom. The modern German Bundeswehr really should play the march again, with its lusty, jolly, striking chords in the first section and radiantly artistic trio which beguiles and captivates the listener. Gottfried Piefke (1815-1884), the most famous Prussian Military Kapellmeister, had finished his composition certainly by 1863. So it rang out often in subsequent years during the autumn manoeuvres of the III Army Corps in the area of Lebus (north of Frankfurt-on-Oder). The Commanding General, Prince Friedrich Carl of Prussia, always called the piece *den Lebuser*. In the following year (1864), the piece appeared as an Army March in the catalogues of Berlag Bote & Bock/Berlin. From there the notes were copied into March Book '1st series' in 1914.

AM II, 183 Marsch des Regiments von Sebastopol

After the freeing of Europe from Napoleon's dictatorship in 1813/14, came the union through marriage of a younger brother of the Russian Tsar with the eldest daughter of the Prussian King. The couple took over the government of Russia in 1825. So there remained a close relationship, with many visits to and fro between the families. In this situation it is easy to understand that Prince Albrecht of Prussia, the youngest brother of the Prussian King, in 1862 undertook a journey to the Caucases as a guest of local Russian troops. At this get-together with the Regiment 'Sebastopol' he obtained the parts for this piece in November 1862 and took it back for this brother in Berlin. In 1864 it appeared as an Army March in Musik Verlag Bote & Bock/Berlin, again in 1914 in the first edition of March Book '1st series'. It was not played a great deal; it has a difficult faltering rhythm. As a Galopmarsch it was occasionally heard. In Russia it remained the March of the Sebastopol Regiment, later numbered the 75th Infantry Regiment, and also the Regimental Quick March of the 14th Georgian Grenadier Regiment 'General Kotljarevksij' – both Imperial Russian Regiments had full infantry style wind bands.

AM II, 184 Liechtenstein-Marsch by Joseph Strauss, arranged by Friedrich Wilhelm Voigt

A true Wiener ('Viennese') from Strauss! The composer (1827-1870) is the second of three sons of Johann Strauss (Father) who let loose the *Dorfschwalben aus Österreich* ('Village Swallows from Austria'). The Liechtenstein-Marsch (Opus 36) he wrote for the fifty years Golden Jubilee celebrations of the Imperial Austro-Hungarian Agricultural Society on 17th May 1857 in Vienna, held there in Ungers Casino, and named after Prince August von Liechtenstein, the President of the Agricultural Society. In Prussia, the beautiful piece became an Armeemarsch in 1864. Possibly the Prussian King got hold of it on 21st-22nd November 1865 from the Austrian Infantry Regiment No 34, whose Regimental Band he heard that night as he was their Honorary Colonel. The troops spent two days in Berlin in celebratory parades and festivities after their campaign alongside Prussian Troops in the war against Denmark for Schleswig-Holstein. The Stabshoboist of the 1.Garde-Regiment zu Fuss and Court Kapellmeister, Friedrich Wilhelm Voigt, was called upon to arrange the parts for Prussian military wind band. Since 1926 the notes appear in Marschbuch '2 Folge' for all German Bandsmen, an arrangement by Armeemusikinspizient Professor Oskar Hackenberger. The copyright since 1864 is held by Bote & Bock/Berlin.

Friedrich Wilhelm Voigt (1833-1894), the first Musikinspizient of the Prussian Army 1887-1890. Previously Bandmaster of the 1.Garde-Regiment zu Fuss 1857-1887 he led them all through the Wars of German Unification (1864-1871). (Archive DGfMM eV)

AM II, 185 Düppeler Sturmmarsch by Gottfried Piefke
&
AM II, 186 Düppel-Schanzen-Sturmmarsch by Gottfried Piefke

The storming of the Düppel Redoubts on the 18th April 1864 in the war against Denmark belongs to this day to the most impressive and famous feat of arms in war. About thirty-seven-thousand Prussian troops were brought together, often said of these soldiers, determined to clinch matters and be the first into the storm, and all under the watchful eyes of the Prussian Crown Prince, Feldmarschall Wrangel and Prince Friedrich Carl. And what is more, the Bands played in the firing line the *Yorck'scher Marsch* for the advance of the four bands massed, namely:-

Leib-Grenadier-Regiment Nr. 8 from Frankfurt/Oder under Musikdirektor Piefke
Infanterie-Regiment Nr. 18 from Guben under Stabshoboist Zikoff
Füsilier-Regiment Nr. 35 from Brandenburg/Havel under Stabshoboist Lübbert
Infanterie-Regiment Nr. 60 from Wriezen under Stabshoboist Thormann.

That was around one-hundred-and-thirty musicians, the Musikdirektor Piefke conducting with his drawn sword. (About an equal number of fifes and drums were mustered with the band – total band and drums nearly three hundred.) Having made such an indelible impression, Gottfried Piefke's (1815-1884) two Düppel Storm marches became instantly recognised Army Marches (1864) and were published by Bote & Bock Verlag,

Berlin. The first of the two marches remembers in its first section, by having five empty bars with only a fife playing, the effect of the exploding grenade during the battle. The other begins with a high trumpet playing the Tattoo signal of the Infantry and has in the trio the folk song *Steh ich in finstrer Mitternacht* by the poet Wilhelm Hauff. Fresh and full of rounded sound it was much played. With the ACO on 31 May 1899, it is ordered to be the Parade Quick March of the Pionier-Bataillon Nr. 3 in Spandau, and continued to be blown by them until the end of the Second World War. Pioneer Klinke of this Battalion was the first of these determined 'stormers' to reach the Düppel Redoubts where, at the age of twenty-four, he met his death. Today his memorial statue still stands in Spandau. The march went into March Book '1st series' in 1914 to all Prussian military musicians; since 1961 the Bundeswehr has it in Volume II. Furthermore it has been suggested that Piefke had composed the two marches already before the storming of the redoubts, and already had them played. Thus he played them during the attack (?). Whatever, the Leib-Grenadier-Regiment Nr. 8 welcomed the King at Flensburg Railway Station on 21 April 1864 with this march, and he expressed a wish that this beautiful piece should have the title *Schanzen-Sturmmarsch*. So it was which could explain why the two marches written by the same composer have such similar titles.

AM II, 188 Düppeler Morgenroth by Friedrich Zikoff

Friedrich Zikoff (1824-1877) belongs to our outstanding Prussian military kapellmeisters. He grew up in the Military Boys Institute at Annaburg (20 km north of Torgau), and at eighteen years of age (1842) became a Bandsman in the Regimental Band of Infanterie-Regiment Nr. 18 whose leadership he took on from 1853-1877. For thirty-five years until his death he belonged to the IR18! With them he was at the campaign to suppress the Polish uprising in Posen in 1848, then in the field campaign against Denmark in 1864, against Austria in 1866, and in the war against France in 1870/71. Often decorated, in 1871 he was made a Director of Music. During the field campaign of 1864, he and his band stood with three other bands under the direction of Director of Music Piefke in the firing line and played the *Yorck'scher Marsch* for the storming of the redoubts. For this high point in his life he wrote his march *Düppeler Morgenroth*, which he immediately dedicated respectfully to the Prussian Crown Prince (later Kaiser Frederick III). In the trio he set the already one-hundred-and-fifty -year-old folk song *Morgenrot, Morgenrot* (with the verses from Wilhelm Hauff from the year 1824). The march instantly became an Army March (1864). Zikoff had good composition abilities. In the years 1853 and 1861 he won, for his entries to the march competition of the Berlin Publishers, Bock, second prize. In 1870/71 he wrote *Über'n Rhein* Opus 58 and the *Siegesmarsch von Rezonville* Opus 59 (both in Verlag Hainer/Breslau), besides which the *Deutschen Kaiser-Marsch* Opus 69, which became the Parade Quick March of the Bavarian 6.Infanterie-Regiment Kaiser Wilhelm, König von Preussen in Amberg, and belatedly it became an Army March (1925) as AM II, 259. Over one-hundred-and-thirty pieces of useful music, including many good marches, appeared from Zikoff. He was keenly played and over the decades has had a good reputation.

AM II, 189 Siegesmarsch by Gottfried Piefke, arranged by Johannes Schade

This is a march about the victory of the Prussians in the Danish War of 1864, written by Piefke. It is no campaign feat march like the other Düppel marches, but a joyful festival celebration piece. In the trio is Spontini's Prussian folk song *Borussia* from 1820, but beforehand in the 2nd section rings out the King's Hymn *Heil dir im Siegerkranz* (tune of 'God Save the Queen'), sung by the King's victorious soldiers in two-part harmony choir and a fresh 4/4 march rhythm. The King immediately took the piece as an Army March in 1865, already overjoyed with and informed about the products and leadership qualities of his Bandmaster from the Leib-Grenadier-Regiment Nr. 8. The parts never reached all troops. It was no parade or street march. So, even the Stabshoboist of the 1.Garde-Regiment zu Fuss in Potsdam, Friedrich Wilhelm Voigt, did not know it, as when he went to the Bohemian campaign in 1866 he wrote his *Königgrätzer Siegesmarsch* with an identical trio. This, too, became an Army March. Now we had two marches with the same trio! And Voigt was twenty-two years the junior of his famous colleague from Frankfurt/Oder in service years. A dreadful gaffe! Both marches were never played outside Potsdam or Frankfurt-on-Oder.Through the war against France in 1870/71, and with the capitulation of Sedan and the 'Entry into Paris', and with the event of the 'Kaiserkrönung' in Versailles 1871, they forgot the victory marches of Düppel and Königgrätz. Alternatives were created by others. The presumably long lost and unavailable band parts of Piefke's *Siegesmarsch* were arranged belatedly by Musik Inspector Johannes Schade of the Bundeswehr in 1977.

AM II, 190 Der Alsenströmer by Gottfried Piefke

It was a matter of course, once upon a time, that Bandmasters should go with the troops into battle. With the development of battlefield technology, especially that of firearms, the practice naturally had to come to an end. The German-Danish War of 1864 was the last time in which the band played in the first line of an advance into the storm of battle. With the attack of the Prussians on the Düppel Redoubts on 18th April 1864, the Director of Music, Gottfried Piefke, with four regimental bands under him, conducted the *Yorck'scher Marsch*. Living through this was the height of this bandmaster of the Leib-Grenadier-Regiment Nr. 8's soldierly career, which led him to write both his Düppel-Sturm marches (*AM II, 185* and *186*). To this very day they are widely known. To the further marches of this campaign belongs the *Alsenströmer*. It remembers the crossing of the Sound over to the Island of Alsen near Sonderburg. The Hungarian style remembers the allied comrades from Hungary who fought alongside the Prussians. In order to find the right tone, the composer used a lightness of touch; the piece is a completely Hungarian-style march. The composer, Gottfried Piefke (1815-1884), is the soldierly and musically prime example of the Prussian Military Bandmaster. He was, for forty years (1843-1884), the Bandmaster of the Leib-Grenadier-Regiment Nr. 8 in Frankfurt/Oder. He went with them on every exercise and campaign. He was highly regarded by his King, the old Kaiser Wilhelm I. Ten marches by Gottfried Piefke are in the Collection, this one went in in 1865. The Bundeswehr play this march today and thereby have a typical Hungarian-style march to perform.

AM II, 191 Der Lymfjordströmer by Gottfried Piefke

Gottfried Piefke (1815-1884), Prussia's most significant military Kapellmeister and Musikdirektor of the Leib-Grenadier-Regiment Nr. 8 in Frankfurt/Oder, had his greatest soldiering and composing era during the German-Danish War of 1864. Outside Düppel he conducted four military bands for the storming of the trenches, and within six months of this campaign had composed five of his best marches which became Army Marches.

The *Lymfjordströmer* is named after the Fjord at Alborg (Jutland) which became the strongly defended northern border of the German occupied area. With the suggestion of the folk song *Schier 30 Jahre bis du alt* it makes reference to the soldiers cloaks, with which the terrible cold of the first winter months stationed in an exposed position in north Jutland were associated. Piefke's march appeared from Verlag Massute/Frankfurt an der Oder. The printed parts as an Army March were placed with and copyrighted by Bote & Bock/Berlin, and from thence in Marschbuch '2 Folge'. Professor Hackenberger newly rearranged the piece in 1926 for use by the smaller bands of the Reichswehr.

AM II, 192 Kärtner Liedermarsch by Anton Seifert, arranged by Georg Goldschmidt

Truly a popular and much played march! It was written by Anton Siefert (1826-1873), Austrian Military Bandmaster of the (Hungarian) 12th Infantry Regiment, who was with them in 1861 in their garrison of Wolfsburg-Kärnten. From 1 May 1846 – not quite twenty years – Seifert led the band until his death in 1873. He was a gifted musician in Prague, and was well-trained by other famous Austrian Bandmasters like Kapellmeister Johann Schubert of the 42nd Infantry Regiment. As a composer he was tireless. This is his Opus 80. He went later with his regiment to Olmütz and finally to Cracow.

Georg Goldschmidt (1823-1903) Stabshoboist of the Prussian 'Königsgrenadiere', the Grenadier-Regiment Nr. 7 in Liegnitz, Silesia, equally gifted as Seifert, was much taken with the march and arranged it for Prussian Infantry Band (different instrumental combination), and his Regimental Royal Colonel immediately made the piece an Army March in 1865. Printed and published by Bote & Bock/Berlin; from 1914 in March Book '1st series' for Prussian Bandsmen and since 1961 in March Book Volume II of the Bundeswehr.

AM II, 193 Krakowiak aus Österreich by Friedrich Wilhelm Voigt

In 1841, Prince Wilhelm of Prussia was given the position of Inhaber (Honorary Colonel) of the Hungarian Infantry Regiment Nr 34 (later Austrian IR. 34 'Prinz von Preussen').

Such honorary positions gave the Inhaber an interest in the individual troops and they in him. The soldierly Prince enjoyed visiting the regiment. In the Danish campaign of 1864 it belonged to the Austro-Hungarian Army Corps. At the request of the Inhaber, since 1861 now King of Prussia, as an honour to the Regiment he arranged for them to parade through Berlin on their return journey. On the afternoon of 21st November 1864, the Regiment was greeted at the Railway Station by the Prussian King and Princes, it jubilantly marched through the bunting-bedecked streets led by the Prussian King, mounted and sword drawn wearing the Regiment's uniform, and found quarters for the night in one of the barracks already vacated by a Prussian regiment still in the field. The 1st Company and Regimental Band accompanied the Regimental Colour party to the Berlin Schloss where the Colours were lodged overnight. The next morning, at 10.30 am, they paraded down Under den Linden to the march *Ungarn und Brandenburg* composed especially by their Regimental Bandmaster, Sigmund Levengly. The Prussian King again wore the uniform of the Hungarian Regiment. To conclude, the officers were guests at Court in the Schloss. Then the King visited the other ranks. They danced for him the 'Krakowiak', a Polish dance from their homelands on the Carpathian-Galician border, the sub-district of Kaschau. The melancholy piece of eight bars twice over gains a sharp rhythm beating on the off beat. Friedrich Wilhelm Voigt (1833-1894), Stabshoboist of the 1.Garde-Regiment zu Fuss, and responsible for Court Music, was requested to make a march out of it. He set the melody in the trio. The sprightly composition became at once an Army March, publishers Bote & Bock printing a conductor's score in 1865, sent to all Prussian military bands. Since 1914 the piece stands in Marschbuch '1st series'. So, here we have a Polish dance in the Army March Collection!

AM II, 194 Marsch von Problus und Prim am 3. Juli 1866 by Heinrich Laudenbach

The district of Problus and Prim lies 12 km west-north-west of Königgrätz. On 3 July 1866 they were part of the critical battlefield of the Bohemian campaign in the Austro-Prussian War. In consequence of the Füsilier-Regiment Nr. 33 being engaged there, their Regimental Bandmaster, Heinrich Laudenbach (1827-1907), wrote this melodious march with its long beautiful crescendo in the trio. It became, in the same year, an Armeemarsch and in 1867 Verlag Bote & Bock/Berlin provided the parts to all Prussian military bandsmen. Since 1914 the piece has stood in Marschbuch '1.Folge', and since 1961 in Volume II of the Bundeswehr.

AM II, 195 Der Königgrätzer by Gottfried Piefke

The composer, Musikdirektor Gottfried Piefke (1815-1884), was Bandmaster of the Prussian Leib-Grenadier-Regiment Nr. 8, and this Leib-Regiment was held in the highest esteem in both war and peace, also, too, it's Band. Piefke had this band for forty long years and led it from 1843 until his death. Piefke was every inch the soldier, musically gifted on all instruments, and understood exactly how to arrange and compose. In the Danish War (1864) before Düppel he conducted the four Regimental Bands involved in the Storming of the Redoubts.

In the war in Bohemia in 1866 before Königgrätz he played the *Preussenmarsch mit der Königshymne* (*AM II, 119*) as the Regiment advanced into battle on 3rd July. The King heard it atop the Roskos Mountain (18 km north-west of Königgrätz) and felt so encouraged that he bid Piefke play it again. After the battle, he bid the Stabshoboist come to him. "Piefke, I will never forget that from you!" Furthermore, on the battlefield, Piefke had composed and written out the parts for *den Königgrätzer*. At the King's Evening Table in the open air, he played the piece unannounced. The King was entranced and he had to play it three times over. With astounding haste the theme and arrangement were put together and all written down with the historic Prussian *Hohenfriedberger* (*AM III, 1b*) as trio added. Further, in the same year it was an Army March but, however, its playing on parade was forbidden! The *Hohenfriedberger* was the exclusive right of the Königin Kürassier-Regiment Nr. 2, the successor regiment to the Bayreuth Dragoons who alone were allowed to play it at great parades. Since 1919, when the old regiments were disbanded, it has been played always and everywhere. It is one of our most popular marches. The Bundeswehr Bands have it in their Volume II.

AM II, 196 Der 30. Januar 1866 by Friedrich Wilhelm Voigt

The significance of the date is unknown to us. It could be of significance to the Voigt family – we simply do not know! One can feel the joy of a late winter's day, skating on the ice near the Marmorpalais in Potsdam in the sounds of this sprightly march.

Karl Friedrich von Steinmetz (1796-1877) (Duncan Rogers)

AM II, 197 Steinmetz-March by Carl Bratfisch

This Army March of 1867 is for one hundred years one of our most used and famous of street marches. All in one, it has a swinging melody, a thumping good rhythm, a playful arrangement, in short, a full, rounded piece. And solidly built: after four bars introduction, follow two sections of 16 bars (with repeat) and a trio of once again 2 x 16 bars (once again repeated). The composer (1829-1901) was born in Riga, the son of a music teacher there. He became a Prussian military Kapellmeister in Glogau, Silesia, then from 1857 to 1860 with the Pionier-Bataillon Nr. 5, then from 1860 to 1869 with the newly-raised Infanterie-Regiment Nr. 58. From there he accompanied them to the war in Bohemia under General von Steinmetz, after whom he named this march as a memorial to the battle near Skalitz on 28th June 1866. The Prussian Field Marshal, Karl Friedrich von Steinmetz (1796-1877), had already as a seventeen-year-old fought in the War of Liberation 1813/14, then all subsequent campaigns for Prussia. As Commanding General of the V Army Corps, he was the victor of the Battles of Nachod and Skalitz 1866.

AM II, 198 Fridericus Rex-Grenadiermarsch by Ferdinand Radeck

This wonderful march came quite unexpectedly in the year 1867. Neither was it the precursor of a further wholesale string of works; for sure, further of such useful pieces were awaited but further pieces from him are not known. But this piece alone stands him in good stead and in all the one-hundred-and-twenty-five years until today.

Ferdinand (August) Radeck (1829-1903) was a Prussian Militärkapellmeister; born in fortified Spandau near Berlin. Being musical, he became a bandsman and at twenty-four-years old, in 1853, he took up the position of Stabshoboist (Bandmaster) of Infanterie-Regiment Nr. 6 in the city of Posen. His predecessor Carl Nerlich (see *AM II,*

53) was dismissed after twenty-six years there! Two years later, the Regiment was sent to be stationed in Glogau (Silesia) for five years. Here the population heaped praise on the weekly string concerts given in the famous White Chamber of the Town Hall (Weissen Saal der Rathauses – destroyed in 1945), which were completely sold out. Great special new musical works appeared in the programmes. After the return to the old garrison of Posen in 1860 such concerts were made into a regular feature, from then on in the town further infantry bands and cavalry Trompeterkorps brass bands performed when stationed there. It was a time when string music was valued highly, as important for the bands then as the usual practice, at that time, of wind music on the barracks drill square. At the same time as his appointment as Stabshoboist, Radeck had married, on 9th July 1853 in Spandau, Mathilde the daughter of Master nail maker Poritz, who gave him sons and daughters until her death in childbirth in 1862. Two years later, in 1864, Radeck married again, this time to Louise, daughter of financial accountant Orlovius in Marienburg. Both wives were, just like Radeck, Evangelical. For Wieprecht's Jubilee of twenty-years-service on 2nd February 1863, he travelled to Berlin. In 1863 he was present for the unrest in Posen (Polish uprising), in 1866 compaigned in the field in Bohemia and was at the battle of Königgrätz (where the Prussians defeated the Austrians, which led to the expulsion of Austria from Germany after eight hundred years dominance, leaving Prussia in charge of German affairs). Radeck transferred in 1867 to the post of Barracks Inspector, and later became the Royal Garrison Administration Controller in Posen. With his old band, and his successor, Stabshoboist Appold, he remained closely associated. The *Fridericus Rex-Grenadiermarsch* quickly triumphed in all Prussian garrisons. In August 1867, when it became an Army March, the Musikverlag Ed. Bote & G. Bock sent the conductor's score to all regiments. So the individual parts remained hand-written in all march books until the 1914 published '1.Folge'. Twenty percent of all Prussian and Baden Infantry Regimental Bands played this as their regimental march. That says more than anything I can write here. After four introductory bars, follows sixteen bars repeated, then to the trio when three themes of the Ballade by Carl Loewe (1796-1869) are included. The ballad is Loewe's Opus 61 from the year 1838, which appeared from Verlag Wagenführ, with text by Willibald Alexis (real name: Wilhelm Häring 1798-1872). Of course, the march had no da capo. After the First World War, from 1920, the piece arose to shine worthily as the whole population sought to hear its tones. The *Fridericus* became demanded, no wind concert without it being called for! Already the first two bars were known by everyone. A whole generation grew up with it. And so it remains. The Bundeswehr has had the march in their Volume II since 1961. And when one hears it played as Hauptmann Kuckertz did in 1988 with his Heeresmusikkorps I in Hanover, from the two sets of four notes of the opening bars until the last theme, played strongly and haltingly, then one can feel 'Old Fritz' returning once more, so that he can help his people once again.

AM II, 199 Lundby-Marsch by Carl Walther

The composer is 'The Great Walther' (1842-1917), Royal Saxon Music Director from the Saxon Infanterie-Regiment Nr. 107 in Leipzig, famous and a wonder with his wind music for the service and his symphonic string concerts. But, at the time of the *Lundby Marsch* he was at the beginning of his career. Carl Walther, born on 29th July 1842, the son of a master shoemaker in Weissenfels, a devout Evangelical, became, on 16th October 1860, a bandsman in the regimental band of the Prussian Infanterie-Regiment Nr. 32 in Halle-

Carl Walther (1842-1901) was bandmaster of Infanterie-Regiment 50 from 1864 to 1872 and then Musikmeister of (8. Sächsisches) Infanterie-Regiment Prinz Johann Georg Nr. 107 (Leipzig – raised 1708) from 1872 to 1901 and absolutely dominated the music scene in Leipzig during those 29 years. He was a tireless arranger of music, and very adept at self-promotion using his little black dog in much of his advertising. There are numerous different versions of Walther postcards depicting him with his little dog which were widely circulated and sold as something well-known in the Leipzig scene in his long era there. (Eagle & Lyre Archive)

on-Saale. The Stabshoboist (Bandmaster) there then was the fifty-eight-year-old Music Director, Joseph Golde, already for thirty-three years having done superb work in this position, and famous through his *Preussenmarsch* (*AM II, 119*) as well as his *Festreveille*. A better teacher Walther could not have found. And so it was that Walther, who was only in his twenty-first year, on 10th March 1864 reached Breslau to take over the position as Stabshoboist of Infanterie-Regiment Nr. 50. His predecessor, Kapellmeister Winzer, should be dismissed, the Regiment's Commander, Colonel von Hackewitz had agreed. Certainly of the troops involved in the campaign against the Danes, the new regiments wanted to prove themselves. On 3rd July, the 1st and 2nd Company were in the fighting near Lundby (30 km south west of Aalborg). Walther wrote the *Lundby-Marsch*, with the Methfessels song from the 1813/14 War of Liberation *Heraus in die Ferne* as the trio. They found themselves in a strange land, their garrison lay over 800 km behind them. The King chose the beautiful *Lundby-Marsch* to be an Army March, the copyright with the Berlin Verlag Bote & Bock. In 1914, the piece was in the March Book '1st Series' and until 1939 all German military musicians had the parts. Walther remained with the Prussian IR50 until 1872. He went to the campaign in Bohemia with them in 1866 (Königgrätz), and to

France 1870-71 (fighting at Weissenburg, Sedan and Paris), and later, when they changed garrison from 1866 to Posen, after 1871 to Rawitsch. He wrote his *Wörther Siegesmarsch* (Opus 40), *Den Sedaner* (Opus 41) and *Die Preussen in Paris* (Opus 44), all published by Bote & Bock. From 1872, Walther led the Band of the Saxon Infanterie-Regiment Nr. 107 in Leipzig for twenty-nine years. In 1901, after forty-one years service and with a chest full of medals, he retired. Musikdirektor Walther was the very image of a musician, a soldier, orchestra builder, and a fabulous man.

AM II, 200 Kriegers Lebewohl by Wilhelm Lücke

Wilhelm Lücke (born 1825) was, in the middle of the 19th century, a Trumpet-Major Bandmaster for twenty-three years in the Guards, an era full of changes in the music for the mounted arm. His proud first appearance in front of his Trumpeter Band of the Guard Hussars was in Potsdam in 1859. The Garde-Husaren-Regiment was stationed in the barracks built by Schinkel on the road that led to Berlin. The wide open space across the street in front of the barracks provided a riding row for the horses, the stables were at the back of the barracks on the banks of the wide Havel River Lake. The four squadrons each had four Trumpeters who together could form a sixteen-strong mounted band. Lücke led his band to Berlin on 2 February 1863 for Wieprecht's 25th Anniversary of Service celebrations. One year later, in 1864, Lücke himself transferred to Berlin to be Trumpet-Major Bandmaster of the Garde-Artillerie-Brigade. The reason? The Mounted Band there had an official establishment of sixty-three Trumpeters/Musicians for this newly-raised branch of service. With such, much could be achieved musically, even when in 1866 in Bohemia and in 1970-71 in France work was disturbed by campaigns on the field of battle. Whilst on campaign in Bohemia, Lücke wrote his march *Kriegers Lebewohl* with the words to a song to go with it. The piece became an Army March in 1867. With the occupation of France, Lücke had an hour of stardom. On the Longchamps, Paris, on 3 March 1871, the Prussian Guard Corps held a Victory Parade. The Prussian King William, since 18 January also 'German Kaiser', rode at the front. Then followed the Artillery, glittering at the front was Lücke and his fifty-strong mounted trumpeter band pealing out *Ich bin ein Preusse!* ('I am a Prussian!'). The Kaiser was pleased and always reminisced about this occasion. Further still, Lücke continued his good soldierly career. He voluntarily transferred in 1872 to the newly-raised 2.Garde-Feldartillerie-Regiment in Berlin. In this mounted trumpeter corps there were ten piccolo trumpets, pistons and cornets, ten Eb Trumpets, four Tenor Horns, two Baritons and five to six Tubas or Helikons. That was thirty-two musicians. After ten years with this regiment, Lücke ended his service in 1882.

AM II, 201 Defiliermarsch über die Ballade »Die drei Liebchen« – Ballade by Wilhelm Speyer – March by Friedrick Wilhelm Voigt

This is a commissioned piece, which is called a march, as Voigt certainly composed it at the request of a person belonging to the Prussian Royal House. Wilhelm Speyer (1790-1878) made a living as a salesman and violinist in the Frankfurt-am-Main area. As a musician he composed duets for violins and for flutes, also chamber music and male voice choir music. His Lieder-songs were charming, from which his *die drei Liebchen* found great popularity. Thus Friedrich Wilhelm Voigt (1833-1894), Bandmaster of the 1.Garde-Regiment zu Fuss in Potsdam, made a march from this song when asked, as Militärkapellmeister Voigt was also responsible for all the music of the Court. Voigt wrote the march in January 1866 as his Opus 36. In the following year (1867), the piece became an Army March. It was not for service use. It is interesting for us as an example of march composition by Voigt, whose knowledge and works and instructional works are fully and still to this day well regarded. Voigt was a gifted composer. Eight Army Marches are from him.

AM II, 202 Königgrätzer Siegesmarsch über Spontini's »Borussia« by Friedrich Wilhelm Voigt

Friedrich Wilhelm Voigt (1833-1894) was Kapellmeister/Stabshoboist in the 1.Garde-Regiment zu Fuss (the 1st Foot Guards), where he was committed with them against Austria at Königgrätz. So after the victorious battle, he wrote this opus 40, in the trio Spontini's Prussian folk song *Borussia* from about 1820. He could not have known that, two years before (1864) the famous and twenty-two years in the service senior to him, Musikdirektor Gottfried Piefke, had also written a Siegesmarsch (Victory March) for the Danish Campaign with the same trio. An unfortunate thing to do! Furthermore, that later Piefke's *Siegesmarsch*, and also Voigt's *Siegesmarsch* became Army Marches in 1867. The responsible General Musikdirektor Wilhelm Wieprecht must have not been paying attention, for two identical pieces should not appear in the Royal Collection. In any event, both marches were played little outside the Frankfurt-on-Oder (Piefke's) or Potsdam (Voigt's) garrisons respectively. The war against France, 1870-71, with the Capitulation of Sedan and entry into Paris, especially the 'Kaiserkrönung' Imperial Coronation in Versailles, quickly led the Germans to have much more than old victory marches from 1864 and 1866. The piece became forgotten. After 1900 it was no longer played.

AM II, 203 Marche Militaire by Pauline Viardot-Garcia, arranged by Wilhelm Wieprecht

Every collection has a piece which became included through special circumstances. So, the march collection of the Prussian king's gained the composition of a French female singer. How did it come to pass? The composer of this march was, throughout Europe, a highly fêted songstress, the daughter of a highly musical Spanish household. Born as Pauline Garcia in Paris in 1821, she obtained the very best and an all-round education and training. With her wonderful alto voice she already had gained success as a sixteen-year-old in Brussels. With concert tours to Berlin, Dresden, Frankfurt-am-Main and Leipzig, she found fame. In London she had her first engagement. To his great joy, after she appeared in the Rossini Operas in Paris, the Director of the Italian Theatre, Louis Viardot, became engaged to her in 1839. Two years later, in 1841, they married and as an Impresario he took her on tour through Germany, Italy, Spain, Russia and England. On the 1st January 1847 she sang Rossini's *Barber of Seville* at the Berlin Royal Opera in the German language and caused a storm of adulation. From 1862 she gave up the stage and made a home in Baden-Baden as a song teacher (voice trainer) and dedicated herself to her many varied compositions. It was here that this 1867 march appeared. It is in five sections and graced with a sharp rhythmic counter to its flowing melody. In order to promote the piece and get it into the famous Army March Collection, she wrote to Wilhelm Wieprecht to ask him to arrange the piece for military music. Her exchange of letters survives and is in faultless German and, naturally, in full German gothic script! A further letter that I have enquires whether it can be dedicated to the Prussian Queen Augusta, and that whether her daughter, Louise, Grand-Duchess of Baden will have the march. Both the composer and Queen Augusta shared a mutual friend of many years standing, the Russian Poet, Ivan Turgenev (1818-1883). The title *Augusta-Marsch* was not permitted. However, as it was the composition of so great an artist, and with a dedication to the Queen, it was, at the beginning of 1870, allowed to be noted as an Army March. Through the safe and correct title 'Marche militaire' the collection now ha two marches of this name; indeed the *Grand Marche Militaire* (*AM II, 138*) a salon piece, which was never a march and thus never played. However, the march by Viardot, in the event, was also not played and remained a dedication only. During the War of 1870-71, the composer was in London. Then she moved to Paris where, in 1910, she died.

AM II, 204 Helmstadt-Marsch by Albert Klaar

In 1860, the internal and foreign political developments of Prussia reached the Infanterie-Regiment Nr. 70 in Trier. Already by the following year it was moved to Saarlouis as (a new) garrison. The leadership of the regimental band was taken up by the twenty-three-year-old Albert Klaar. He became Stabshoboist forthwith. He had been born in Berlin in 1837. In 1866, the Regiment had its first campaign. It was then it had its baptism of fire. It was in the Würzburg area against Bavarian troops who had allied themselves with Austria against Prussia. Stabshoboist Klaar named this beautiful march, which he had written at this time, after the victorious battle on 25 July at Helmstedt, 16 km west-south-west of Würzburg. The Prussian King first heard this march later. He also took to it. So in 1870 it became an Army March, the score was printed and posted by the copyright holders, Musikverlag Schlesinger in Berlin-Lichterfelde. Over sixty years later (1933) the march was placed by Heeresmusikinspizient Professor Hermann Schmidt in his published band book Notenheft 4. Folge to all German military musicians. The composer Klaar had further been (with his regiment) on campaign in 1870-71, and it was in 1873 that he retired from the service.

AM II, 205 Salus Caesari nostro Guilelmo (1871) by Friedrich Wilhelm Voigt

This march with the hymn from Handel's *Judas Maccabeus* was not meant for use in barracks or for parades. It appeared in 1871 as *Sieges-Festmarsch* – a victory festival march – to glorify the German Kaiser's Coronation and Kaiser Wilhelm himself on 18th January in the Palace of Versailles. The beautiful chorus from Handel's Oratorio is worked into the trio, the Latin title further enhances the festive atmosphere. So what lay behind this Opus 61 by the composer – who was the composer? Friedrich Wilhelm Voigt (1833-1894) was, from 1857 to 1887, Bandmaster and Director of Music of the 1.Garde-Regiment zu Fuss in Potsdam. Apart from this high profile position in the service, Voigt was much more besides. His father served as an energetic and well-regarded bandmaster for about thirty years with Infanterie-Regiment Nr. 30. However, the highly-musical son, Friedrich Wilhelm, did not want to become a soldier. Thoroughly trained as a musician by his father, he took his Konservatorium examination in Cologne with a recommendation to go to Berlin where he soon gained the Grand-Silver medal from the Royal Academy for Art and Science for his choral symphony *Ein feste Burg ist unser Gott.* At the same time, he was busy playing in the Royal Opera Orchestra and in the relative orchestras of the music directors Bilse and Liebig. Voigt was a musician and violin player through and through. Then in 1857 the position as Bandmaster with the 1st Guards Regiment became vacant. Director of Music, Engelhardt, retired after forty years service. Nobody from the Band was ready to take over, and nobody from outside the Band was suitable because this Regimental Band, along with its normal service requirements, had to play all the Court Music for State Occasions. So the King, searching for a suitable successor, turned to Wieprecht who proposed his Opera Orchestra colleague, Voigt. So the twenty-four-year-old Voigt next became a recruit and four months later, on 12th September 1857, became a Stabshoboist – a Bandmaster. Good music was thus guaranteed as a result of the disciplined upbringing under the old and dependable Bandmaster, this the Regimental Commander Colonel Freiheerr Hiller von Gärtringen and Voigt's visiting father, having a nostalgic conversation with one another, could agree upon. Thus began for Voigt his thirty-year-long restless occupation. Apart from which, he wrote over one hundred compositions, of which many were marches, eight of which became Army Marches. His marches came, like those of Piefke, previously unheard into the Collection. Many are pieces for special occasions. The *Salus Caesari* became an Army March straight away in 1871. The piece appeared in the Feldquartier before Paris, one can excuse the 1st and 2nd sections, which are quickly passed over before the festive trio. And no-one would seek to outdo Handel's Chorale to begin with! With his 'Kaiser and King' Voigt came to have the most familiar relationship, further both shared the same birthday (22nd March), so that at every Birthday Parade he received a Royal expression of good wishes. Voigt's position was significant. In 1887 he became the first ever Army Music Inspector.

AM II, 206 Versailler Festmarsch zum 18. Januar 1871 by Friedrich August Trenkler

The composer Friedrich August Trenkler, born in Dresden in 1836, died there in 1910, was an important personality! At thirty-one-years-old (1867) he took over as Bandmaster the newly-raised Saxon Grenadier-Regiment Nr. 101 Regimental Band, out of which he created a first-class wind band and string ensemble. His grasp and touch as a conductor was full of deep understanding. As patron of the Regimental Band stationed in Dresden, the capital of the Kingdom of Saxony, and with the King of Prussia as Honorary Colonel of the Regiment from 1868, he and his band of forty musicians actually took part in the war campaigning in France in 1870-71. Trenkler was a good soldier, an agreeable apparition, and a great musician. When after seventy years of toil and hope, on the 18 January 1871, a united Imperial Germany was created, joy was everywhere and numerous festive marches were composed. Trenkler could place his directly in front of the Kaiser in Berlin as his Regimental Colonel-in-chief, and it was immediately made an Army March. The score was naurally by Trenkler personally, the publication of the parts followed soon from the Berlin music publisher Schlesinger on 1st July 1871. The piece enjoyed universal popularity, which through its rhythmicality, 'die Moral der Musik ist'. It was eagerly played in Saxony as well as Prussia. From 1926 it was in the March Books (2nd Series) of all German bands (until 1945). Trenkler undertook a four-week tour with his band to Westphalia, the Rhineland and Holland in 1873. The eight appearances in the garden of the Volkspalast in Amsterdam found a captivated public. In 1874 the band played before Kaiser Wilhelm I and his wife, the Kaiserin, in Schloss Babelsberg in Potsdam. The 1870s were Trenkler's greatest era, which he himself said. On 19 April 1879, he was named as a Royal Saxon Director of Music, and in 1889 he retired. Trenkler had composed much – dances, songs, marches. His *Sedaner Siegesmarsch*, his Opus 102, his *Versailler Festmarsch* his Opus 106, and his *Wettinger Jubiläums-Marsch* of 1889 (for the six-hundred year jubilee of the Saxon Royal House of

Friedrich August Trenkler (Duncan Rogers)

Wettin) entered the HM collection in 1933 as *HM IIIA 66*. Often Trenkler visited the Court Theatre and concerts by foreign performers in order to broaden his own knowledge. It must also be pointed out that Trenkler, after leaving military service at the age of fifty-five years, took over the leadership of the Dresdener Gewerbehauskapelle. Capable and tireless he brought the previously failing orchestra to a peak of perfection, out of which, in 1903, the Dresden Philharmonic was created. The young Oskar Hackenberger played as a trombonist in the Gewerbehauskapelle under Trenkler before he became a Prussian military musician, Bandmaster and later Chief Inspector of Army Music!

Friedrich August Trenkler was a person of note!

AM II, 207 Bombardonmarsch by Heinrich Saro

The composer, Musikdirektor Heinrich Saro (1827-1891), belongs to our most useful of military band masters. At the express wish of the Crown Prince (later Kaiser Frederick III), he was changed in 1859 from Stabshoboist of Infanterie-Regiment Nr. 11 in Breslau, Silesia to the Kaiser Franz Garde-Grenadier-Regiment Nr. 2 in Berlin, whose Band he led until 1887. Of Saro we have a good impression, as still valid today is his 'Instrumentations-Lehre für Militär-Musik' of 1872 (288 large format pages with guidance notes to scores). Saro's marches are likewise prime examples. This Opus 107 is after motifs from the Opera *Das Goldene Kreuz* by Ignaz Brüll, an Austrian composer (1846-1907). Already by the following year, this version from Saro became an Army March and the score came out from the Berlin music publishers, Bote & Bock, who still today can sell you the parts for this Opera, arranged for wind band with an arrangement for the saxophone to play the lead. Of the march Saro composed, further words are superfluous, one cannot do better than hear what Saro arranged and shaped.

AM II, 208 Die deutsche Kaisergarde by Friedrich Wilhelm Voigt

This march goes directly back to the year 1869, as the Prussian Crown Prince (later Kaiser Friedrich III) took part in the opening ceremony of the Suez Canal, the Crown Princess with her children had a long stay in Cannes. Particularly her eldest, the ten-year-old Prince Wilhelm, lived life to the full in this strange flora (and fauna) and freedom, and along with the other boys enjoyed it when the military marched through the resort with their glittering (French) clarion-bugles. When fourteen year later in Potsdam, he was riding to Exercises at the head of his Battalion of the 1.Garde-Regiment zu Fuss, behind the Regimental Band, he spoke to Musikdirektor Voigt, asking why such a happy high blaring sound was never played by us? The full-blooded musician Friedrich Wilhelm Voigt (1833-1894) wrote thereupon his Opus 66 *Die deutsche Kaisergarde*, the trio of which he set in the key of the bugles (Signalhörner) so that the Buglers (Hornisten) of the Fife/Bugle and Drum Corps players (Spielleute) could let rip with their bugles, playing with the Band, overlying the D major chords of the trio. The march appearing in 1883, which immediately became an Army March, sought to remember the Regiment's baptism of fire at Grossgörschen seventy years previously (2nd May 1813). The copyright belonged to Bote & Bock of Berlin. In 1914, the march went into Marschbuch 1. Folge to all Prussian military musicians, (and) in 1961 in the Volume II of the Bundeswehr.

AM II, 209 Drei Kaiser-Marsch by Friedrich Wilhelm Voigt

For all receptions and festivals at the Prussian Court, de facto the Imperial German Court, the Honour Company (Ehrenkompanie) of the 1st Garde-Regiment zu Fuss with the Regimental Band turned out, and Friedrich Wilhelm Voigt (1833-1894) was the Director of Music of this band from 1857 to 1887. For thirty long years he lived his life never far from the next display of political and military ceremonial, and sometimes composed a march for the event. And so this piece appeared to mark the visit of the Austrian Kaiser Franz Joseph I and the Russian Tsar Alexander II (5th – 12th September 1872) to the German Kaiser Wilhelm I in Berlin. It was a friendly meeting of the three monarchs and a great event for the population. Voigt's march was well received at the free public concerts, with its trio from the Austrian national anthem (by Haydn) and also the Tsarist Russian anthem (by Lvov) ringing out, together with Germany's *die Wacht am Rhein*, a song which was more than just an anthem. The exalted visitors actually did not get to hear the march. Very soon such a piece of the moment was no longer playable, overtaken by events, forgotten. But fifteen years later, on 22nd March 1887, it was called back to life. Every year, Director of Music Voigt played a 'birthday greeting serenade' (*Geburtstagständchen*) for his Kaiser, on this occasion, his 90th birthday and Voigt's swansong as Director of Music of his Band. On 29th April he took up the new position as Army Music Inspector in Berlin. There followed a discussion about Voigt's compositions and particularly this piece. The old Kaiser thought back to happier times when, in 1872, his nephew Alexander II, his sister's son, reigned in Russia but who, in the intervening period in 1881 in St Petersburg, had been murdered by an assassin. And so, after fifteen years, the *Drei Kaiser-Marsch* became and Army March with the score being published by Schlesinger Buch-und Musikhandlung (Robert Lienau) Verlag on 1 July 1887. The piece is not widely known; however, at the time of the 'Three Emperors Gathering', it had entranced everyone.

King Karl I of Württemberg (1823-1891) (Eagle & Lyre Prints Collection)

AM II, 210 (see *AM III, 69*) ***Der Torgauer Parademarsch*** – a cavalry march

AM II, 211 (see *AM III, 70*) ***Schwedischer Reitermarsch*** – a cavalry march

AM II, 212 König Karl-Marsch by Carl Unrath

The most widely-known March from Württemberg, even today! Written by Carl Ludwig Unrath (1828-1908), the Royal Württembergische Stabshoboist, for twenty years (1851-1872) with the 4.Württembergisches Infanterie-Regiment (later re-styled the Füsilier-Regiment Nr. 122) in Stuttgart, whose garrison from 1852 was Ludwigsburg and from 1866 transferred to Ulm. The march appeared in 1868 in Ulm, the copyright granted in 1869 to Musikverlag Adolph Fürstner in Berlin. The piece was dedicated to King Karl I of Württemberg (1823-1891) who came to the throne in 1864. His death occasioned the much-loved march to be given his name, and in 1892 was taken into the Prussian Army March Collection, newly-arranged by Friedrich Wilhelm Voigt (1833-1894) already well known as Prussian Army Music Inspector. Since then the piece has been played universally, indeed by many regiments as their Parademarsch until 1939. The German Kingdoms which joined together to create the German Empire in 1871, which lasted until 1918, were the kingdoms of Prussia, Bavaria, Saxony and Württemberg. The consort of the previously-mentioned King Karl was Queen Olga (1822-1892), a Russian Grand Duchess and niece of the Prussian King Friedrich Wilhelm III and Queen Luise. The composer Unrath retired from the regiment in 1872 when they changed garrison to Ludwigsburg. He became a Chancery Clerk and from 1887 was on the Finance Executive of Württemberg War Ministry in Darmstadt. In 1898 he retired. Unrath wrote many marches. He died in Stuttgart.

AM II, 213 (see *AM III, 72*) ***Des Grossen Kurfürsten Reitermarsch*** – a cavalry march
AM II, 214 (see *AM I, 55* **and** *AM I, 70*)

AM II, 215 Marsch by Prinz August Wilhelm von Preussen (1722-1758), arranged by Carl Frese

Prince August William of Prussia was the younger brother of Frederick the Great, and as the Great man had no children, also Crown Prince and his successor as King. Two marches by the Prince wer resurrected after more than 144 years (in 1893) and taken into the Army March Collection, this one and also *AM II, 218*. They had been laid up in the music archive of the Berlin Schloss and brought to light by the cataloguing work of Dr Thouret. The composition is from 1751. It is a concert piece of its time, with a form and content based on a strict set of rules, which seems stilted today. It was never intended that the piece should be a military march; neither for the attack nor on parade. Kaiser Wilhelm II desired that the composition should be taken into service use and live on. So on 27 January 1893, the 2.Garde-Regiment zu Fuss in Berlin had it bestowed upon them as their Präsentiermarsch in an arrangement by the talented Carl Frese (1831-1903), Bandmaster of the Garde-Füsilier-Regiment in Berlin. The inclusion of the Army March in volume II of the Collection was an error by Army Music Inspector Professor Rossberg, it should have gone into volume I. After two-and-a-half years, on 7 November 1895, the Regiment was presented with *AM I, 56* and *AM I, 57*, of which *AM I, 56* was played (to 'Present Arms'). The march by Prince August William was, from then on, no longer played.

AM II, 216 Marsch des Infanterie Regiments von Thiele Nr. 46 arranged by Carl Frese

This march too was found in the Berlin Stadtschloss when Dr Thouret was working there making a catalogue of the music archives in 1890. One can say for certain that the march was played from 1795, as their Regimental March, by Infanterie-Regiment Nr. 46 whose Chef from 1794-1806 was General von Thiele, their garrison being Warsaw. (In the third partition of Poland, the Polish capital became temporarily part of South Prussia). Kaiser Wilhelm II put the piece in front of one of his favourite Directors of Military Music, Carl Frese (1831-1903), to arrange it for modern military band. The beautiful march was solidly put together with eight bars in the first section, sixteen bars in the second section, and still no trio. Dr Thouret came up with a Piano arrangement, and both versions from Frese and Thouret joined the already one-hundred-year-old 'thin' arrangement which had been for six to ten oboists. The music publishers Breitkopf und Härtel of Leipzig undertook the publishing and copyright. With the ACO of 27th January 1893, the piece became the Präsentiermarsch of the Kaiser Franz Garde-Grenadier-Regiment Nr. 2 in Berlin. The 'Franzer' were created in 1814 in part (amongst others) from the Grenadier companies of the Regiment von Thiele who had campaigned in the Silesian Wars (early 1740s) under Frederick the Great. During the years of peace before the First World War, the Kaiser Franz Garde-Grenadier-Regiment Nr. 2 always performed the 'Present Arms' to this old Prussian march, all Berliners knew it, along with the fact that the Austro-Hungarian Kaiser Franz Josef was the Chef of the Regiment. Finally the march-past would take place to their Regimental Quick March (Parademarsch), the Radetzky March!

AM II, 217 Marsch des Infanterie Regiments Prinz Ferdinand Nr. 34 arranged by Carl Frese

An old Prussian march from before two hundred years ago that we can still use and play today thanks to the research work of more than one person and a stroke of good luck. Two regimental marches are known of the 'old Prussian' Infanterie-Regiment Prinz Ferdinand Nr. 34 whose peacetime garrison had been in Brandenburgish Ruppin (4 km north-eastwards of today's Neu-Ruppin) played since 1750 was AM I, 73, and this march AM II, 217 since 1790. The score of the latter was filed away in the Berlin Stadt Schloss by the musically-interested and able Prussian King Friedrich Wilhelm II (1744-1797). The parts lay there undisturbed during the following decades through the period of French occupation and were in the forgotten music archive rediscovered by Dr Thouret (1855-1924) in 1889. Together with ten further, also rediscovered, Prussian military marches, Dr Thouret rearranged the sparsely-scored pieces for a few oboes into an edition published by Verlag Breitkopf and Härtel in Leipzig for the Piano-forte in 1892. Kaiser Wilhelm II (1859-1941) commanded that ten of these eleven pieces be arranged for full Prussian Military Band instrumentation by Bandmaster Carl Frese (1831-1903), to be then conferred upon named successor regiments as their 'Präsentiermarsche'. The arrangements, too, were published by Breitkopf & Härtel, and they are still available today. The marches entered the Army March Collection as II, 214-223, whereas the Army Music Inspector should have included them in either volume I or III of the collection (a clerical error). This march, AM II, 217, was bestowed upon and played as their Präsentiermarsch by the Garde-Füsilier-Regiment in Berlin until the First World War.

AM II, 218 Marsch by Prince August Wilhelm of Prussia (1722-1758) arranged by Carl Frese (1831-1903)

Prince August Wilhelm of Prussia was the next youngest brother of Frederick the Great. This march became the Präsentiermarsch of the Prussian 3.Garde-Regiment zu Fuss in 1893 in much the same way as the other marches rediscovered in the Berlin Castle Library.

AM II, 219 Marsch Composed by The Duchess Philippine Charlotte of Brunswick-Lüneburg (1716-1801), arranged by Carl Frese

The composer was a sister of Frederick the Great. The march – it is a concert piece, a concert march. She wrote it in the year 1751 for her brother, Prince August William of Prussia, who was also an able composer. In those days it was Princely practice to be proficient in the realms of art and music. Music stood under the influence of Johann Sebastian Bach and on a basis of a rigid set of rules. The construction and typical modulation, the melody and repeats were stylised. Such concert marches were not used by troops in attack (Angriff) or for movement on parade. Also the band of a regiment was only made up of four to six musicians, all called 'Hoboists' – after the principal instrument of the ensemble, the oboe. This march was set for two oboes, one bassoon and one trumpet. In 1889, the long-lost score for this march was rediscovered in the Berlin Schloss, and at the command of Kaiser Wilhelm II was arranged for modern military band by Bandmaster Frese (1831-1903) and in 1893 was conferred upon the 4.Garde-Regiment zu Fuss in Berlin as their Präsentiermarsch. The Regiment was less than happy at being lumbered with this piece. It is only ever played now for historical interest.

AM II, 220 Marsch des Infanterie-Regiments von Möllendorff Nr. 25 arranged by Carl Frese

In Prussia there was, from 1782 to 1806, the Infantry Regiment von Möllendorff Nr. 25 with Berlin as its garrison. It played until 1796 two of its own marches, this the first, the more junior (the second AM I, 64). They were 18th century marches for the slow tempo of that time. In the years of Napoleon's conquest and occupation at the beginning of the 19th century the notes were lost. For the first time in 1889 all these old regimental marches were found in a cupboard of the Berlin Stadtschloss. Kaiser Wilhelm II was very interested in the historical research of Dr Thouret and decreed that on 27th January 1893 all these pieces should be given to Regiments who had descended from these old regiments as Präsentiermärsche. This march belonged thus to the Grenadier-Regiment Graf Kleist von Nollendorf (1.Westpreussisches) Nr. 6 in Posen. Carl Frese (1831-1903), Stabshoboist of the Garde-Füsilier-Regiment in Berlin, was given the task of arranging these old marches for the then Prussian Band instrumental composition. The Kaiser had a good opinion of this bandmaster. Music Inspector Gustav Rossberg (1838-1910) had the responsibility for compiling the register of Army Marches in the Army March Collection. These old slow marches, quite wrongly, went not into the collection I for slow marches but into collection II for quick marches. The mistake was not corrected so that still today eight slow Präentiermarsche have the numbers AM II, 215-222. There is a new arrangement by Hackenberger in his 1926 (2 Folge). Included by the Bundeswehr in their 1962 Volume I as no. 17.

AM II, 221 Marsch des Infanterie Regiments von Treskow Nr. 17 um 1800 arranged by Carl Frese

A wonderful piece! The old two section march of the Infanterie Regiment von Treskow Nr. 17 in Danzig from about the year 1800. It is quite possible that this march is a good deal older, having been established as the Regimental March by that time. Another rediscovery by Dr Thouret, it was passed to Carl Frese like the others found in the Berlin Schloss. On 27th January 1893, it was bestowed upon the Grenadier-Regiment Nr. 10 in Breslau by Royal Order in Cabinet as their Präsentiermarsch. In 1897, the regiment moved to a new garrison in Schweidnitz in Silesia. From that time, it was heard at every parade in Schweidnitz, also in the days of the Weimar Repulic's Reichswehr, and the Wehrmacht whose Infanterieregiment 7 continued the tradition. Every citizen of Schweidnitz knew it, and it was indelibly associated with the two regiments for fifty years until 1945.[7]

AM II, 222 Marsch des Infanterie-Regiments Jung Bornstedt Nr 20 arranged by Carl Frese

The peacetime garrison of the Infantry Regiment Jung Bornstedt Nr 20, between 1786 and 1793, was in Magdeburg. It had two particularly outstanding, pretty regimental marches. The first, the older (now AM I, 74) was in two sections; the second, younger, namely this one was in two sections with a further two section trio from 1792, all sections run along calmly with eight bars. One wants to play both pieces in 4/4 time. In the Napoleonic Wars which followed the notation was lost. These two marches were found again in 1889, along with other old Prussian marches, and tucked away in a cupboard of the old Berlin City

7 Today Schweidnitz is in Poland, the German population having been expelled between 1945 and 1955.

Grand Duke Friedrich von Baden (1826-1907)

Schloss. Dr Thouret took the trouble to find out their historic identity. Kaiser Wilhelm II then bestowed them as Präsentiermärsche on the successors to the old Regiments. These reached Infanterie-Regiment Nr. 27 in Magdeburg on 27th January 1893, and had been arranged by Carl Frese (1831-1903), conductor of the Garde-Fusilier-Regiment in Berlin. Frese stood in Imperial favour for his good music. The score had quite properly been issued in 1890 by the office of the Army Music Inspector, Gustav Rossberg (1838-1910). He had the responsibility for compiling the register of Army Marches in the Army March Collection. These old slow marches, quite wrongly, went not into the collection I for Slow marches but into Collection II for quick marches. The mistake was not corrected so that still today, eight slow Präsentiermärsche have the numbers *AM II, 215-222*. In 1933, *AM II, 222* went into March Book '4th Series' to all German military musicians, and since 1962 the Bundeswehr have had it in their Volume I.

AM II, 223 (see *AM III 83*) **Marsch by Prince August Wilhelm of Prussia** – a cavalry march

AM II, 224 Marsch Infanterie Regiment Grossherzog Friedrich von Baden **by Carl Haefele**

It is, quite rightly, a much-loved and much-played march; a street march, parade march and concert march. It is a march of long sounds, of whole and half notes. From the third bar, sumptuous long chords from the horns hang in the air under the whole thing. Above, happy music emanates from the flutes, oboes and many clarinets, these also in long chords and soft tones. The rhythm belongs to the trombones and bass instruments. Everything flows in a winning style, including the jubilation of the happy trumpets in rounded tones. Nothing is forced, stark or hard-hitting. Jazz trumpets had never been heard of then. The march is from 1893. The composer, Carl Haefele (1848-1924), was, on the 4 March 1863 (at fourteen years old, in fact!) taken into the 8th Württembergish Infanterie-Regiment Nr. 126 in Ludwigsburg, then there he became Sergeant-Hoboist (Band Sergeant) in 1879, and then Stabshoboist (Staff Musician-Bandmaster) in 1887, then Musikdirigent (Conductor-Bandmaster), and in 1905, Musikdirektor (Director of Music – but still of NCO rank). After forty-seven years in the Regiment, he retired in 1910. In his time as Kapellmeister he created a Regimental Band with an establishment of thirty-five personnel plus a number of supplementary people.

The instrumentation was as follows:

2 flutes
1 Oboe
1 or 2 bassoons
2 Eb clarinets
8 B clarinets
4 horns
2 tenor horns
1 Euphonium
5-6 trumpets
2 flügelhorns
4 trombones
1 bass trumpet
3-4 tubas
1 helikon
3 percussion

The field campaign against Prussia in 1866 (including the Battle of Bischofsheim, Prussia v. Württemberg/Bavaria/Austria), and then the 1870/71 campaign against France, Haefele undertook as an ordinary musician with the band. From 1891 the Grand Duke Friedrich of Baden was the Chef (Honorary Colonel) of the Regiment and the Regiment was restyled the 8.Württembergisches Infanterie-Regiment Nr. 126 Grossherzog Friedrich von Baden. The garrison of Strasbourg in Alsace, from 1871 on, was dreadful. In the heavily occupied city there were a further six infantry Regimental Bands, two cavalry 'Trompeter' Brass Bands and two Battalion Bands, who all attempted to augment their finances outside their army pay by giving concerts. The march came out in 1893 and was immediately an official Army March; copyright Bote and Bock of Berlin. It was dedicated to the regiment who from then on played it as their Parademarsch. In 1914 it appeared in Marschbuch 1. Folge for all Prussian troops and from 1961 is in Volume II for the Bundeswehr. Das Musikkorps der Kommandantur Berlin (in effect the band for ceremonial 'Public Duties' in Berlin) under Musikmeister Ahlers often played this piece at 'Changing of the Guard' between the two World Wars. A wonderfully beautiful march.

A march composed to celebrate the alliance of Germany and Austria-Hungary at the outbreak of war in August 1914. Note the German imperial colours of black-white-red and the Habsburg colours of black-yellow on the cover which depicts Kaiser Wilhelm II and Kaiser Franz Joseph I. This march did not get into the collection and did not gain approval for parade use. (Eagle & Lyre Archive)

AM II, 225 (see *AM III, 89 Praesentiersmarsch des Leib-Kürassier Regiments Grosser Kurfurst Nr.1*) – a cavalry march

AM II, 226 Hohenzollern-Marsch by Otto Berger

It would have been an unknown piece, if Infanterie-Regiment Nr. 67 in Metz had not had it as their Parademarsch (regimental quick march). The composer, Otto Berger (1837-1910), was Lieutenant General and Commanding Officer of the 58th Infantry Brigade in Mülhausen, Alsace, whose Opus 43 the Kaiser had laid before him, and at Royal command on 26th November 1896 was named an Army March. General Berger originated from East Prussia, had his training from 1855 with the Infanterie-Regiment Nr. 13 in Wesel and served as a Captain and Company Commander in the Infanterie-Regiment Nr. 53 during the 1870-71 campaign, being awarded the Iron Cross 2nd Class. Later he was with them, as Battalion Commander, until he took over the command of the Füsilier-Regiment Nr. 86 in Flensburg on 9 September 1890 at the request of the Kaiserin, Queen of Prussia, who was the Regiment's Honorary Colonel. After four years as a Brigade Commander in Mülhausen he retired. The inclusion of this composition in the Army March Collection indicates a keen personal interest by the Kaiser in the old General, and in good Marschmusik.

AM II, 227

This is *AM II, 52*. Through an adminisrative error by the Music Inspector this march is wrongly included again.

AM II, 228 Marsch des Hannoverschen 5. Infanterie Regiments (1866) by Carl Merkel

This Royal Hanoverian regimental march with its resounding trumpets was heard in the garrison of Lüneberg until the disbandment of the regiment in 1866. The piece had been composed by Carl Merkel (born 1808), the Musikmeister of the Regiment from 1848-1866. Then in 1900, now listed as a Prussian Army march, this rare march was bestowed upon the 2nd Hanoverian Infanterie-Regiment Nr. 77 in Celle (Nr 77 in the Prussian Line as Hanover had been annexed in 1866), from where it ultimately was also played by the Reichswehr and Wehrmacht as a Parademarsch. It has become a piece forever associated with Celle.

AM II, 229 Marsch des Hannoverschen 2. Infanterie-Regiments (1866) by Carl Neumann

With the All-Highest Cabinet Order (AKO) No. 7 of 27 January 1900, the marches of the former Hanoverian Army were given to Prussian Regiments in order to continue their traditions. Until then these were not listed as Army Marches. In a further AKO, No. 85 of 24 March 1900, these marches were placed in the Army March Collection and given numbers. The ensnaring of the Hanoverian marches was not completed with the usual Prussian care, as it was overlooked that the march *AM II, 229* was already listed as AM II, 143 as a Prussian Army March. There lies, therefore, a double entry in a single collection! Similarly, it is the same case with *AM II, 227*, although with a Trio, and the *AM II, 52* (without trio). Besides these, the very beautiful *Marsch des Hannoverschen 7. Infanterie-Regiments (1866)* (also known as the *Fünf Eichen Marsch- 'The Five Oaks March'*) by Thomas was completely overlooked and not included as an Army March at all.

AM II, 230 Marsch des Hannoverschen 4. Infanterie Regiments (1866) by Julius Gerold

Julius Gerold (1808-1876) was, during the middle of the 19th century, for the Kingdom of Hanover what Wilhelm Wieprecht was for the Kingdom of Prussia. Yet both were very different. Wieprecht was a bustling, impulsive, inexhaustible apparition; Gerold was calm, mature, and he was a soldier. Entering the Garde-Jägers in the capital of Hanover, he became for twenty years, from 1830 to 1850, their Bandmaster until the highly-qualified Louis Oertel succeeded him in 1850. In the meantime, King Ernst August, whose mounted statue still stands before Hanover's main railway station, named Gerold, on 20th July 1847, as Armee-Musik-Direktor, whereby all Hanoverian military musicians would be under his supervision. And so Hanover had an active, reliable personality in this position. Gerold was already declared to have inherited a great feel for music and was held up as an example as a composer and arranger. Further, after the death of King Ernst August in 1851, the new King Georg V, highly musical himself, upon assuming power did not end the special appointment. The march listed above, Gerold wrote in 1862 as the *Georgs-Marsch*. It must be stated that already by 1844 Gerold's very delightful *Paulinen-Trabmarsch* was a Prussian Armeemarsch (*AM III, 34*). With the abolition of the Hanoverian Army in 1866, Gerold left the service. The newly-raised Prussian troops, who were determined to continue the Hanoverian tradition, had already by 1867 called themselves 'hannoversch' in the subtitles of their Regiments. But the beautiful Hanoverian Regimental Marches were not officially carried forward. Naturally they continued to be popularly played, particularly as Musikverlag Louis Oertel (the above-named successor to Gerold as bandmaster) in Hanover worked hard to have them included. Indeed they were eventually taken on as Army Marches and linked to their respective Regiments. Principally, Kaiser Wilhelm II must be remembered for his ACO of 27th January 1900 which ordered this. Then appears a mistake by the Armeemusikinspizient, the already since 1848 to hand *AM II, 143* was re-included as AM II, 229. Just as he had in 1893, eight old slow marches from the 18th century numbered as Quick marches II, 215 to 222. Gerold's much-loved, highly artistic *Georgs-Marsch*, the old march of the Hanoverian 4th Infantry Regiment in Stade, was taken on by the Prussian (5th Hanoverian) Infanterie-Regiment Nr. 65 in the Harz mountains (part stationed in Goslar, part in Quedlinburg) as their Parademarsch. The name of the once-enemy King Georg was avoided. The Bundeswehr has this good march used by all Bands.

AM II, 231 Marsch des Hannoverschen Garde Jäger Bataillons (1866) by Wilhelm Nedderhuth

The Hanoverian rulers were so interested in their Jäger Troops that their regiments had to go through many disbandments and new raisings. They raised themselves after the end of Napoleon's occupation in 1816 a Jäger-Garde-Bataillon which already, four years later in 1820, became a full Garde-Jäger-Regiment, and in 1833 again cut back to a Garde-Jäger-Battalion. But they always remained in their garrison the capital city, Hanover, and as their Präsentiermarsch played the piece by Nedderhuth. It was in 1804, during the days of the Anglo-German Legions, that the piece emanated from Nedderhuth, a Bugle-Major in the Music-Band of the 1st Light Battalion of the British King's German Legion, and constructed on the English 'Hunting Song of the Chase' belonging to the Hampshire Hunting Club. The arrangement hails from Julius Gerold (1808-1876) who was the twenty-year-long (1830-50) Kapellmeister of the Regiment/Battalion. The piece is in two sections (twelve and eighteen bars) and stands in 6/8 time for the slow pace. Three months after the abolition of the Hanoverian Army on 27 September 1866, there was founded a new cadre in Potsdam, which was to muster the Prussian Jäger-Battalion No. 10 with the help of the Prussian Guard Jägers, Guard Schützen and Jäger Battalions to rebuild a Hanoverian Jäger tradition but within Prussian service. Their garrison was to be Goslar, from 1890 Colmar in Alsace, 1901 Bitsch, and from 1909 again in Goslar. In Prussian service the Battalion made no further changes in structure despite, however, three changes of garrison. In 1900 all four former Hanoverian Battalion's Jäger marches were selected for the collection. The 10th played this march *AM II, 231* as their Präsentiermarsch for Presenting Arms, for Parademarsch *AM II, 58* for marching past in quick time (once the march of the Hanoverian 1st Jäger Battalion).

AM II, 232 Marsch des Hannoverschen 2. Jäger Bataillons (1866) by Christian Ehrengott Meyer

The aforementioned-named Batallion began in 1833 as a Light Battalion and was, in 1857, turned into the 2nd Jäger Battalion with their last station in the capital, Hanover. With the end of the Hanoverian Army this Battalion too was abolished. As with the other Hanoverian Jäger Battalions, its traditions were taken on by the 10th Prussian Jägers (Jäger-Bataillon Nr. 10). This piece remained in memory of the 2nd Jäger Battalion. It had been composed by Christian Ehrengott Meyer (1803 – ?), Bandmaster of the Battalion from 1840 to 1846 in their then garrison Einbeck. The march is in four sections, three sections of eight bars and a closing section of sixteen bars. It was the Parademarsch of the Battalion. The copyright of all Hanoverian marches was Musikverklag Louis Oertel in Hanover, later Grossburgwedel, whose proprietor was Bandmaster of the Hanoverian Garde-Jäger Battalion until 1866. Also A. Kützing from the same firm did much to promote Hanoverian marches and song.

AM II, 233 Marsch des Hannoverschen 3. Jäger Bataillons (1866) by Johann Michael Moscherosch

The Hanoverian 3rd Jäger Battalion's final base was in Göttingen, until abolished in 1866. Their Parademarsch hailed back to the old Landsknechtlied by Johann Michael Moscherosch (1601-1669), the secret service agent and writer known under the pseudonym of Philander von Sittewald. The piece sprang along in 4/4 time without break through thirty-five bars. After 1866, the surviving NCOs and Other Ranks of the four Hanoverian Jäger Battalions were pressed into the Prussian 10th Jäger Battalion in Goslar. The aforementioned march of the 3rd Jäger Battalion rang out only at concerts from then on, especially in Minden and Göttingen, the one-time garrison of the Battalion. With its declaration as an Army March in 1900, the piece has been handed down to us today.

AM II, 234 Marsch der Hannoverschen Pioniere (1866)

This march speaks for itself. It is short, clear and wonderfully festive in rhythm; two sections of eight bars and a trio of likewise eight bars. The origin is possibly from an incomplete and long-abandoned folk dance; in any event it is a popularly played piece. Once the march of the Hanoverian Pioneers until 1866, it was given to the Prussian 'Hanoverian' Pioneer-Bataillon Nr. 10 in Minden, who keenly continued Hanoverian traditions. The copyright of Hanoverian marches was and is held by Musikverlag Oertel in Hanover, later Grossburgwedel. The Bundeswehr has the piece in their march books.

AM II, 235 (see *AM III 113 Kreuzritter –Fanfare*) – a cavalry march

AM II, 236 Kaiserin Auguste Victoria-Marsch by Eduard Funck

On 9th September 1890, Kaiser Wilhelm II appointed his consort, the Kaiserin Auguste Victoria (1858-1921), to the position of Chef (Honorary Colonel) of the Schleswig-Holstein Füsilier-Regiment Nr. 86 in Flensburg. Thereby honouring the Regiment stationed in the most northern garrison in Germany and the Province of Schleswig-Holstein, especially as the Kaiserin was born a Princess of Schleswig-Holstein-Sonderburg-Augustenburg before the 1864 frontier with Denmark was established. On the river Alsen lay the homelands of Augustenburg and also Sonderburg, where the III Battalion was stationed in the castle's barracks (on the bank by the bridge which led to 'Castle ' island). A relation of mine (son-in-law of my Father's Aunt) was there in 1913/14, commanding the 10th company. The interest of the Kaiser in the sea, was matched by that of his wife the Kaiserin with their journeys to the north (Norwegian Fjiords) and joint interest in their Navy. With regard to the composer, the able Stabshoboist Eduard Funck (1861-1927) took over the Band of the Regiment on 1st November 1899, writing this march as soon as 1902 (his Opus 145), within which the song *Schleswig-Holstein, meerumschlungen* is interworked. The song is by Carl Gottlieb Bellmann (1772-1862), a Kantor in Schleswig and is still often heard today in Schleswig-Holstein. The march became immediately an Army March (AM) and the Präsentiermarsch of the Regiment. The copyright belongs to Lehne & Co./Hanover which is today owned by Musikverlag Rolf Budde/Berlin, Hohenzollerndamm 54A.

AM II, 237 Marsch des Sibirischen Grenadier Regiments, Fassung 1905 arranged by Heinrich van Eyken

This march was in its original 1817 form as *AM II, 14*. In that form it had already endured many changes. Originally a Langsame Angriffsmarsch (slow attack-march) in tempo circa seventy-five paces to the minute, after its importation in quick time at the beginning of the 19th century it was transformed into a Geschwindmarsch. In this new version, titled above, we find a later-composed trio tacked on and naturally the instrumentation arrangements of the year 1905. It was undertaken by Heinrich van Eyken (1861-1908), really a song composer, who was Professor at the Berliner Hochschule für Musik between 1902 and 1906. In 1933, with the publication of the newly-titled *Deutsche Heeresmärsche*, the march was correctly placed under the Präsentiermärsche with the number *HM I, 7.* In its slow form it sounds as in this edition.

AM II, 238 Marsch des Hessischen Leibgarde Infanterie-Regiments 115 by Hugo Hauske

The Grand Duchy of Hesse's troops possess two noteworthy beautiful Geschwindmärsche (quick marches) (*AM II 238 and 262*), each were put together by combining two old, slow, Electoral Hesse marches from the 18th century and set in tempo 114. For the wondrous version of this march in 1907, we can thank Obermusikmeister Hugo Hauske (1866-1938), who, from 1907 until its abolition in 1919, was Kapellmeister of the (1. Grossherzoglich Hessisches) Leibgarde-Infanterie-Regiment Nr. 115 in Darmstadt, and where this march had been the Parademarsch of the Regiment. Unfortunately, through a new arrangement in 1933 by Professor Hermann Schmidt, the imposing first bar was destroyed, the unified chord by all instruments in half notes now elaborated with eighths and sixteenths. On records from before 1933 it is still possible to hear the original version. For the first and second sections the Marsch des Landgrafen Ludwig VIII of 1744 appears, for the trio (also in two sections) the march of the Hessischen Leib-Regiments zu Fuss from 1790, all masterfully woven together in tempo 114. Immediately (1908) the march was taken into the Army March Collection, and from 1921 it continued being played traditionally by the 1st (Hessian) Battalion of the Infanterie-Regiment 15 in Giessen, and in 1961 the Bundeswehr put it in their Band II. With the ACO (All-Highest Cabinet Order) of 29th June 1908 the piece was officially assigned to the Leibgarde-Infanterie-Regiment Nr. 115 as their Parademarsch.

AM II, 239 Marsch der Freiwilligen Jäger aus den Befreiungskriegen arranged by Heinrich Homann

We do not know how old this march really is (although its title is from the Napoleonic Wars, translated 'March of the Volunteer Jägers from the War of Liberation'). In Russia it was already known at the time of Suvorov, the Generalissimus who died in 1800. (The march is still played today in Russia and called *Yegerski.*) Anton Dörfeldt did not place the piece in his 'Imperial Russian' March Collection of 1809-1816. Also, later, it did not become a Russian Regimental march. Germany travelled along with the swinging melody through the Wars of Liberation, bringing it back in 1813-15 to a Fatherland liberated from French domination and plunder. In this process, one wishes the Jägers, as crack-shots, good shooting and success. Unconscripted, they were formed of volunteers. From the Russian border in East Prussia, to beyond the Rhine, they had to throw the enemy back. It was a titanic struggle and huge movement of troops, who were together encouraged on their way by easy melodies with which to march to. On our southern border in Switzerland, the piece is well-known as the *Sechselläutenmarsch.* At the yearly Spring Festival it rings out in Zürich and is regarded as typical from that city. On the other hand, German Jäger Battalions regard it as their own. The Stabswaldhornist of the Pomeranian Jäger-Bataillon Nr. 2 in Kulm (West Prussia) from 1874-1900 was Heinrich Homann (born 1841 – ?). He wrote the arrangement for the instrumentation of a Jäger Band. In 1899 Kaiser Wilhelm II bestowed the march on his Garde-Jäger-Bataillon and the Jäger-Bataillon Nr. 2 for big parades. Since 1911, it is an Armeemarsch. In 'Marschbuch '1 Folge' it has stood for all German Bandsmen. The Bundeswehr has it in their volume II. A happy, old and widely known piece, with a 'soldier's text' – sung by the Salvation Army!

The 2.Jäger-Abteilung (as it was then styled) in Greifswald had a close association with Prince Bismarck (the old Iron Chancellor, who had united Germany under Prussia's leadership), as it was with them from October 1838 he had began his almost lifelong service in the military. Still in 1896, the Waldhornistenkorps from their garrison then in Kulm, West Prussia, travelled to his seat at Friedrichsruh in order to serenade the old Chancellor on his birthday morning in his grounds. From 1914, the 2nd Jägers were named the 'Fürst Bismarck' Battalion.

AM II, 240 Preussens Gloria by Gottfried Piefke

This was a people's march, for the following reasons:

The piece emerged during the war of 1870/71, and the famous composer Musikdirektor Gottfried Piefke (1815-1884) at the war's end in 1871 played the Leib-Grenadier-Regiment Nr. 8 home into their Garrison town of Frankfurt/Oder to the sound of this march. After

Gottfried Piefke in old age. (Eagle & Lyre Prints Collection)

Piefke's death in 1884, his successor, Stabshoboist Rudolf Glasneck (born 1857) continued to have the march played within the regiment. Hauptmann (Captain) Elstermann von Elster, who was Officer Commanding the 11th Company there between 1892 and 1899, confirmed that the piece was heard often in Frankfurt-on-Oder. However, it was not widely known, unlike Piefke's *Düppel-Schanzen-Sturmmarsch* and his *Königgrätzer* played by all Prussian troops. It was first published by Verlag Arthur Parrhysius/Berlin in 1898. When in 1909, now Oberst (Colonel), Elstermann von Elster became the Commanding Officer of the 3.Garde-Regiment zu Fuss, he requested its use so that now it was heard at Changing of the Guard in Berlin too. The Infanterie-Regiment Nr. 64 in Prenzlau/Mark had it bestowed upon them as their Parademarsch by the King (e.g. the Kaiser; to Prussian Regiments he remained known as their King, 'the Kaiser' only to non-Prussian Regiments) on 26th October 1911, because of which it entered the Army March Collection on 11th November 1911. Now we find that the brother of Kaiser Wilhelm II, Grossadmiral Prinz Heinrich (Grand Admiral Prince Henry of Prussia) had fallen for the march. As General-Inspekteur of the Imperial German Navy, he made the piece well known in Kiel and Wilhelmshaven, so that it was often played as a Navy march. In 1914 the score was published in the Prussian Marschbuch 1st Edition that from 1921 all troops of the Reichswehr and later the Wehrmacht were supplied with (i.e. throughout all German Länder, not just Prussia).

After the collapse of Germany in 1945, I heard that a ban was being considered for this march. (It was indeed banned in the Soviet Zone, later in the DDR it was the subject of a SED Party ban). Its title was unmentionable or unacceptable in conversation. In 1961 the Bundeswehr got the march into their Volume II in 1961 thanks to Musikinspizient

An attractive cover of a collection of marches from the Prussian collection and the other minor German states arranged by Fr. R. Richter for pianoforte. A portrait of Kaiser Wilhelm II framed by the imperial tricolour of black-white-red adds patriotic appeal. (Eagle & Lyre Archive)

Wilhelm Stephan's insistance. It thereafter became widely played in West Germany, but remained banned in the DDR until 1989. The structure of the composition has a first and second section, each of eight bars and, after four linking bars, a calm trio of two sets of sixteen bars of long notes and well put together rhythm. The composer of 'Prussia's Glory' was Prussia's most significant Militärkapellmeister.

AM II, 241 Schwedischer Kriegsmarsch (Björneborganes)

The Finnish port of Björneborg on the Bay of Bothnia (in the Baltic) lies 230 km north-west of Helsinki. The Finnish march originates from the end of the 18th century when Finland belonged to Sweden. In origin a French contre-dance, it was probably arranged as a march by Christian Fréderic Kress. During the Finnish struggle for independence in the Swedish-Russian war of 1808-1809, the march became a national tune and remained so even when the country became part of Russia. Already by 1892-1897 German regiments were playing it merrily. Concert tours by Finnish orchestras and choirs made the piece well known. With the publication of 27th March 1912, it became an Army March arranged by Armeemusikinspizient Professor Theodor Grawert (1858-1927), copyrighted by Arthur Parrhysius in Berlin. In 1926 there appeared a new arrangement by Armeemusikinspizient Professor Oskar Hackenberger (1872-1929) in Marschbuch 2. Folge for all German bandsmen, in 1961 for the Bundeswehr in their Volume II.

Der Schwedishe-Finnländische Reitermarsch (*AM III, 70*) (Swedish-Finnish Cavalry March) and this Swedish-Finnish War March have much in common. Both originate from the 17th/18th century when Finland still belonged to Sweden. Both begin with two bars (eight paces) of kettle-drums/infantry drum before the music begins. Both have a short first and second section of eight bars and a short trio. And both stride along joyfully, with dignity, without wide expansion, and in a calm flow. Imperial Russia had assigned both marches as Regimental marches for their Finnish troops. With this Kriegsmarsch (War March), the Drummers could play along during the whole piece. The key for military band is set to that of the Fifes (Spielmanns-Pfeifen), so that the Military Band and Fife and Drum Corps are often heard playing this together. Finally, the piece is a much-used march for the Fifes and Drums (Spielleute). Altogether it was a famous and versatile march.

AM II, 242 Frontmarsch by George Kirchhof

A completely unknown piece! No one can say that they have ever heard it! Indeed, in even over fifty years of asking about it. The march originates from 1913 and was, by Imperial decree through the War Ministry, made an Army March on 16th December in the same year. It is possible that the composer laid the piece before the Kaiser on the occasion of his 25th Jubilee on 15th June 1913. The music publishers Arthur Parrhysius of Berlin listed the parts among their publications, however not named for use by any particular Regiment but for general purchase. Half a year later, the 1st World War began. Who bought these scores in the last few months of peace, the individual instrumental parts that is, tried them out, and used them in their repertoire? The composer, George Kirchhof (1837-1918), was seventy-six years old and still actively a composer. In the campaign of 1870-1871, he had been a Captain and Company Commander in Infanterie-Regiment Nr. 20 from Wittenberg, and then from 1884-1887 was Lieutenant Colonel of Jäger-Bataillon Nr. 6 in Oels, Silesia, then from 1887-1889 Colonel of Infanterie-Regiment Nr. 129 in Bromberg, Province Posen. Finally, he commanded the 11th Infantry Brigade in Brandenburg-on-

Havel, where in 1892 he retired having reached the rank of Lieutenant General. The march consists of twenty bars with repeats and, after two linking bars, a two-part trio follows.

AM II, 243 Der Jäger aus Kurpfalz by Johann Gottfried Rode

Johann Gottfried Rode is the founder of our Jägermusik, that means the music of our Jäger (Huntsman) and Schützen (Sharpshooter) Battalions. Military music (German) had from the early 19th century until 1945 three distinctly different sound ensembles, Harmoniemusik of the Infantry (with woodwind, brass instruments and complete 'Janissary' percussion), Trompetenmusik of the mounted troops (brass instruments with kettle drums, no French horns or woodwind), and Jägermusik (sometimes called Hornmusik, brass instuments alone, led by the French horns, with no percussion at all).

In the year 1935 there arrived a fourth type of music, Luftwaffenmusik (Harmoniemusik, but with a large range of saxophones added and dominating the sound. (For a short time in the late 1930s there was a fifth type – Panzermusik, essentially infantry instrumentation but with extra brass added to try and compete with the noise of the roar and rattle of the tanks.) The Bundeswehr copies the former Luftwaffe style for all bands of the Army, Luftwaffe and Navy (1956 – date).

Johann Gottfried Rode (1797-1857) was already, in his early years, an excellent musician on the clarinet, on the flute, on the trumpet and on the violin. On the 'Inventions-Waldhorn' (the first 'French' Horn with valves) at the age of twenty he was a virtuoso, so much so that the Commander of the Garde-Jäger-Bataillon in Berlin, Major von Neumann, called on Rode in Eisenberg to ask if he would fill the vacant position of premier Horn player. With the Garde-Jäger-Bataillon, Rode began his military service in 1817, the Battalion in the same year being re-stationed in Potsdam. The Band of the Battalion, which in the Jägers is called the 'Waldhornistenkorps' (literally 'Woodland-horn-corps' – we would say French Horn Corps. Ed.) was well-formed and in fine condition. They had been built up and were led by Stabshornist August-Heinrich Neithardt (1793-1861), but he did not go with them to Potsdam, being transferred to the Garde-Schützen-Bataillon in order to build up a similar band there. The new Kapellmeister of the Garde-Jäger-Bataillon was Carl Heinrich Schumann (1786 – ?) until the capable Rode took over as his successor in 1827. It was the age of the first tentative use of valves for brass instruments, so that the instrumental make-up of the ensemble was forever changing; as they became available, more chromatic instruments were being included. So the last to arrive, in 1835, was the much waited for and vaunted useful Bass Tuba, with it Rode's ensemble comprised:

9 – 10 'French' Horns
3 Kenthorns (Keyed bugles) – from 1847 replaced by cornets
3 Trumpets
1 Althorn
1 Tenor horn
1Bass Trombone with valves
2 Tubas

That is twenty musicians. The predominance of the Horns gave it its 'Jäger-ness'. With this ensemble came Rode's compositions and arrangements. He was tireless. It included over three thousand works all in Jäger-Huntsman character. He was teacher to Prince Carl of Prussia on the French horn. The Russian Tsar Nicholas presented him with a golden tabatiers for a Jagd composition in 1833 (and of course in 1838 Bismarck was a

Professor Theodor Grawert (1858-1927) Chief Inspector of Army Music 1908-1924 (Archive DGfMM eV)

new recruit in a Jäger Battalion). In 1842, he gained the Allgemeine Ehrenzeichen, 1849 the Hohenzollern-Medaille, and on 15th May 1855 he became 'Königliche Musikdirektor' (Royal Director of Music). He also founded the Widows and Orphans Fund for the Potsdam Cavalry Regiments and the Garde-Jäger-Bataillon. For the Silver Jubilee of his service, and later for his twenty-five years as a Bandmaster, he was showered with praise and gifts from the Officer Corps. After forty years service in the Battalion, and with thirty years as their Stabshornist, Rode died on 8th January 1857. The world that followed had much to thank him for. The bustling Wieprecht could not wait to cut the 'Waldhorn' ensembles of the Jägers; as a trombonist and friend of Cavalry style music he did not care for the warm warbling of the Jäger sound. The official History of the Garde-Jäger-Bataillon does not say a single word about music. Rode, who for forty years long shaped the Band was, above all, not named. And only one composition of Rode's became an Armeemarsch, namely this one on 19th December 1913, two years after (15th December 1911) the Garde-Jäger Battalion had been bestowed with it as their Parademarsch. At the outbreak of war in 1914, half of all Jäger Battalions played the march as their own. It is a beautiful piece, in the trio of which is the song of the Carmelite Father Martin Klein (1735-1795), 'Tutor in Residence' to the children of Wilhelm Utsch, the original 'Jäger aus Kurpfalz', whose memorial stands today in Soon-Wald (25 km west-south-west of Bingen).

AM II, 244 Rigauer Einzugsmarsch by Karl Hagen

This is the last march that the King of Prussia took into his Army March Collection. It appeared in the Great War 1914-1918, when the whole world fell upon the Germans and the anxiety of it did not allow attention to any other matters. In the north of the Eastern Front, Riga could be taken, and Kaiser Wilhelm II travelled with his brave troops. At a march past, eye to eye, on 6th September 1917 he saw the gratitude of his soldiers and they his gratitude to them. The last Regiment to march past, the Reserve-Infanterie-Regiment Nr. 59, had no Regimental march connected with them and played the latest from their Obermusikmeister Hagen created for the entry into Riga. The Kaiser, always with an open ear for a good march, with a short rise of the hand said 'Ha, what's new, a teasingly attractive march!' and said to his Flügeladjutant, Graf Moltke, next to him that Grawert should be interested in this one. Armeemusikinspzient Grawert sat there in Berlin, had to toil long and hard under the circumstances, amongst the various and ever-changing troops abroad, to find the Regiment and Band with this march that the Kaiser meant. In between, there were others important ones. The matter of this march remained. Finally, on 23rd June 1918, by Imperial Decree, the composition by Obermusikmeister Hagen, as the *Rigaer Einzugsmarsch*, became an Army March. The Musikverlag Breitkopf und Härtel in Leipzig had printed and published the score. In 1933, all German military musicians took on the piece in the new march book (4th series). The composer Karl Hagen (1867-1941) had attended the conservatory in Sonderhausen as a pupil, (then) at twenty-one years old had his training in Potsdam with the 3.Garde-Ulanen-Regiment. The twenty-seven man strong Trompeterkorps had been led by the experienced Stabstrompeter Kühne for the previous twenty-five years. Hagen played althorn, flugelhorn and Eb cornet. On 1 May 1900, Hagen took over, as a fresh new Stabstrompeter, the twenty-four Trumpeters of the newly-raised Feldartillerie-Artillerie-Regiment Nr. 52 in Königsberg, East Prussia. There he changed in March 1906 to Kürassier-Regiment Nr. 3, with them he became Obermusikmeister on 20th February 1909, and in 1914 went with them in the Field. From 1916 he led the Band of the Reserve-Infanterie-Regiment Nr. 59. After the war, Hagen proved to be most helpful, serving for many years as *Verbandsführer des Reichsverbandes ehemaliger Musikmeister der Armee und Marine* (Union Leader of the National Union of former Bandmasters of the Army and Navy) in Berlin.

Select Bibliography

Pre-1945 Publications

Arnold, Kurt, – *Findeisen Wir zogen in das Feld – Bilder aus Geschichte des deutschen Soldatenliedes und der Marschmusik* (Reutlingen: Enßlin & Laiblin, 1939)

Degele, Ludwig, – *Die Militärmusik Ihr Werden und Wesen, ihre kulturelle und nationale Bedeutung* (Wolfenbüttel: Verlag für musikalische Kultur und Wissenschaft, 1937)

Hierse, G., – *Der Musikmeister Handbuch für der Musikmeister der deutschen Armee und Marine und für Militärmusiker, die sich dazu vorbereiten wollen nebst Auszügen aus den Exerzier-Reglements, soweit Sie den Dienst der Musikkorps und Spielleute betreffen.* (Berlin: Parrhysius, 1911)

Kalkbrenner, August, – *Wilhelm Wieprecht, Sein Leben Und Wirken* (Berlin: E Prager, 1882) (Photocopy of Library of Congress Microfilm courtesy David E Clark)

Kalkbrenner, August, – *Die Organization Der Militärmusikchöre Aller Länder* (Hannover: Verlag Louis Oertal, 1884) (Photocopy of Library of Congress Microfilm courtesy David E Clark)

Kredel, Fritz, – *Wer will unter die Soldaten – Deutsche Soldatenlieder mit farbigen Bildern* (Leipzig: Insel-Verl, 1934)

Panoff, Peter, – *Militärmusik in Geschichte und Gegenwart* (Berlin: Siegismund, 1938)

Prager, Emil, – *Militair-Musiker-Almanach 1886 für das Deutsche Reich* (Berlin: Prager, 1886)

Parrhysius, Arthur, – *Militär-Musiker-Almanach 1899 für das Deutsche Reich* (Berlin: Verlag der Deutschen Militair-Musiker-Zeitung, 1899)

Parrhysius, Arthur, – *Militär-Musiker-Adreßbuch 1909 für das Deutsche Reich* (Berlin: Verlag der Deutschen Militair-Musiker-Zeitung, 1909)

Parrhysius, Arthur, – *Militär-Musiker-Adreßbuch 1913 für das Deutsche Reich* (Berlin: Verlag der Deutschen Militair-Musiker-Zeitung, 1913)

Parrhysius, Arthur, – *Militär-Musiker Notiz und Taschenbuch 1909* (Berlin: Militair-Musiker-Zeitung, 1909)

Schmidt, Hermann, – *Verzeichnis der Präsentier-und Parademärsche* (Berlin: Parrhysius, 1940)

Silcher, Friedrich, & Friedrich Erk, – *Allgemeines Deutsches Kommersbuch* (Lahr: Schauenburg, 1929)

Wieprecht, Wilhelm F., – *Die Militair-Musik und Die Miltair-Musikalische Organization Eines Kriegsheeres* (Berlin: C. Habel, 1885) (Photocopy of Library of Congress Microfilm courtesy David E Clark)

Modern Publications

Blankenburg, Gudrun, & Hans-Joachim Blankenburg, – *Deutsche Marschkönig Hermann Ludwig Blankenburg in seiner Zeit 1876-1956* (Bad Langensalza: Verlag Rockstuhl 2011)

Brixel, Eugen, Günter Martin, & Gottfried Pils, – *Das ist Österreichs Militärmusik von der "türkischen Musik" zu den Philharmonikern in Uniform,* (Styria: Edition Kaleidoskop, 1982)
Bunge, Fritz, – *Musik in der Waffen SS* (Osnabrück: Munin Verlag GmbH, 1975)
Busch, Heinz, – *Vom Armeemarsch zum Großen Zapfenstreich : ein Lexikon zur Geschichte der deutschen Militärmusik* (Bonn: Verlag Der Kurier, 2005)
Deisenroth, Friedrich, – *Deutsche Militärmusik in fünf Jahrhunderten – Die Entwicklung von der Feldmusik zur Militärmusik* (Wiesbaden: Erdmann, 1961)
Höfele, Bernhard, – *Die Deutsche Militärmusik* (Köln: Luthe, 1999)
Martin, P.C. (Ed. Hans Bleckwenn), – *Die Musik Der Spielleute Des altpreußischen Heeres Band 1. – Das Altpreussische Heer 1713-1807 Teil V* (Osnabrück: Biblio Verlag, 1976)
Moormann, Peter, Albrecht Riethmüller & Rebecca Wolf, – *Paradestück Militärmusik – Beitrage zum Wandel staatlicher Repräsentation durch Musik* (Bielefeld: transcript Verlag, 2012)
Müller, Reinhold, Manfred Lachmann, Wolfgang Friedrich, & Doris Garscha-Friedrich, – *Spielmann – Trompeter – Hoboist : aus der Geschichte der deutschen Militärmusiker* (Berlin: Militärverlag der Deutschen Demokratischen Republik, 1988)
Obermair, Gilbert, – *Lieder der unvergessenen Heimat: Volks und Heimatlieder aus Mittel und Ostdeutschland* (München: Heyne, 1981)
Ringelmann, Kurt, Wolfgang Steinmetz, Martin Heidler & Walter Ratzek, – *'500 Jahre Militärmusikgeschichte' Das Ausbildungsmusikkorps der Bundeswehr eine Dokumentation* (Bonn: Verlag Der Kurier, 1999)
Schramm, Michael, (ed) – *Militärmusik im Diskurs: Hans-Felix Husadel – eine Schriftenreihe des Militärmusikdienstes der Bundeswehr* (Bonn: Militärmusikdienst der Bundeswehr, 2006)
Schwenk, Hans, – *Marschmusik vom Kriegsruf zum Großen Zapfenstreich* (Munich: Feder Verlag, 1965)
Sollfelner, Anton Othmar, & Christian Glanz, – Die *österreichische Militärmusik in der II.Republik 1955-2000* (Graz: Austria Medien Service, 2000)
Stein, Hans-Peter, – *Symbole und Zeremoniell in deutschen Streitkräften vom 18. bis zum 20. Jahrhundert* (Augsburg: Militärgeschichtliches Forschungsamt, Weltbild-Verlag, 1992)
Suppan, Wolfgang, – *Lexikon des Blasmusikwesens* (Freiburg im Breisgau: Blasmusikverlag Fritz Schulz, 1973)
Thurmair, Elisabeth, – *Alte Deutsche Reiter Lieder* (München: Universitas-Verl., 1983)
Toeche-Mittler, Joachim, – *Armeemärsche, Bd. I –III,* (Stuttgart: Spemann, 1966-75)
Toeche-Mittler, Joachim, – *Musikmeister Ahlers 'Ein Zeitbild unserer Militärmusik 1901-1945'* (Stuttgart: Spemann , 1981)
Ullrich, Günter, – *Soldatenlieder im Wandel der Zeit* (Beckum: Vogel-Druck, 1989)
Vajda, Stephan, – Mir *san vom k.u.k .... Die kuriose Geschichte der österreichischen Militärmusik* (Wien: Uebereuter, 1977)
Waldmann, Friedrich, – *Militär- und Blasmusik der bewaffneten Organe der SBZ/DDR. SBZ/DDR-Schallplattenproduktion 1946-1989* (Niedestetten, 1996)
Waldmann, Friedrich, – *Marschmusik : volkstümliche Blasmusik "Soldatenlied"; Blasmusik d. Arbeiterschaft der Alt-BRD ; Musikkorps d. Deutschen Bundeswehr, d.*

Polizei (Werksorchester, Chor), zivile Blasorchester auf Schallplatten/Tonträger 1945 – 1990, (Niederstetten: Waldmann, 1999)
Waldmann, Friedrich, – *Marschmusik u.Lieder auf Schallplatten von 1898–1945 in Deutschland* (Niederstetten: Waldmann, 2002)
Woche, Kurt-Rainer, – *Vom Wecken bis zum Zapfenstreich: Die Geschichte der Berliner Garnison* (Potsdam: Kurt Vowinkel-Verlag, 1998)

English Language Sources

Döll, Karl Anton, (English translation by Anne Corrie), – *Old Comrades – Alte Kameraden – Vieux Camerades*, (Homburg: Carl Teike Verlag, 1971). A Biography of the composer Carl Teike written by his nephew.
Conradi, Peter, – *Hitler's Piano Player: The Rise and Fall of Ernst Hanfstaengl, Confidant of Hitler, Ally of FDR* (London: Gerald Duckworth & Co, 2005)
Mantle, Robert, – *Military Music in the Campaign of 1866* (Solihull: Helion & Company, 2009)
Matthews, Brian, – *The Military Music & Bandsmen of Adolf Hitler's Third Reich 1933-1945* (Winchester: Tomahawk Films, 2002).
McKenzie, Stuart, – *Collecting Third Reich Recordings* (Church Stretton: Ulric Publishing, 2001)
Murray, David, – *Music of the Scottish Regiments* (Edinburgh: Pentlands Press 1994, Mercat Press, 2001). Covers in detail the German influence on British military music.

Military Music Periodicals, Archives and useful Websites consulted

Mit Klingendem Spiel – Zeitschrift der Deutschen Gesellschaft für Militärmusik (*Journal of the German Military Music Society*)
Website: www.dgfmm.de
Associated; Traditionsmusikorps 1.Garde-Regiment zu Fuss (a superbly musical re-enactment pre-1914 style infantry band well-uniformed)
Website: www.traditionsmusikkorps.de
Associated; Trompeterkorps Husaren-Regiment Kaiser Nikolaus II. von Rußland (1.Westfälisches) Nr. 8 "Buke Husaren" (Paderborn) (a superbly musical re-enactment pre-1914 style cavalry band well-uniformed)
Website: www.husaren-buke.de
Zeitschrift für Heereskunde. Especially the articles written by members of the *'Arbeitskreis Militärmusik'*
Band International (Magazine of the International Military Music Society)
Websites: www.imms-online.org (International – over 30 countries have active groups, and there are civilian and military members in many more)
www.immscanada.ca (Canada)
www.immsfrance.fr (France)
www.imsitalia.it (Italy)
www.imms.nl (The Netherlands)
www.imms.pl (Poland)
www.imms-uk.org.uk (United Kingdom)
Drummers Call (the Journal of the Corps of Drums Society – UK charity for the promotion of traditional military drum, fife and bugle music – largely civilian or ex-

Army, but has strong links with serving British Army Infantry Battalions' Corps of Drums) Website: www.corpsofdrums.com

Ancient Times (the Journal of the Company of Fifers and Drummers- USA based, but worldwide following. Concentrates on 18th century military style fifes and drums in period uniforms)

Website: www.companyoffifeanddrum.org

Eagle & Lyre Archive – Founded in 1997 by Tony Dean and Ian Smart, an archive with a library of all the above listed books and several hundred more on the subject of German, Austrian and Worldwide military music and musicians' uniforms. The archive holds recordings of over 4,500 German & Austrian march titles on MP3, CD, Vinyl and Shellac dating from 1898 to 2013: Over 800 pre-1918 photographs, prints and postcards; A large collection of period equipment of the German Spielleute; fifes, drums, bugles, swallowsnest wings etc..: Between 2006 and 2010 the Archive had a trading arm owned by Mrs Jenny Dean, Eagle & Lyre Publications and Recordings, most of whose products are still available from Discurio Ltd (UK) and Berliner Zinnfiguren (D). Most importantly, the archive has an extensive collection of sheet music and band parts available for loan to wind-bands making recordings using German march arrangements; to date made use of by the Band of The Royal Lancers, The Royal Tank Regiment Cambrai Band and The Honourable Artillery Company Regimental Band: Archive Email: eagleandlyre@btinternet.com

Index

Personages & Publishers

Place Names

Music Titles by Keywords

German Military Units 1815-1919

Index of Non-category specific words

Authors' biographies

Antony Dean – Editor-in-Chief and Translator

Tony was born in 1956, the son of an Historian and former Chaplain of Christ Church, Oxford, Michael Dean MA (Oxon). From 1968-74 Tony studied French Horn under former Grenadier Guards musician Frank Watson. In more recent years Tony has studied side-drum, Bb military flute (fife), bugle, trumpet and other brass instruments under Major Mike Hall (late Coldstream Guards), former State Trumpeter David Edwards (late The Life Guards) and former Guards Division Senior Drum Major Peter Foss (late Scots Guards). Regularly appearing at the Lord Mayor's Show and other public events, in 1999 Tony was selected to perform on the military side-drum in a massed military and civilian Corps of Drums at the last Royal Tournament at Earl's Court. During the 1970s Tony spent extended periods studying German language, history and culture living with families in Hamburg and Berlin. He returned to qualify as a history teacher in Britain, but pursued a political career, first as a parliamentary candidate whilst earning a living as an advertising manager, but then later as a full time professional political agent and advisor at regional and later national level at Westminster working for David Steel and then Paddy Ashdown. After leaving politics in 1989 he became head of a civil litigation team in the Electricity Industry, being seconded to the Share Information Office set up in the City by merchant bankers Kleinwort Benson to advise on privatisation of the industry. In 1994 he returned to teaching for eight years in his home county of Berkshire, but ten years ago began working for Berkshire Magistrates' Courts. Tony has a wife, Jen, and an adult step-daughter, Vicky.

Joachim Toeche Mittler (3rd March 1907 – 5th June 1996)

Toeche Mittler spent his early years in Offenbach-on-Main and then later moved to Berlin with his parents. He was educated in the capital and after leaving school applied to become an Army officer. In 1926 he was accepted as an officer aspirant in a mounted artillery unit. After officer training at Jütebog, in 1930 he was commissioned Leutnant and posted to Schweidnitz. Toeche Mittler married in 1934 at the age of 27, which then required special permission. On 1st April 1935 he changed service and joined the newly formed Luftwaffe. Due to his army training, he was assigned to anti-aircraft artillery units. He served in several air force garrisons in Germany, and was eventually selected for General Staff training in 1940. After graduating from the Air Force Academy in Berlin-Gatow he served in Brussels, Northern France, and as a battalion commander in the Soviet Union. In 1944 he was transferred to the General Staff of the Commanding General Air Force for Training and Operations. His rank at that time was that of a Lt. Colonel (General Staff). He was imprisoned by the Soviets, but managed to escape after only a few days. After the war he took over his father's company, which was well-known in Germany for chemical engineering the field of the fine arts. It was after the war that his interest in German military music – which had always been prevalent in his life – really became a field of main emphasis. Consequently he published several books on German military music, the first one of this three volumes dedicated to *Armeemärsche* was published in 1966. Later followed a biography of *Stabsmusikmeister Ahlers*. The further two volumes of *Armeemärsche* appeared in 1971 and 1975. These three volumes of *Armeemärsche* are recognised as the standard work on the subject in the German language, copies of which are held by all major reference libraries around the world. He was one of the founding fathers of the Arbeitskreis Militärmusik which evolved into the Deutsche Gesellschaft für Militärmusik (The German Military Music Society). Towards the end of his life, Toeche Mittler unfortunately contracted hearing problems and sadly was no longer able to listen to music.

Werner Probst

Werner Probst was born in Schweinfurt (Northern Bavaria) on 10th November 1938. He studied to be an interpreter and translator in Munich graduating with the so-called "public examination". He was drafted into the West German Air Force (Bundeswehr-Luftwaffe) in 1959. He undertook various national and international assignments at command levels, including at the West German Ministry of Defence, Bonn. His last position was as Assistant Director Air Force, German Armed Forces Intelligence Office as Oberstleutnant (Lt.Col.) (General Staff). He developed an interest in German and international military music at an early age, winning a TV quiz show in this field in 1956. He has had numerous articles printed in domestic and international specialized magazines. Co-author (with George Foeller) of *Bands of the Austro-Hungarian Empire* (1987), he is now a free lance journalist on wind bands for the Westdeutscher Rundfunk (West German Broadcasting Corporation), Cologne, since 1985. He is the representative for Germany on the International Committee of the International Military Music Society and the Vice Chairman of the Deutsche Gesellschaft für Militärmusik (The German Military Music Society).

David Murray

Lt. Col. (Retd) David Murray was born at Kuldana in the Murree Hills of the Punjab, now in Pakistan. His interest in the Armies of Imperial Germany was kindled by his father's stories of service in the Legation Guard in North China, where Germany also maintained a contingent. His fascination with military music began when the outstanding BBC Military Band, now long defunct, broadcast a series 'Pictures in the Fire' in the years before 1939. Trained as a piper by two of the great names in piping, Pipe Majors Robert Reid and Willie Ross, in World War II he served in the 1st Battalion, The Queen's Own Cameron Highlanders, in which he had been born, the third generation of his family to serve in the battalion. With it, he took part in the operations in Assam and Burma. He retired from the army in 1968, having commanded the last battalion of the Cameron Highlanders. His connection with the Edinburgh Military Tattoo began in 1948, when the first 'Military Display' took place on the Esplanade of Edinburgh Castle, with illumination provided by the headlights of military vehicles, and continued intermittently until 1980, when he finally stood down as Deputy Producer. David is the author of *Music of the Scottish Regiments*, published in 1994, and again in 2001.

Robert Mantle

Robert Mantle died suddenly on 24 September 2009 at the early age of 61 years. He leaves a widow, Sue, who has encouraged this project to proceed as she knows Rob would have been delighted for it finally to be published. Rob was born in Kenilworth on 14 September 1948 and spent his childhood at school in Coventry. He gained a BA in English at Sheffield University and a post graduate qualification as a Librarian from the College of Librarianship, Aberystwyth. He spoke and read fluent German, undertaking much original research with many visits to German and Austrian cities. He began his career at Whitechapel Library in 1973 before gaining promotion to become the National Director of the Library Inter-loans Service. This post he held for many years, until nearing retirement, he chose to return to what he really enjoyed, frontline contact with customers, when he was invited to launch the new library at the Canary Wharf development. He retired in 2008. Since an undergraduate he was heavily involved with the re-enactment movement, which saw an explosion of interest from the early 1970s. He was a member of the Napoleonic Association, establishing its first demonstration "Prussian" unit and publishing his first work in 1976, *Prussian Reserve Infantry 1813-15*; so thorough, it is still regarded as the standard work in the English language on the subject thirty years on. In 1984 he suggested the creation, and was a founder of the Great War Society. This became widely respected for its thorough research and historical accuracy and helped the BBC organize their human experience *Trench* TV series of the 1990s, re-enacting in trenches in Belgium the lives of the Hull Pals using modern youngsters drawn from the same area. Robert was interested in military music for most of his life and collected military recordings for over thirty years. His primary interest was the music of nineteenth and early twentieth century Austria-Hungary and Germany, and the men who composed and played it. He was a member of several historical research societies, much in demand as a speaker, delivering amusing and learned lectures on the 'Life and Work of Gottfried Piefke' and on 'The Music of the 1866 Campaign', most recently at the Continental Wars Society (1815-1914) meetings at the Polish Institute, Lancaster Gate.

Ian Smart

Ian Smart has been following bands since before he can remember and a band member since the age of eleven. The only son of a Baptist Minister and a Leicester school teacher, he grew up in the North of England receiving a thorough grounding in reality at Central School, Darlington. The love of history he formed listening to his parents and grand parents was honed there by the gifted and dedicated staff. After attending the VIth form at Hemel Hempstead and surviving the culture shock he went on to graduate with a BA in History from Kings College, London. After working as a kitchen porter and school caretaker he found his niche in the Civil Service where today he is employed with the Department of Transport, Local Government and the Regions in Hastings. He resides in the Bohemia area of that town. He is a playing member of the City of London Corps of Drums, the Hastings Corps of Drums and the John Kensit Memorial Flute Band, as well as the UK wide charity the Corps of Drums Society, and the International Military Music Society. Ian plays both bass drum and side drum with equal skill and relish! He is an active member of religious fraternal organisations and a dedicated member of the Baptist Church. Outside bands his interests are military and police history, horses and ska music.

Tunes of Blood and Iron

German Regimental and Parade Marches from the Age of Frederick the Great to the Present Day

Volume 1 - Infantry (Part 1)

- Prussian Military Music from Tilsit to Versailles 1807-1871
- Royal Prussian Army March Collection 1817-1918 – Quick Marches
- Index

Volume 2

- Cavalry, Artillery & Panzers – Inspection marches, Walk marches, Trots & Canters 1819-1945
- Infantry (part 2) – General Salutes 1817-1945, Quick marches 1925-1929
- Field Music of Fifes, Drums & Bugles
- Regimental lists for Infantry and Mounted Troops – nicknames & marches
- Index

Volume 3

- Schützen & Jäger
- Kaiser Parades
- Prussian Guards Bandmasters 1900-1914
- Imperial Music Services
- Great War Gallery
- Index

Volume 4

- The March Collections and their Legacy – The Story of German military music 1817 to 2012. Includes later Wehrmacht & Waffen SS marches. March compositions of the East German Nationale Volksarmee and West German Bundeswehr 1956-1989. Post Re-unification Bundeswehr 1990-2012
- Navy & Colonial Forces – Bands and Repertoires
- Luftwaffe March Collection - 1935-1945
- Bundeswehr March Collection (1961) and Truppenmärche (1998)
- Index
- Series Bibliography
- Biographies of contributors

Helion Studies in Military History

No 1 *Learning from Foreign Wars. Russian Military Thinking 1859-73* Gudrun Persson (ISBN 978-1-906033-61-3)

No 2 *A Military Government in Exile. The Polish Government-in-Exile 1939-45, a Study of Discontent* Evan McGilvray (ISBN 978-1-906033-58-3)

No 3 *From Landrecies to Cambrai. Case Studies of German Offensive and Defensive Operations on the Western Front 1914-17* Capt G.C. Wynne (ISBN 978-1-906033-76-7)

No 4 *Playing the Game. The British Junior Infantry Officer on the Western Front 1914-18* Christopher Moore-Bick (ISBN 978-1-906033-84-2)

No 5 *The History of the British Army Film & Photographic Unit in the Second World War* Dr Fred McGlade (ISBN 978-1-906033-94-1)

No 6 *Making Waves. Admiral Mountbatten's Radio SEAC 1945-49* Eric Hitchcock (ISBN 978-1-906033-95-8)

No 7 *Abolishing the Taboo. Dwight D. Eisenhower and American Nuclear Doctrine 1945-1961* Brian Madison Jones (ISBN 978-1-907677-31-1)

No 8 *The Turkish Brigade in the Korean War Volume 1. Kunu-Ri Heroes (November-December 1950)* Dr Ali Denizli (ISBN 978-1-907677-32-8)

No 9 *The Diaries of Ronnie Tritton, War Office Publicity Officer 1940-45* Edited by Dr Fred McGlade (ISBN 978-1-907677-44-1)

No 10 *The Thinking Man's Soldier. The Life and Career of General Sir Henry Brackenbury 1837-1914* Christopher Brice (ISBN 978-1-907677-69-4)

No 11 *War Surgery 1914-18* Edited by Thomas Scotland and Steven Heys (ISBN 978-1-907677-70-0)

No 12 *Counterinsurgency in Africa. The Portugese Way of War 1961-74* John P. Cann (ISBN 978-1-907677-73-1)

No 13 *The Armed Forces of Poland in the West 1939-46* Michael Alfred Peszke (ISBN 978-1-908916-54-9)

No 14 *The Role of the Soviet Union in the Second World War* Boris Sokolov (ISBN 978-1-908916-55-6)

No 15 *Generals of the Danish Army in the First and Second Schleswig-Holstein Wars, 1848-50 and 1864* Nick B. Svendsen (ISBN 978-1-908916-46-4)

No 16 *A Considerable Achievement. The Tactical Development of the 56th (London) Division on the Western Front, 1916-1918* Matt Brosnan (ISBN 978-1-908916-47-1)

No 17 *Brown Waters of Africa. Portugese Riverine Warfare 1961-1974* John P. Cann (ISBN 978-1-908916-56-3)

No 18 *Man of Steel and Honour. General Stanislaw Maczek. Soldier of Poland, Commander of the 1st Polish Armoured Division in North-West Europe 1944-45* Evan McGilvray (ISBN 978-1-908916-53-2)

No 19 *The Gaysh. A History of the Aden Protectorate Levies 1927-61 and the Federal Regular Army of South Arabia 1961-67* Frank Edwards (ISBN 978-1-908916-87-7)

No 20 *The Whole Armour of God. Anglican Army Chaplains in the Great War* Linda Parker (ISBN 978-1-908916-96-9)

No 21 *Wars, Pestilence and the Surgeon's Blade. The Evolution of British Military Medicine and Surgery during the Nineteenth Century* Thomas Scotland & Steven Heys (eds.) (ISBN 978-1-909384-09-5)

No 22 *With Trumpet, Drum and Fife. A Short Treatise covering the Rise and Fall of Military Musical Instruments on the Battlefield* Major Mike Hall (ISBN 978-1-909384-17-0)

No 23 *Battlefield Rations. The food given to the British soldier for marching and fighting 1900-2011* Anthony Clayton (ISBN 978-1-909384-18-7)

No 24 *Railroads and Rifles. Soldiers, Technology and the Unification of Germany* (new edition) Dennis E. Showalter (ISBN 978-1-909384-19-4)